Travel Page

Every publication from Rippple Books has this special page to document where the book travels, who has it and when.

Greetings from

Campbell Jefferys

Rippple
Books

First published in 2017 by
Rippple Books

Cover design: Claudia Bode
Editor: Jeff Kavanagh
Layout: Susanne Hock

Rippple Books
Rippple Media
Postfach 304263
20325 Hamburg
Germany
www.rippplemedia.com

A CIP catalogue record for this book is available from the British Library.

ISBN: 978-3-9816249-4-6

Acknowledgements

The stories in this collection span two decades of travel. Some evolved into or out of published articles, which appeared in print and/ or online form. In those cases, credit shall be given to the various magazines, newspapers and websites.

A version of *Out of the Blue* was published in *The Globe and Mail*, Canada, which also published the story about skiing in British Columbia detailed in *Winter Sting*. Versions of *Berlin Underground* and *The Prussian Peasant* appeared in *The Sunday Telegraph*, London. Under different titles, *Auschwitz-land* was published by the *European Journal*, and *Romans, Rieslings and Riders* by *Decanter Magazine*. *Digital Enlightenment* appeared in *Living Now Magazine*. A much shorter version of *The Uggstralian Diaspora* was published by *Scoop Magazine*. The online news site www.thelocal.de published versions of *Paradox Island*, *Silver Harz* and *Red Island Cricket*, while *There's Something in the Wasser* and *Vainglorious* are on the www.purathletes. org blog in different form.

For stories involving personal experience, the names have been changed to protect the innocent and to avoid shaming the guilty, and in one special case, reduced to a single letter.

Postcard from Lanzarote

Dear Neil,

Well, here we are on lovely Lanzarote in the Canary Islands. No doubt you've heard about this place because almost everyone has been here. We threw caution to the wind and took a one-week package tour. The flight was fine. When we arrived, we had a lovely view of the airport while we sat in the bus for an hour waiting for other people to board. As a special treat, we were given a two-hour sightseeing tour of Puerto del Carmen, as the bus drove all over the city, dropping people off at their respective resorts.

The reception area of our resort is very comfortable and, on arrival, we sat there for a couple of hours while our room was cleaned and disinfected. There was some confusion as our bedroom not only faced the main road, but also had some mould on the walls, but the receptionist was very friendly and professional, and we were moved across the street to where our bedroom was as dark as a cave and our terrace faced the main street. How nice it is to sit on the terrace and watch the cars, trucks, vans, scooters and buses roar past; it saves me from making conversation with the missus.

We spent the first day at the pool. What a view! In front of the ocean backdrop, many well-fed British and German people were lounging on the complimentary green deck chairs. We couldn't get a free sun chair though, because they were all taken, either by a person or by a towel spread over the entire sun chair.

The water was brisk to say the least, and only the well-insulated children were brave enough to jump into the pool. Oh, how they screamed and splashed, kicking balls here and there, and calling out across the pool to their parents, who were too busy playing with their phones or sleeping to look up. There were quite a few kids who didn't seem to have parents at all.

For dinner, we were in the restaurant with everyone else at seven on the dot. The wonderful food is included in our package tour, but you have to pay for drinks. The beer tastes like it has been diluted with water, but that only makes it more refreshing.

The buffet was excellent, with plenty of deep-fried fish, calamari swamped in batter, and chips dripping with oil. The salads went mainly untouched, while there were plenty of guests who skipped dinner and went straight for the desserts. There was red and green jelly, wobbling in great mounds, and those fabulous puddings of strawberry and banana where you add milk and water to a powder. How quickly it disappeared. The bowl of fruit looked highly unappetising and most stayed away from that.

The best thing about the restaurant: the people. It's funny how the couples sit there and stare at each other, looking around the room and watching what others are eating to see what's popular. Because the tables are low, many of the men have to hunch over to eat. From behind, it looks like they're not even using cutlery. The kids run around, darting between the tables and knocking stuff over, having a great time. And just like at the pool, it seems these kids don't belong to anyone.

After dinner, it was time to hit the town for some nightlife. Puerto del Carmen is a long, stretched out resort following the coastline. Most of the bars and clubs are close to the main beach, Playa Grande, and it's here that the tourists congregate every evening. We thought six euro was pretty good for a fancy cocktail, which came with a bright sparkler and a couple of little umbrellas. They think of everything here, even the best soundtrack. With the music, I lost fifteen years and it was 1989 again.

Some people danced, but we preferred to sit on the cane chairs on the terrace and people-watch. The tourists really dress in their finery for their holidays. The men favour tracksuit pants and aren't shy about advertising the football team they support. Hoop earrings are popular, as is pasted-down hair. The women parade around in short skirts of denim or polyester and halter tops that keep falling down, which require two hands and a shimmy to get back up. Their hairstyles also match the soundtrack. You can tell the Germans from way off, because of their tapered jeans and their preference for hair cut short at the front and long at the back. Their faces are well-tanned, thanks to regular visits to the sun studio back home in Stuttgart.

We got to bed after midnight and fell asleep straight away. The sound of the traffic was a soothing reminder of the city we'd left behind. How well we slept, and how thankful I was for the en-suite bathroom, as the watered down cocktails ran their course.

In the morning, the shouted conversation of the Spanish cleaning women made the perfect alarm clock, waking us for breakfast. The sun was out, and what better way to start the day than with fried eggs, bacon, baked beans and fried tomato. As with dinner, the fruit went untouched, with everyone wanting a hot breakfast to fortify themselves for a long day of sleeping by the pool.

The coffee machine was a great place for a quick chat, as the line was long and slow to move, and people kept cutting in where their friends or partners were standing. Like us, other guests had hauled their summer clothing out of mothballs. There were plenty of garish shirts, and white legs and knobbly knees poked out from baggy shorts. Those who had been here longer had perfect sock tan lines and shiny pink faces, and their tattoos stood out against the brown of their skin.

We met a lovely couple that first morning. By mistake, we had sat at their regular table. They asked us to move, but we got talking anyway, and the missus and I moved over to the next table to keep the conversation going. But that turned out to be another couple's table, so we chatted with them before moving on once more. We marvelled at what a great way this was to meet people, and decided to do it again during dinner.

Like yesterday, all the sun chairs at the pool were taken, mostly by towels, so we headed for the beach instead. Playa Grande is a long beach of coarse, golden sand covered with orderly blocks of sun chairs. The friendliness of the people was apparent as everyone sat very close together. The kids splashed happily near the rocks and the adults swam out far from the breakers, looking for a rip to float in. We preferred the sand to the inexpensive sun chairs and lay down to bake our shrivelled winter bodies in the sun. How nice it was, to feel the sun on our skin, and how funny the parent-less kids were as they ran over our towels, covering us with sand.

We were then warm enough to try the water. It was invigorating and oily, but the strong current and smashing waves soon made us forget how cold we were. We splashed and struggled, swimming into the current for exercise, and playing a game of avoiding the rocks as we tried to catch waves. A stray soccer ball thumped one swimmer in the head and this was very funny.

We spent the whole day at the beach, until it was time to wash off the salt and oil and head for the restaurant, getting there bang on seven with everyone else. As planned, we sat at a couple's regular table and were glad to get chatting with them. We talked about what a great language Spanish is and shared the words we'd already learned, such as *Frito* (fried), *Cerveza* (beer) and *Bar* (bar).

From there, the days just flew by, each one exactly the same as the last. We thought about venturing inland to explore some of the island, but most of the guests we spoke to didn't recommend this. Buses were limited and nobody spoke a word of English. And why would you journey away from the beach? So we did like the others, slothing between the beach and the restaurant, listening to Rick Astley in the discos and drinking the thin cocktails with the sparklers inside.

Before we knew it, the week was over and we were sitting in the reception area waiting for our bus to take us back to the airport. We knew most of the other one-weekers and swapped stories about how we had spent our days. One adventurous couple had taken a local bus to the capital Arrecife. They were much braver than us, but they said the town was a disappointment, a run-down Spanish wasteland. It had none of the beautiful white high-rise apartment resorts which populated Puerto del Carmen. So, we were thankful we hadn't wasted a day. One week is a short time, and every moment in the sun has to be savoured. We knew our friends back home would gauge the success of our holiday by the depth of our tans.

The package gave us the holiday feeling right to the very end, with another sightseeing tour around the city. We picked up other guests and were able to see the places where we had spent our money recklessly and danced the night away to Banarama. I thought I saw the Irish bar where we had watched the football one afternoon, but I wasn't sure if it was the right one; there were so many, and most of them looked the same. But it didn't matter. I will know for sure when I download the photos from the ten memory cards I filled.

So, Neil, I fully recommend a visit to Lanzarote, and especially to the delightful resort of Puerto del Carmen. It will take years off your life. We all miss the glory days of the eighties, and here you can be whisked right back to them. And to top it all off, you will have a genuine Spanish cultural experience. Give my best to Beryl and the kids.

Your partner in fun,
Noel

Looking for Wolfgang

In three hundred years from now, what music will have stood the test of time? Which of our post-war pop icons will generations far down the line cling to and revere? Will people gather in ornate halls to hear renditions of the Beatles, or to see another performance of The Who's *Tommy*? Surely no one will put on their fancy duds centuries from now and attend an orchestral concert of Robbie Williams or Beyoncé. So why is it that Mozart has survived the ordeal of time so well? Why is he normally the first thought of at any mention of classical music?

Mozart was the man. Sure, Beethoven, Bach, Haydn and the others were all pretty good, but they're in the carriage behind. Mozart's up front. He's the one we know, his compositions so light, uplifting and graceful, so often used in film scores and as background music for dinner parties. Mozart's concert sonatas are a perennial Christmas gift and are always well received. Any cultural education begins with an appreciation of Mozart, but the best way to learn about the man is to go to where it all began, to Salzburg, where the hills were alive with the sound of music well before Julie Andrews got there.

The Austrian city is close to the German border and sliced down the middle by the Salzach River, with the hills of Kapuzinerberg and Mönchsberg flanking the city and providing natural protection. Looming over it all is the Hohensalzburg Fortress, built in 1077 and the largest preserved citadel in central Europe. From here, one can look down on the city that gave birth to a genius and which inspired him throughout his life. And who wouldn't be inspired? With the towering turrets of churches, the flat-topped houses, Italian architecture, winding streets and sprawling squares, Mozart's melodies resound within these historic walls. The numerous staircases patter with feet like rising and falling crescendos, the leaves flutter with rhythmic grace, and the small alleyways and courtyards hold secret duets and dramatic denouements.

The overture begins at Mozart's Birthplace on Getreidegasse. The tourists gather here in great numbers to photograph the building, but surprisingly few venture inside. They miss out on learning fascinating details about a remarkable man, including the complicated relationship he had with his musician father. Mozart was perhaps the first child star, a prodigy who at age three could pick out tunes on the piano and was composing by the time he was six. But like many young talents, he fell victim to an overbearing and ambitious parent intent on living through his offspring. He also succumbed to the demands of celebrity.

The house, modest, comfortable and in the heart of the old town, befitted the means of the moderately successful Vice-Kapellmeister, Leopold Mozart. Single-minded and with enough success and training to proclaim judgement over his son's gifts, Leopold set out from the beginning to take young Wolfgang to the top. He began by turning his virtuoso son into a travelling sideshow, visiting courts all over Europe. Poor little Wolfgang grew up on tour.

The museum, which has original instruments, compositions and portraits, also details young Mozart's life on the road: the nature of travelling at the time, the long hours spent in carriages and the impact of being denied anything remotely like a normal childhood, which comes through in various letters and documents. Mozart would, like so many child stars to follow, struggle in adulthood and always remain something of a child. It's interesting how, of the many Mozart-related things people can buy in Salzburg, the most popular are Mozartkugeln, round sweets made of marzipan, nougat and dark chocolate, introduced a century after his death.

Standing at Mozart's clavichord and looking at his first violin, one can imagine the long hours of practice he put in, with his father staunchly behind him, waiting for mistakes, pushy and anxious, while outside children frolicked by the river, playing games in the sun or throwing snowballs in winter. As a child, Mozart was extravagantly praised, but never able to get the respect or admiration from the one he sought the most. His bitter relationship with his father was in stark contrast to the style of music he produced. Perhaps he sought resolution and happiness in the make-believe world of opera, in costumes and crescendos, where relationships came crashing down with a thump of drums, and declarations of love were met with light strings and a flutter of high keys.

Across the river on Makart Square, near the Mirabell Gardens, is Mozart's Residence, where he lived from 1773-1780. The first floor museum focuses on the life of the Mozarts at this time, including the death of his mother in 1778, but is not quite as revealing and fascinating as Mozart's Birthplace.

Walking distance from the house is the St. Sebastian Cemetery, where Leopold and Constanze Mozart, Wolfgang's wife, are buried.

In as much as Salzburg was Mozart's inspiration, it was also his undoing. The city never had a ruling royal family. In Mozart's time, it was governed by the archbishops as a Roman principality. The lack of royals meant there were no patrons who could offer Mozart high-paying court jobs. As a disgruntled organist in Salzburg, perhaps feeling he deserved more, he was soon dismissed. He then city-hopped from Prague to Paris to Vienna in search of the lucrative position he felt was his due. He died in 1791, aged thirty-five. Always bad with money and somewhat destitute at his time of death, he was given the cheapest funeral possible and buried in St. Marx Cemetery in Vienna in a common grave that has never been found.

How Mozart conducted his life and where he was laid to rest are not nearly as relevant as his music. For it is the music that is remembered and played. The man himself has been lost in the annals of history. Salzburg offers many different avenues to enjoy the music of Mozart. Most interesting is the Marionette Theatre, which performs *The Magic Flute* and other Mozart operas with puppets to recordings of the world's leading orchestras and vocalists.

Concerts are also held in the Marble Hall of the Mirabell Palace, in the magnificent state rooms of the Hohensalzburg Fortress, and in the music hall of the Salzburg Palace. The Mozart Chamber Orchestra performs popular concerts in the exclusive setting of the Salzburg Residenz. The concert season culminates in summer with the Salzburg Festspiele, from late July to September, and in winter with the Mozart Festival held at the end of January.

After his death, Mozart's popularity rose considerably. So, not only was he the first child star tarnished by early celebrity and fame, he also died before his time, and in death became more famous and valued than in life.

Though buried in Vienna, his legacy remains in Salzburg. There's a Mozart connection at just about every turn, including the Mozart statue on Mozartplatz in front of the tourist office. This square is a good place to finish a walking tour of the old town, and to sit down, drink a coffee and look into the stone eyes of the great man who remains the benchmark for classical music and who also provided the blueprint for the rock'n'roll lifestyle that would be copied centuries later.

Perhaps Mozart's story is less about the perils of celebrity or the problems of being a boy-genius, and more about fathers and sons. Or even parent and child.

Was Leopold Mozart ever proud of his son, beyond the appreciation received for Wolfgang the virtuoso child? From what I can gather in Mozart's Birthplace and Residence, their relationship was strained, difficult and distant. But somehow, Wolfgang rose above this and composed music that remains timeless.

I conclude that Leopold was jealous. Or perhaps he was deeply conflicted, feeling love, pride and envy all at once.

Even among genius composers, family relationships are complicated.

This is rather reassuring.

Baltic Riviera

The arctic wind blustering over the water is teeth-chattering cold. It's messing up hair, disconnecting men from their hats, and causing umbrellas to flutter, shake and turn inside out. Far into the distance, the wide beach is peppered with angular specs of grey and black; brave souls well rugged up and walking sideways into the wind. Some rigidly toss tennis balls for retrieving dogs.

The sand is white and frozen, with some marks of bare feet.

Further along, past the old-timers playing bocce and a wet-suited man struggling to rig up his windsurfer, a derelict concrete edifice looms high over the beach. It has a multi-levelled terrace that looks out over the Baltic Sea, but there is no glass in the window frames, and the walls are covered with fading graffiti. The building has long been abandoned, with the light fittings hanging from the ceilings like broken spider webs.

Venturing inside, broken glass cracks underfoot. I carefully climb the stairs to the top floor of the terrace, half-expecting some Latvian hobos to appear from the shadows and chase me off their territory, and worrying the whole building might come crashing down.

In what was the dining area, the few remaining tables have been pushed against the wall. It offers an incredible view; the sand stretching into the distance in both directions, and the Baltic, cold blue and rocking to the rhythm of the wind, appearing endless. It seems from here that life has no limits. The world is huge, and the beach and the sea stretch forever.

The wind blows through the vacant window frames. In my fantasy, it's a warm breeze.

I'm seeing summer, decades ago. The dining area is full, with adults laughing between mouthfuls of black bread and jam. The kids poke at their breakfasts, impatient for the sand and the water. The day is warm and the radio plays bright Russian music, summer songs of lakes and fields and long days. One by one, the eaters leave their tables to join the throng on the beach.

Until there's no one left. And time speeds up. Glasnost, Perestroika, the fall of the Berlin Wall, the end of the Iron Curtain. The tables get hauled away or pushed to the sides. The windows get smashed. Vandals paint their names on the walls. There's no money to fix it all up and make it new again. And no one wants to, because no one is coming back, leaving a building that is cold and empty, stale with the smell of damp concrete. Every exposed piece of metal is rusted brown by Baltic salt. The beach is deserted, but for a stubborn few, and this Soviet edifice is now an eyesore and a window to a forgotten era.

This is Jurmala (Latvian for "seashore"), the centuries-old resort twenty-five kilometres from Riga. This was once known as the Baltic Riviera, with over thirty kilometres of uninterrupted white-sand beach. It was here that Soviets from all over the Union holidayed in the relatively prosperous 1960s and 1970s. One year, there were over six million visitors. Communist party officials were frequent visitors, including General Secretaries Leonid Brezhnev and Nikita Khrushchev. Ex-military men retired here and built large homes in the Art Nouveau style. But the flow of visitors was reduced to a trickle following the fall of the Soviet Union, with many resorts and buildings falling into disrepair.

Standing on this terrace, I don't see it staying that way. It's too nice a spot, even in winter. I conclude the Baltic Riviera will bounce back. Someone will come along, knock down this edifice and build something new and better. It's just a matter of when.

Away from the beach, Jurmala is in better shape. The streets are lined with well-kept Art Nouveau houses of pink, green, yellow and blue. Security gates open to German automobiles and immaculate gardens.

Clearly, there's still some money here.

Jurmala's architecture makes it a city of historical importance. Over one-third of the twelve thousand buildings are considered historic, with one thousand protected by UNESCO.

I waste my time wandering up and down the streets of Majori, in the heart of Jurmala. A failed attempt at communism may have bankrupted the Soviet Union, but not before party officials could spend some cash on these very nice houses.

But I wonder: what was a Soviet summer like? How was it in this place, say, in August, 1964? Communism was always depicted as drab, the people dour, the life miserable; but, look at the colours of Jurmala. This doesn't strike me as a place of misery and suppression. I'm seeing house parties, lights on all night, music playing, campfires, kids running down the streets, impromptu games of soccer on the beach. I'm seeing youth, bright and beautiful, and being smiled at by the adults watching. I'm seeing fit young men out of their military uniforms, and long-legged girls in heels and bikinis.

I've always been something of a closet communist. Not hardcore red, but often questioning why a wealthy person should live extravagantly while others live in poverty. When it comes to wealth distribution, I would like a bit more balance and fairness.

It occurs to me that Jurmala, circa summer 1964, may have been the Soviet version of an unfair distribution of wealth, more suitable to the capitalist West. While the rich and European flocked to the French Riviera and Italy's Amalfi Coast, the rich and Russian escaped to Jurmala. Perhaps the chosen few built all of this using state funds, while all their other comrades toiled in factories and mines, in places cold and grey.

Cold myself, I enter a small café and have a steaming bowl of solyanka. What looks like watered-down motor oil with large slices of sausage is rather tasty and warms me up inside, enough to steel me for a second walk along the beach.

The wind has dropped and the sun has come out. The windsurfer is now a coloured spec motoring along the horizon. The bocce men have been replaced by Tai Chi enthusiasts. A couple of runners pound the sand with sneakers on. Owner-less dogs dart around. One man, clad only in a pair of dated swim trunks, and he has these pulled up very high, is slowly edging himself into the water.

At Bilduri, I cut through the pine forest and head for the train station. The forest borders the beach the whole thirty kilometres. The houses here are more modest than in Majori, but still the colours are bright and just a little garish.

The Soviet-era train rattles into the station and slows to walking speed. You have to jump on while the train is still moving, which the older people, locals surely, are rather adept at doing. It makes me wonder if the train would start again, if it came to a full stop.

Pulling out of the station, the train barely picks up any speed. It may even be faster to walk. The train rocks and shudders, the rivets threatening to pop. Every clickity-clack vibrates through the wooden seats and up my spine.

I'm suffering, but I'm also appreciating the history, and this time machine has a very Soviet price: 0.50 lats, which is like spending chocolate coins.

We leave the beach and pine forest behind and pass over the

Lielupe River. It takes forever for the train to cross the bridge. Then there is a section of swampy marshland, overgrown and rotting, an unwanted area stuck between two rivers. It looks like people have tried, at some point, to use this land, as I can see the ruins of small houses and rusted, abandoned machinery. There are also leftover fences, which mark out what were once fields for farming or keeping animals. It's all empty now, more water than land.

Closer to Riga, getting there at crawling speed, the view out the window becomes the kind of impoverished sprawl particular to former Soviet and communist cities. There's not much going on here, not much industry, not much endeavour, but there are plenty of remnants of what had been going on in the Soviet era, as these outskirts were home to factories, industrial areas and warehouses. All closed up now and left to waste, but still with people living out here in the boxy tenements built specifically for the comrades working nearby and their families.

On the streets, I see mostly old women, hunched over and pulling those ugly, two-wheeled shopping trolleys behind them. The old men gather in small groups, and sit and smoke. It looks grim.

The train crosses the bridge over the Daugava River and pulls into the station. When it stops, the final hiss I hear sounds like a sigh of relief, or pride.

Seen from inside the old town, Riga is a busy, cosmopolitan metropolis, much more European than Russian. It all looks pretty good, with the Riga Castle and the Guild Halls, and other impressive buildings that were somehow spared the Soviet wrecking ball. This includes the famous Art Nouveau building at Strelnieku 4a, built in 1905, which was a student hostel during the Soviet years and now houses the Stockholm School of Economics.

The old town has been painstakingly restored. A lot of money has gone into this restoration, to show the city's most beautiful side and return the Latvian capital to its pre-war glory as the "Paris of the Baltics". It doesn't appear that the money went beyond the old town's walls. What remains is almost a two-faced city: half Latvian, half Soviet. There are quaint cobblestoned streets and wide-laned boulevards built for military parades, Art Nouveau buildings and high-rise, pre-fab apartment blocks, and fashionably dressed young women with designer label handbags and old women pulling shopping trolleys.

This duality is captured rather well by my hotel, which is just outside the old town. Half of the hotel has been renovated; the other half is a construction site, but there are no workers. The receptionist informs me that the owner has run out of money, for now. The way he says it makes me think he's the owner himself.

So, it's just been left. I do some exploring and find my way into this construction area, getting through a door that's not terribly well locked. The structure and layout make me think this building was always a hotel, perhaps for a hundred years. The yet-to-be-renovated rooms are much like they were thirty or maybe fifty years ago, the furniture and furnishings still remaining.

I wonder what kind of people stayed here. Were they dignitaries, party officials, ambassadors, celebrities? Something tells me this was once a posh hotel. The rooms are large. The ceilings are high and ornately decorated, though dirty and stained. And while there's a lot of work to do to make this inhabitable again, it still holds the echo of luxury and exclusivity. Perhaps another example of unfair wealth distribution in the Soviet Union.

The hotel will eventually be finished, but for now, it's half-way there, like Riga. All the ingredients are here: beaches, buildings and boulevards. The only thing missing is money. Chocolate coins might buy tickets on creaky old trains, but they can't be used to renovate hotels or turn beachside edifices into five-star resorts.

Mendocino Man

Leonard was short and stocky, in his sixties. He wore thick glasses and had a full beard, trimmed short, much more salt than pepper.

Leonard was laughing very loudly. He seemed a merry sort, the kind of person who placed both hands on his belly when he laughed, whose cheeks turned quickly pink with mirth, and whose laugh sounded like of joyful scoff.

He was laughing at Justine.

The two had shared a ride from San Francisco to Caspar. She was an actress from New York visiting friends in California. He was a natural therapist from the Netherlands who now lived in Oakland. He'd also spent some time in Sydney, and it meant he had a strange accent, saying different words in different ways, pronouncing them with the accent of where he'd learnt them.

The three of us were in the communal kitchen of the Caspar Youth Hostel. Leonard was laughing because of this exchange between me and Justine.

Me: "I'm going to make dinner. Do you guys want some?"

Justine: "Oh, yes. This I have to see. A real Australian man making dinner."

Me: (Filling a pot with water and placing it on the stove) "Just simple stuff, but I can make it stretch for three."

Justine: "What's with the water?"

Me: "It's for pasta."

Justine: "Is that gonna be, like, a side dish?"

Me: "No."

Justine: "Oh."

Me: (Cutting some vegetables) "All I've got is what I brought with me."

Justine: "So go outside."

Me: "Huh?"

Justine: "Go out and catch something. You're an Australian. I thought you'd catch dinner for us."

Me: "Well, let me just change into my loin cloth first."

And Leonard began his fit of joyful scoffing.

"I saw it on TV," Justine said, using her stage voice to drown out Leonard's laughter. "They live off the land down there. They eat bugs and snakes. They do."

14

"Sure, some do," I said. "But most of us live in cities. In fact, nearly all of us do. San Francisco isn't so different from Sydney. You've got water, hills, parks and sunshine, some homeless people, a big bridge everyone knows."

Leonard was nodding. "Some things the same, other things different. Here, dinner is normally from a microwave or a telephone book. Down there, they catch it."

And he laughed some more.

"You can't catch dinner in cities that are mostly suburbs," I said.

Dinner was quickly made. As I served them both, Leonard produced a bottle of red wine.

"Our contribution to the feast," he said. "We detoured through Napa on the way up here and stopped at some wineries."

"Great. Pop the cork."

Through dinner, Leonard proceeded to drink much more than he ate. Justine pecked at her food like a bird. I wondered if she really would've preferred a hunk of game killed by an Australian-made spear and skinned on the youth hostel's kitchen table.

Leonard wanted to know my story. There wasn't much to tell. I was hitch-hiking up the coast, from Los Angeles to Vancouver.

"You're insane," Justine said. "Do you have any idea what kind of whackos are out there?"

"Just the usual Americans," Leonard said.

"I'm serious. He could get hurt. Taken off to some barn somewhere."

"Hasn't happened yet," I said. "They've all been pretty normal folks so far."

"Like what?" Leonard asked.

"You know, people who want some company on the drive. Others who feel sorry for me, for whatever reason. If I don't feel good about a ride, I turn it down."

"Did that happen?"

I shook my head. "No whackos. Yet."

"All that risk just to save a few dollars," Justine said.

"I'm not doing it to save money. I'm in it for the experience."

"Good for you," Leonard said. "It's important to do things for the right reasons."

We chatted some more. Justine was something of a bulldozer, ploughing through our conversation.

When we got around to the topic of what we were doing in Caspar,

15

I explained I'd spent the day in Mendocino, exploring the city and watching the very small Fourth of July parade. Justine ploughed in, saying Mendocino was where *East of Eden* was shot, the film that launched James Dean's career. And she went on, almost shedding a tear as she said how tragic it was that he had died; she mentioned other actors and actresses who had died young, including some people she knew, and that Mendocino for her would always be a place of tragedy, loss and sadness. When she paused, I said Mendocino would always remind me of the Beatles, because there was a drunk guy on the parade's one float singing *Eight Days a Week,* Karaoke style, over and over again, as that one float circled the town all afternoon.

Leonard laughed at this.

"I'm here to see some friends perform tonight in Mendocino," Justine said.

"Shakespeare, yes?" Leonard asked. "A befitting tragedy."

"No. Improv. Kinda crazy stuff. They take prompts from the audience and run with it. Really out there. Experimental, you know. It starts at nine. You're both coming, right?"

And the way she asked made it sound more a given than a choice. Leonard smiled and nodded. I had nothing else planned.

So off we went to Mendocino. In day time, the town had presented itself as an attractive settlement perched on a cliff; a bit hap-hazard, with some of the buildings and houses placed wherever they could go without any thought given to symmetry or integration. It was home to a thriving artistic community, according to the tourist office. By night, it was quiet and dark. Only a few streets were lit. I could hear the surf pounding against the rocks below. The theatre, as the sole building with lights on, seemed to be the only place open. Inside, a dozen people were spread around the tables, in groups of two or three. On stage, the troupe was warming up. One actor was actually stretching, first pulling each ankle up to his behind to stretch his quads, then pushing against a wall to loosen his calves. He stretched like an actor pretending to be an athlete, which made him look completely unathletic, and funny.

Justine waved at that actor as we took seats at the table furthest from the stage. There were small squares of paper on the table, and we were to write strange sentences on these squares, which would then be randomly plucked from a hat to prompt the improvisation.

The show began.

The troupe aimed for comedy, reaching so hard for laughs that it was sometimes painful to watch. If they'd been a little more self-aware, they might have attempted to pull off something so unfunny that it became funny. But in the end, Leonard got his wish; we watched tragedy, improvised.

During the intermission, free wine was served, perhaps in the hope of lubricating the vocal chords of those present, to get them laughing.

It didn't work.

But we stayed to the end, as did everyone else in the audience.

During the final applause, Leonard said, "A reunion of friends and family, I think."

As the people dispersed, Justine lingered to chat with her actor friend. He had a small towel around his neck and was dabbing at his forehead with one end of it. We were introduced. His pleasure at how well the improv had gone was funny.

As he spoke earnestly of what had "played" with the audience, it was difficult to hold in my laughter. Leonard was smiling too.

Justine drove us back to the hostel, then she went to bed. I made myself a cup of tea while Leonard helped himself to the wine we hadn't quite finished at dinner. He'd left the bottle on the table for other guests to drink, with a note, but it appeared the three of us were the hostel's only guests.

Leonard drained the bottle. He'd drunk quite a lot over the course of the evening, including plenty of free wine during intermission, but he seemed anything but inebriated.

"Don't get the wrong idea," he said. "About Justine. We're not together. I just gave her a ride up here. Friend of a friend type thing."

I held up both hands. "No judgement passed."

"It's more correct to say that she's a friend of a client. A patient. Someone I'm helping through a rough time." He placed a pager on the table. "I have this in case she calls."

"Is she suicidal?"

Leonard shook his head. "Lonely. And alone. Not a good combination."

"True. People think the two things are the same."

"No, they're very different. Take you. You're travelling alone, but I don't get the sense that you're lonely. Some people, they like to be alone. This is healthy. To be lonely, that's something close to desperation. It's reaching for something. Wanting."

That last word seemed to hang in the air. It was a prominent childhood theme I was still in the process of reconciling with in young adulthood. The cycle of wanting things out of reach was proving hard to break.

Leonard seemed pleased with the closure his last word gave and said no more. He drained his wine and went to bed.

I sat in the kitchen, alone with my cup of tea and my lies.

The truth was that I hadn't even started hitch-hiking yet. I'd flown from LA to San Francisco, and taken a handful of buses to get to Caspar. I was scared shitless about sticking my thumb out on the American highways, and Justine's talk of whackos and secluded barns and something bad happening echoed my own fears.

Because it was more wanting: to be a world-weary traveller and a seasoned hitch-hiker, the guy that's been everywhere and done everything and has all these amazing stories to tell. The guy with the deep set eyes and three-day growth who's had some kind of epiphany out on the road, and who knows things about life that other people don't. The guy who doesn't say much, but when he does talk, he imparts a kind of folksy wisdom that everyone listens to and it makes them all stop and think. The guy who breezes into people's lives, has a telling impact, and is gone the next day.

I could already talk a bit like that guy, but was far from being him, and not even close to giving a convincing impersonation. Tomorrow, I was supposed to take my first steps towards becoming that guy. The plan was to go to Fort Bragg for the Fourth of July Salmon Barbecue, then start hitching north for Leggatt.

My main motivation to get started, despite my fears, was that I might stop being the guy I was and become more like the guy I wanted to be.

Wanting a self. To be liked and admired, maybe even to inspire a quiet awe.

***

The next day, Leonard decided to come with me, and promised to drive me out to a hitch-hiking point afterwards. It was very generous of him, but it also meant that I would be impelled to start.

"I've heard about this barbecue," Leonard said in the car. "Thousands of people. They come from all over."

"Yeah. Should be fun."

Justine wasn't with us. Leonard said she'd gone to Mendocino for brunch with her actor friends. In her absence, there was a decidedly different vibe between me and Leonard. He seemed more relaxed; less like an unwilling chaperon and more like a potential travel buddy. He was more talkative, playful and energetic.

When we got to the barbecue, there was already a long line of people snaking around and between the picnic tables, which were set up in rows, with narrow gaps between them, and nearly every space was taken. There was an army of kids running around and chasing each other. The younger kids had balloons of red, white or blue. A band was setting up, doing a sound check. The air was thick with the smell of barbecued salmon and corn cooked on the grill.

Leonard led the way, moving with the assuredness of a local. We joined the back of the line. It edged forward steadily, as there were a dozen barbecues going. As we shuffled forward, Leonard got talking with some folks nearby, his joyful scoff ringing out loudly and making people turn. Despite our accents giving both of us away as clearly being not from Fort Bragg or anywhere in the vicinity, we were well accepted. By the time I had a slab of salmon on my plate, along with a cob of corn, some vegetables and a fluffy-looking roll, we were being taken to a table by a family Leonard had befriended in the line. We squeezed onto the wooden benches and jostled elbows as we ate.

The band started playing, the kind of country-bluesy rock you'd expect at such an event. People got up and danced. Adults danced with children. Dogs ran between the dancers and barked.

The sun was warm and the food was fantastic.

While eating and taking in the scene, I'd missed much of the conversation that was taking place between Leonard and the people we were sitting with. I caught up quickly, because Leonard was speaking with an Australian twang and referring to me as his son, which made us objects of particular interest, with our table partners ramping up the friendliness to show America's true colours on this day of national import.

Someone brought us beers.

Someone brought us dessert.

Someone took our dirty plates away.

A few hours passed. All the while, Leonard held court about Australia, answering questions the likes of which Justine might have asked. No, we don't wrestle crocodiles, but we sometimes eat them. Yes, we have electricity and running water and television and fast food, but Burger King is called Hungry Jacks, even though they offer all the same stuff. Oh, there certainly are dangerous snakes and spiders, and you don't want to mess with them.

The locals loved it.

At one point, I was champion surfer, according to Leonard. Then, when different people sat down, I was a jackaroo. Then a driver of road trains. I'd seen the whole country, apparently, and it was big and marvellous and beautiful, and I was now in America to do the same thing. Leonard explained that, as my concerned father, he'd come over to the States to help me get started on the journey.

The locals really loved that. The tight bonds of family. The togetherness.

One guy offered me a job on his farm. Another had a construction company that was in need of an extra truck driver. And another asked me very seriously if I knew how to dry-wall, because he needed urgent help.

Leonard politely turned them down, saying I was on holiday.

All through these exchanges, I said very little, because I was always at the point of bursting out laughing.

As the barbecue started to wind down, with the band playing slow rock so the couples could dance close together, and with the picnic tables getting folded up and packed into a large truck, there was talk of me and Leonard joining some others to keep the party going, at some shindig in a barn somewhere. Leonard said it was time I got out on the road. After heartfelt (if slightly superficial) goodbyes, the people dispersed to various pick-up trucks and Leonard drove me in his little hatchback out of Fort Bragg. We stopped at the turn-off to Highway 101. I started to get nervous.

"The Americans," Leonard said. "They sure can be friendly when they want to be."

"Yep."

"Sometimes, all you need to do is say the right things. Tell them a story they'd like to hear. Or better, tell them a story they'd like to be part of."

"Right."

"It has been good to meet you. Short, but interesting." Leonard looked at the road and pointed at an area just past the turn-off that had plenty of space for a car to pull over. "That looks like a good spot. Maybe you should try standing over there."

"Thanks, Leonard."

I got out and lifted my backpack and guitar from the boot.

"Good luck." Leonard said. "No need to be scared. Whoever picks you up, try to find some common ground, even if that requires a bit of lying."

I nodded.

As I walked to the spot Leonard had pointed at, he turned his car around and drove back towards Fort Bragg.

It was late afternoon, still warm. I was a bit drunk.

I looked down the greyish road, my first stretch of American highway.

The third car stopped and I was on my way to Leggatt.

Berlin Undergound

Downstairs, in Berlin's Gesundbrunnen train station, there is a green door which thousands of people pass every day, completely ignorant to what lies on the other side.

This door leads to a network of tunnels and bunkers. Special guided walking tours take small groups down there, into the darkness.

Eleven of us, including two guides, pass through the door and go down a long staircase.

At the bottom, the lights are out, but the luminous paint still glows, marking the ways and exits. A sign can be made out: Room 14 – 38 persons. In other rooms, there are old toilets, triple-bunk beds, exposed pipes, old egg-shaped lights with steel frames, and even a *Wehenzimmer* (labour room) for pregnant women.

I imagine frightened people shuffling in with battered suitcases, pots for helmets and small stools to sit on. I see women, children and old people, crowding together, their eyes looking upwards as the city thumps and groans with the rhythm of the bombs.

The rooms are dank and claustrophobic, with low ceilings and thin air. A hand-powered ventilator from World War I is still in working order; it was used to thwart the lethal gases used in that war. The old word for toilet, *Abort*, is used because *Toilette* sounded too French. There are old tubes from the pneumatic dispatch system, remnants from underground breweries, and a railway cart that was used by the *Trümmerfrauen* (rubble women) to move debris to special rubbish hills after World War II. Berlin, once a flat city set along the River Spree, has many such hills.

The Berliner Unterwelten Society has prepared these bunkers for exploration. Every Saturday, they conduct informative tours, with each of the three bunkers set up to explain a different section of history: from World War I through to the Cold War. I find it fascinating to learn how the bunkers were modified and updated over the years to cope with modern war technology, and how the underground train system was used as an air ventilator and later as a means of escape by people from East Germany.

Because the Gesundbrunnen bunkers were left untouched after the construction of the Berlin Wall in 1961, you get an immediate sense of the past. Nothing has changed. It's a time capsule.

The Berliner Unterwelten Society has also prepared the nearby Humbolthain air raid tower, the last of Berlin's three World War II flak towers, for public viewing. The other two were destroyed, with one now a large hill in Friedrichshain (the Grosse Bunkerberg), and the other incorporated into the Berlin Zoo.

There are more than a hundred bunkers in Berlin. Many are underground, like the four-level bunker at Alexanderplatz, in the centre of the city. One also enters that bunker from an inconspicuous door in a train station. It is open to the public and houses art exhibitions. Indeed, the location is as interesting as the art.

This bunker is also amazingly well preserved, untouched since World War II. It feels like it has only been given a once over cleaning before opening for exhibition. The rooms are bare, with rusted steel door hinges and frames. I imagine the civilians huddled in here during air raids, down so deep at the fourth level they only just feel the tremors of bombs, and maybe panicking, because it feels like the walls are closing in; even the least claustrophobic person would become anxious down here. I do, and I'm in here to look at art.

Hitler had grandiose plans for his bunkers. From 1940 to 1944, there were over a thousand in Berlin. Included was an extensive network of underground tunnels, with one running from the government sector in Mitte to the airport in Templehof. Hermann Goering could ride in his car the seven kilometres from his Luftwaffe building on Wilhelm Strasse to the airport in secret. Connected to this tunnel was the famous Führerbunker.

After the fall of the Berlin Wall in 1989, historians excavated Hitler's bunker, where he had orchestrated "total victory or total annihilation", married Eva Braun when all was lost, before taking his bride's life and his own. From 1961 to 1989, the bunker had remained untouched in no man's land at the border between East and West Germany. When historians went in, they found of wealth of treasures: dinner menus, Nazi paintings, hair brushes, plates, and some rooms left exactly as they were, including the children's room of the family Goebbels, with the wire bunk beds unmoved, as if the children were coming back to sleep there that night.

Worried the site would become a Nazi shrine, the German authorities destroyed the bunker and built office buildings and apartment blocks over it. The large Holocaust Memorial was placed nearby, where nearly three thousand concrete slabs fill an area the size of a city block. A great historical find was lost, but for sound reasons. The German people struggle hard with their legacy, and the world transpires to never let them forget. Some Germans believe that current and future generations should be held accountable for the actions of past generations, while other Germans distant themselves from the past.

What makes exploring Berlin's bunkers so fascinating is that they were the bunkers of ordinary citizens; the people who perhaps held no political ideology and just got caught in the middle. Every war has millions of such people.

Many of the remaining bunkers are located in suburban areas, surrounded by apartment buildings and offices. Interestingly, while the city has been built around these bunkers, they don't really look out of place. People walk past these buildings every day without giving them a second glance; they are as much a part of Berlin's cityscape as any building.

Such is the case with the aboveground bunkers on Palais Strasse and Reinhardt Strasse; you have to look hard to find them. They are still perfectly intact and are used for special art exhibitions, discussions and theatrical performances. The bunker on Reinhardt Strasse has a rather poignant red cross painted above the back entrance, and is located across the street from a university cafeteria.

Another suburban bunker, located at Anhalter Bahnhof, is open to the public all year round. It houses the Gruselkabinett (Cabinet of Horrors), a grisly exhibition of medicine practices in the Middle Ages, replete with screaming people and cracking bones. In the underground level, there is an excellent display of the bunker's history: with newspapers from wartime, an outline of the last days of the Führerbunker, and air recordings from allied planes.

Sadly, with most of Berlin's bunkers privately owned, trying to visit them all presents a bit of a headache. There is no such Berlin Bunker Tour. Other underground areas of note include the radiation-proof bunker located under the Story of Berlin museum, an underground hospital in Wannsee, and the ghostly rebuilding of the abandoned Potsdamer Platz train station.

Several underground stations in Mitte, which were left unused between 1961 and 1989 as the borderline cut the network in half, are also quite unnerving, even though they have been refurbished and are in use today. When Berlin fell in 1945, many citizens fled into the underground network to escape the street-fighting. The Russians blasted the canal walls of the Spree River and flooded the network, killing thousands. Many still believe the underground is haunted. BVG, the Berlin public transport company, runs tours every Friday night in an open topped train.

No other city in the world captures twentieth century history quite like Berlin, and all the remnants remain to warn, remind and educate.

The Cheese Factory

Let me say right off the bat that I'm a complete idiot, a buffoon, a moron of such stupendous magnitude that I should be locked away in a crazy house sharing a room with a gorilla named Gerald. I am a colossal fool, completely uncultured, uneducated, poorly dressed, but fortunately not quite ugly enough to have to put a bag over my head.

You see, I was in Italy, taking in the sights, marvelling at the churches and galleries, drinking wine with my meals, and eating spaghetti with a fork and spoon like the locals do. I thought I was cultured. I thought I knew Italy. But when I rolled into Parma, I realised how ignorant I am.

The train station was inconspicuous, with most trains arriving and departing late, while a cast of derelict extras bandied about, as is the norm in Italian cities. I wandered towards the old town, along Via Giuseppe Verdi and then under the towers of the enormous Pilotta Palace, which looks more like a prison than a former royal residence. A narrow bridge took me across the Parma River and into the Parco Ducale to see another palace. I took a turn around the garden. Parma certainly was a delightful place, and I liked the green areas, the water, and the slow pace. A negative was that the city had a rather strange smell.

I meandered back into the old town and passed the famed opera house, the Regio Theatre. There was to be a concert that night. *La Traviata* it was called, by some guy named Verdi. I assumed he was perhaps a local of note and so bought a ticket. I then spent a sufficient amount of time in the cathedral admiring the altar and ceiling. Though I must confess that after several weeks of seeing churches in all parts of Italy, I couldn't help but feel they all looked the same. I kept seeing fat cherubs when I closed my eyes, like they were sunspots.

My humble hotel was nearby and I checked in. The receptionist advised me to eat at such and such a restaurant and to try the Pesto di Cavallo. My word that sounded good, and you can't go wrong with pesto. I headed for the restaurant, consulting my phrasebook on the way. Cavallo was horse. I think the receptionist was having a joke with me. But I still walked towards the restaurant he recommended, down the shopping stretch of Strada della Repubblica and across the Piazza Garibaldi. There's a statue of Garibaldi too, looking proud, earnest and somewhat rotund, with a head full of hair. I wonder who he was.

The restaurant was empty. Perhaps I was too late; it was almost seven. The waiter looked at me with consternation, as if I'd walked in when the restaurant was closed. Unperturbed, I took a seat. Pesto di Cavallo was on the menu, but I ordered anolini, described as beef filled pasta served with gravy. I asked the waiter for the house wine and he served me a cold, bubbly red called Lambrusco, so fizzy it was like drinking sherbet. But I nodded approvingly, trying to convince him what an aficionado I am. He then served my meal and rather impudently splashed parmesan all over the top. I looked at him with surprise.

"I didn't ask for that," I said.

"Everything comes with cheese," he said, walking away.

"Why?"

The waiter knitted his bushy eyebrows together and cocked his head slightly. "This is Parma, home of Parmigiano."

"What's that?"

The waiter's mouth dropped open and I could see his tongue was velvet red. He came over to me and thrust the small cheese bowl in my face.

"Parmesan," he said.

"Really? I always thought it came from America."

The waiter took a short step backwards. The cheese bowl clattered on the table, but none was spilt. He began to laugh, his shoulders bouncing up and down. He slipped into the kitchen. There was a brief silence, then more loud laughter, and coming not just from the waiter.

The anolini was good, but the cheese tasted the same as parmesan does everywhere. They were still laughing in the kitchen, but I was determined not to be embarrassed. How was I to know parmesan was from Parma? The waiter came out with the chef in tow. Both of their faces were red and the waiter's eyes were glistening. They spoke in a frenzy of Italian, pointing at me as they talked and laughed. The chef kept shaking his head in disbelief while the waiter ducked behind the bar. He came back with another bottle of Lambrusco, different to the one he had poured for me, and then both men sat down at my table.

"You Americans are so stupid," the waiter said, pouring glasses for himself and the chef, and pouring a new glass for me.

"Hey, I'm Australian."

The waiter shrugged his shoulders as if this made no difference.

The cook then started babbling incoherently and the waiter nodded his head.

"He say you shall go to the factory."

"What factory?"

"The Parmigiano factory." He said something in Italian to the chef, who laughed so hard, small drops of Lambrusco came out of his nose. He wiped them away with the back of his hand.

I paid, left and went to the opera.

The next morning, I set off in search of a parmesan factory. The woman at the tourist office explained that tours had to be booked twenty days in advance, but given that it was winter, there might be a chance. She made a few quick phone calls. I could do the tour tomorrow.

I killed the day, visited the palaces again, the Stuard Gallery and the Farnese Theatre. Parma was very nice, even with the smell, but without the crowds of places like Florence and Rome. Indeed, there didn't seem to be any tourists here at all. I had the Stuard Gallery pretty much to myself. I assumed I wasn't the only one ignorant about the origin of the local cheese.

The factory tour the next day was fascinating. And what an aroma. The tour was free, took two hours and followed the entire process of making parmesan. The guide explained intently, as if outlining the creation of life, that they add rennet, an enzyme from the stomach of calves, which causes the milk to curdle. Then, a balloon whisk called a *spino* is used to stir the curdled milk and make it smooth. The cheese is then heated, lifted from the cauldron, and placed in a special mould for three days. The blocks are then salted in brine for twenty days and aged for two years.

I had thought the factory might be run by some mad recluse dolled up like a cartoon character, a Willy Wonka of cheese, who had spent years locked away perfecting this cheese-making process. But no, the factory was very organised and far from eccentric. They've been making the cheese the same way for over eight hundred years.

Stepping outside, I thanked the tour guide and asked some more questions about parmesan and Parma.

"Of course," he said, "we can't forget the ham. We cheesemakers are not the sole gastronomical kings of Parma."

"What ham?"

The guide gave me a look similar to the one the waiter had given me, somewhere between confusion and mockery.

"Why, Prosciutto, Parma ham. You can buy it everywhere in the world, and you can tour the factory where they make it."

"You're kidding me. Prosciutto is from Parma too?"

Romans, Rieslings and Riders

The vineyards cling to the steep cliffs, extending upwards in harmonious symmetry, shimmering with green and gold. The air is alive with the scent of corks two thousand years old. Paths lead to mediaeval hamlets crammed onto hairpin river bends.

Clicking through the gears, the river bank rolls by. There's a tempting route through a vineyard, to perhaps taste another boutique drop made by a tenth generation local. A fine dry Riesling it will be, part of the recent shift of Moselle vintners towards making dry whites with a mineral soul.

The *Radwege* (cycle paths) are flat and smooth, winding from Trier to Koblenz. They hug the river or meander through vineyards. Historic villages, some with wine-making dating back two millennia, appear as each bend is skirted. The blue-grey slate church towers rise from the centre and the ruins of a castle sit on the hill above. Each *Weinberg* has its own name, its own particular taste, character and history.

"The roots run deep into the soil," says Raimund Prüm of S.A. Prüm. His family has owned vineyards here since 1156. For the Moselle, where the Romans were the first vintners, this is not unusual.

Doors are open for tastings and vintners talk eagerly with passing cyclists about heritage and harvests, about the new dry Rieslings of which they are so proud. They readily admit global warming has had an impact, but the current generation is paying closer attention to detail and balance. Yes, those shrill wines of a decade ago are long gone.

The proliferation of bikers means more street traffic. Vintners are ready to show their wares. They look down the narrow alleys for approaching pedal-pushers and litter the cycle paths with signs pointing to their estates. For bikers, these worthy diversions make the kilometres drift away and each day leads to something undiscovered.

Day 1 – Trier to Trittenheim

Trier to Koblenz requires four relaxed days of cycling, and it's ever so slightly downhill. The Moselle cycle route begins in Metz, France, but the most popular stretch starts in Germany's oldest city. The former capital of the West Roman Empire has a bevy of sights, including the second century Porta Nigra, and the day begins with a few lazy loops of the old town. Leaving Trier, the path runs through an industrial area that, past Mehring, gives way to the beauty of the Moselle as the river starts to curve and reveal its splendour.

It's so peaceful. The only motors are small tractors and monorail trains going up and down the steep hillsides, or maybe a boat. Small specks of workers weave between the vines, their heels digging into the slate. It's tempting to stop at each village and vintner, but Trittenheim awaits. There, wine from the south-facing vineyard, Trittenheimer Apotheke (pharmacy), is reputed to have therapeutic qualities.

The village sits on a thumb of land. The steep cliffs across the bank have been carved into terraces. There are dozens of estates, but Niko Schmitt, at thirty-four years old part of the young generation of local vintners, says competition raises the level of quality.

"We're friends," says the manager of Claes Schmitt Erben. "We always test the wine together. When one of us makes a good wine and the rest of us learn, that's good for all of us. That's good for the image of the Moselle."

Niko and I sit at a long slate table, on the hillside among his vines, and look down on Trittenheim as we sip wine. It's late spring, warm, and the sun slowly sets over the village. Niko explains that the wine he makes is best drunk at leisure, outside, in small sips.

After a day of riding, I should be downing sports drinks and replacing electrolytes and all that rubbish. Well, you can keep that. The best recovery drink is a slowly consumed glass of Moselle Riesling.

Day 2 – Trittenheim to Traben-Trarbach

The Moselle is an amazing river. Somehow, it turns, loops and bends back on itself, coiling like a snake. Villages straddle either a straight stretch or are wedged onto a sharp bend. Often, two are joined as one. The first hyphenated village is Neumagen-Dhron, Germany's oldest wine town. The epicurean Romans left their mark here. There is a replica of a Roman wine ship in the harbour, while a stone version adorns a wine dealer's third century grave. Across the river in Piesport, there is a giant Roman wine press at the base of the vineyards of Piesporter Goldtröpfchen (drops of gold).

A rare straight section leads past Castle Lieser, then down to the Moselle's most popular double-barrelled village, Bernkastel-Kues. The red and brown half-timbered houses crowd the mediaeval market square and lean on the point of collapse. The steep vineyards here are called Bernkastler Doktor, the most esteemed being the estate of Dr Loosen.

Bernkastel-Kues is best described as a giant jewel box. It's a fairytale village made real, a very popular stop for the tour-bus crowd, and rightly so.

The coming vineyards have great names: Graacher Himmelreich (kingdom of heaven), Wehlener Sonnenuhr (sundial), Kröver Nacktarsch (naked bottom). Raimund Prüm, who has his estates on the sundial, is quick to say that the cyclists have been good for business.

"Of course," he says smiling, "they need to know something about wine or they won't stop."

Knowing about the estates makes this bicycle trip more fulfilling. As a wine dunce, it's a pleasure for me to talk with the vintners, to test their wine and hear their opinions on industry shifts and climate change.

"We don't really have bad vintages anymore," says Jan Klein of Staffelter Hof, one of the oldest wineries in Germany, established in 862, and with vineyards in Kröv, Piesport and Dhron. "We have the problem that the grapes get too ripe. In 2005, we made dry whites with up to fourteen per cent alcohol."

After all the tastings, the bike is a little shaky on the last stretch to Traben-Trarbach, the day's final hyphenated town. The late afternoon sun shines on the village's distinctive Art Nouveau buildings. On the terrace of the Hotel Bellevue, the glasses of Riesling glimmer and sparkle – dry whites with slate at their heart.

Day 3 – Traben-Trarbach to Cochem

After two days of riding, tasting and savouring, the trip has attained a pleasant rhythm. The villages seem close together at the start of the day, but drift further apart as the legs start to tire. Bridges are few, but small ferries fill the void, taking you and the bike across the river for one euro.

From the base of Marienburg, one ferry crosses to Pünderich, where, this morning, the streets fanning out from the sixteenth century town hall are deserted. It's another jewel box of a village, impeccably kept, and typical of many that line the Moselle. Zell is another. The vineyards there are called Zeller Schwartzer Katz, and the town's main square has a snarling black cat on top of a wine barrel.

Further north in Bremm is Europe's steepest vineyard. The crisp, dusty wines of the Calmont have a mineral quality that makes you smack your mouth after swallowing.

"The vineyards are special because of the slate," says Ulrich Franzen of Weingut Reinhold Franzen, "and because they're sixty-five degrees steep."

In Beilstein, the cliffs are just as dramatic. Numerous German movies have been filmed in this exceedingly picturesque village, including *Der Schinderhannes* with Curd Jürgens. But what really takes the breath away is skirting the last bend to Cochem. Sitting on a vineyard-covered hill above the town, Castle Reichsburg could be the setting for every fairytale ever written.

In the old town, the narrow alleys are quaint and packed. Cochem gets almost three million visitors a year. This incredible setting is a just reward for the day's ride.

Day 4 – Cochem to Koblenz

Leaving Cochem, the bike goes forward with reluctance. The path ahead isn't terribly inviting. How nice was the stretch from Trittenheim to Cochem, when the solitary, tree-lined path cut through vineyards in full, fruit-scented bloom.

There are still charming villages and castles, including Burg Thurant in Alkan, and the exquisite Burg Eltz, a little way off the path near Moselkern, but the path follows the highway and the rustle of vines has unfortunately been replaced by engines. Closer to Koblenz, the river straightens and industrial areas fan out with ugly consistency. The path ends at the Deutsches Eck (German Corner) in Koblenz, where the Moselle meets the Rhine.

Koblenz has an attractive castle, but the rebuilt old town is given over to consumerism, making it seem like a ye olde shopping mall. The Rhine is wide and straight, but can't compare to the vineyard-lined cliffs of the twisting, curving, snaking Moselle. There also isn't the enchantment of places like Bernkastel-Kues or Beilstein. People drinking wine here do so quickly, with large sips. It's not quite the slow savouring that Niko Schmitt called for in Trittenheim.

It's the heart of the Moselle that captures the imagination and exhilarates the palette. Those small villages nestled onto river bends, where vines grow in slate on sheer cliffs. There, the afternoons are long and dinners are drawn out celebrations. The legs have a pleasant weariness from the day's ride, and each glass of crisp, fresh Riesling is apt reward for effort. Time dissipates, heartbeats slow, and the coolness of a wine glass tickles the tips of your bike-sore fingers.

The Cage

There's an outdoor basketball court at Washington Square in New York City that's surrounded by a very high mesh fence. A bit like a prison yard, though that's probably not the best comparison. The pick-up games go on all day, either half court or full court, but really get going in the afternoon and on weekends. People hang on the fence and watch. An awful lot of talking goes on, from the spectators, the players and the guys hanging court-side waiting (or wanting) to play.

I was in New York in September. It was warm and muggy. I had no intention of playing basketball. I didn't have baggy shorts or any kind of team jersey. I had only a pair of running shoes and tennis shorts.

I found the court by chance, while wandering around Soho, the West Village and Noho. Watching the games, I thought I'd be able to hold my own, if they let me play.

The court had a small entrance which was sort of guarded by two guys. They were big, but not athletic, and they seemed to be just watching the game, except they would sometimes turn approaching players away by shuffling together and blocking the entrance, or part slightly to allow entry to a selected few others. I wondered if they were just buddies with some of the guys already playing, guarding the entrance so their pals could get more court time.

I approached the entrance and stood there until I got their attention.

"What you want?"

"I wanna play."

They both laughed. The guy on the left put a fist to his mouth and laughed into it. They even high-fived.

"You think you can run with these guys?"

"Yeah, I reckon so."

"What's that accent? Y'all from Canada?"

"Australia."

"No shit?" More laughing. "I didn't think you Crocodile Dundees played basketball."

Another high-five.

"This one does."

"Let him in. He'll make a fool of hisself."

"That's right. Get his ass kicked."

"Yeah, well, we'll see about that," I said.

The two guys parted just enough to let me past.

"Ain't no money out here, boy."

"I'm no hustler. I just wanna play some ball."

I skirted the court, walking slowly to where three other players were waiting. I tried to walk along the court like I'd done it a thousand times, like I belonged here, but I didn't think I was very convincing. The other guys eyed me suspiciously, clearly wondering what I was doing here.

And what was I doing here? Why wasn't I in line for tickets to a Broadway show or art-gazing at MoMA and the Met? I was in New York City, and all I wanted to do was play basketball? I didn't even have any insurance. What if I got hurt? What if I got into a fight? What if I got my arse kicked?

Seeing the physicality of the game up close, getting hurt appeared the most likely. It had all seemed much slower and placid from behind the mesh fence.

But I was court-side; there could be no turning back. This was where the action was. Come on, NYC, let's play ball.

While brutal, the game was scrappy and disorganised. No players were willing to share the ball, or to pass and move, or to set screens and make space, or to sacrifice their own game in order to spread the floor. If a player got the ball, he stood there dribbling, took a shot or tried to make a move off the dribble. All the right-handers went right, while the left-handers went left. With the shot missed or the ball turned over, the other four players would berate the player on the way back down court and tell him to "Pass the ball, fool."

Of course, in pick-up games like these, you normally get five guys playing in a team who have never played together, so it's hard for them to develop any teamwork or cohesion. However, it's also in games like these that guys just want to score and show-off.

Defenders took the linebacker approach: blocking the space, hand-checking, holding and pushing guys out. There was no help defence, no switching, no hands in the passing lane. There was a lot of hacking, with guys calling fouls on every hack and the hacker denying it, claiming "That was all ball."

Scores normally came from turnovers, defensive mistakes and fast-breaks, or from circus shots that somehow found the metal net. A two-pointer was worth one and a three-pointer was worth two.

The game was a total brick-fest, a clang-a-thon. It was taking a fair while for either team to reach the required eleven points.

When the score was nine-eight, a tall, brawny guy entered the court. He was a head taller than me (and I'm pretty tall), cut, and wearing a very white singlet, like it was straight out of the packet. He walked up to me.

"Hey, you got next?" He had a deep, smooth voice. The Barry White of basketball.

"What?"

"Y'all got next?"

"Who? Me? Nah. I just got here."

"Well, I wonder who got it."

I pointed to the guy at the front of the line. "Maybe he has."

"Yo! Y'all got next?"

"Yeah. I got it."

"Then, we be running with you."

The guy looked at me, then at the big guy. "I got you, but I ain't takin him."

The large man placed a very large hand on my shoulder. "We's both running with you."

"Yeah, aight. Yeah, okay."

That was easy, I thought. The hand patted my shoulder a few times.

"You throw me the rock, white boy. Every time."

Ah, so that was the catch. He wanted a feeder.

When it was point-game, I started to do some stretching. I was nervous, which was good, because it meant I was ready to play. While not as athletic and physical as the other players, working in my favour was that I had smarts and that I'd played some seriously organised basketball. I had been well-coached and knew what to do, where to run and how to be sneaky. I was also fit, confident that I could run these guys off the court.

People think that basketball is all about shooting, jumping and quickness, but smarts, awareness and sneakiness also get you a long way. One example: a guy can't score if he doesn't have the ball, so don't let him get the ball. Another: most guys never know where to look or how to see the whole court, so move when they take their eyes off you. And finally: basketball is a team sport that requires five guys to work in unison at both ends of the court, so always put the team first.

A voice spoke from behind the fence. "You gonna get killed out there."

Again the big guy came to my defence. "I got ya back. Keep it close and throw me the rock."

"Alright. Got it."

Perhaps he figured that I could play simply because I had been allowed to enter the cage.

"You from California or somethin?"

"A bit further west. Australia."

"Hell no." His face lit up, his eyes widening and his mouth opening in a broad smile to reveal perfect and gleaming white teeth. "I always wanted to go there."

"You should."

Point-game lasted another five minutes or so, as guys hogged the ball and threw up ludicrous shots in the hope of hitting the winning basket. I talked with the big guy; we exchanged names.

From St Lucia, James was working in New York as an actor and model. He confessed he mostly did modelling, as he was too tall to be an actor and only got roles as muscle, thugs or heavies. I had the feeling he could play a little, and not because of his size and his demand that I throw him the ball. He looked comfortable standing on the court, had something of a relaxed swagger. Or was it an act? James getting into his basketball character, replete with his straight-out-of-the-packet white singlet.

The game was finally over. The winning team stayed on court, while the losers walked off, all berating and arguing with each other. There was a bit of pushing. A fight nearly broke out. But these guys were all bluster and show, which was also why they sucked at basketball; they just wanted to score and look good. They couldn't do the little things that mattered.

The guy who had "next" assembled his team. There were no introductions.

"Give me the ball," he said. "Aight? Pass the rock to me."

The winning team got first use of the ball. Before it was checked, the talking began.

"Hey, lookie here, we got Larry Bird playin."

"Yeah, but this Larry Bird ain't got shit."

The player I was defending gave me a shove, then got in my face. "You don't belong out here, white bread. Why don't you go back to playschool?"

I was never one for heckling, but I thought, hey, this is New York. Why not get involved?

"Mate," I said, "you are not even gonna touch the ball."

He laughed. "Listen to country boy talkin trash. Hey, yo, gimme that rock."

The ball was checked and I got into a defensive position, but moved a little more ball-side. As the pass was (reluctantly) thrown to my direct opponent, a lazy, looping pass at that, I put a hand in the passing lane and knocked the ball forward. I reacted the quickest, picked the ball up on the dribble, beat the lazy transition defence down the other end and laid the ball up.

One-zip.

On the way back, James gave me a high-five. "Good hustle, Sam."

"It's Cam."

"Ain't no thing. Keep hustlin."

From then on, it was all about positioning and reading the play. My opponent never touched the ball, because I overplayed him on defence and kept putting a hand in the passing lane. He wasn't smart enough to go back door, or to try to lose me by setting a screen or two and getting a switch. When he tried to get in the post, I shuffled him towards the baseline, taking him out of position and preventing him from getting his feet set. He got frustrated and started pushing me in order to get free. He even threw a couple of elbows, which I managed to evade. But by that time, I'd already intercepted four passes and scored off them, and his teammates had stopped throwing the ball to him. That meant I could step back a little and play some sneaky defence. This included stealing the ball from behind a player and picking up rebounds off wayward shots. With rebounding, if you're not blanketing a player and you've got more time on defence, you can read the ball off the rim and get into the right position. Great rebounders are always in the right position, and they're not necessarily the tallest players on the court. They move when the other players are ball-watching.

I was having a blast. The better I played, the more trash-talk was thrown my way.

When we had a half-court offense going, I gave the ball to James. I also tried to move, set screens and maintain good spacing. The other guys in my team seemed to pick up on the effectiveness of this and started doing it too. They even started passing the ball, which was good because I was always wide open.

A neat, highly useful basketball trick is losing your opponent on offense the second he takes his eyes off you. It's easy enough, especially with guys who have never played organised ball, with guys who are more interested in playing offense than defence and with guys who ball-watch. You get to a position on the court (I always used the baseline corners), and wait for your direct opponent to start turning his head. And he will turn his head, in order to keep an eye on you and an eye on the ball; he might even ball-watch the whole time, thinking that you're out of the play on the weak-side. Let him do it a few times, get him thinking he's got you covered, then move when he's looking at the ball. By the time he looks back, you're standing under the hoop, wide open. If you're playing with the right players who know about spacing and ball movement, you'll get the ball and take an easy shot.

In this pick-up game, where every player wanted to score and no one was willing to pass, it took four "blind cuts" and me standing under the basket waving my arms in the air before a teammate finally passed me the ball. And that teammate was James.

I used the same strategy to get a couple of offensive rebounds as well, which I laid back in.

We won eleven-four and I scored eight of our points. James got the other three.

The game being finished didn't stop the trash-talking. But I wasn't listening. Winning is the most telling trash-talk of all.

The losing team left the court and a new team came on.

We won that game too. The team was starting to click; the other guys started passing the ball to me more. Despite using the same tricks over and over, no one got wise, and I continued my sneaky tactics to great success.

Another team, another victory.

As the afternoon wore on, the level of the players got progressively better. But while the skills improved, the basketball intelligence stayed about the same. The games were closer and more intense, but we still won.

When it was too dark to play and everyone started drifting away, the five of us sat with our backs against the mesh fence. James was all right, but the other three were so exhausted and thirsty, they couldn't speak. A water bottle was being passed between them and they were really sucking from it.

James had sweated through his first singlet and had already swapped it for a fresh one. And they were straight out of the packet, because his bag was full of packaged singlets. He saw me looking and said, "I did a shoot for them last week. You want one?"

My own shirt was drenched with sweat. I took it off and gave it a few rings. "Yeah, I do. If you've got one to spare."

James smiled. "Extra large. Little big for ya."

"I'll take it." I ripped the packet open and put the singlet on.

As the other three players got to their feet, slapped our hands and walked away, James and I stayed sitting there, talking. I bet we looked like an odd couple, both of us in our white singlets. Mine seriously baggy.

James was funny, yet his voice was always low and deadly serious, which seemed to make him even funnier.

He told me about some recent shoots, and about how hard it was to make a living in New York. He explained basketball was an outlet for his anger and frustration. He also said that this afternoon was the best he'd ever played.

"You got skills, man," he said.

"Thanks. But I never would've got on the court without you stepping in."

"Ain't no thing." James paused, then said, "You played, right?"

"Played what?"

"Come on, man. Someone like you, playing in this cage. The way you play. You got to have game."

"Just enough to beat these guys."

James laughed a little. "The games are tougher on the weekend. College kids and old pros. Hard to even get into those games."

"I'm leaving on Friday anyway."

"Too bad."

"But I'll be down tomorrow afternoon, for another run."

"Shyeah, if they let you in."

Romeo, Juliet and Me

"There is no world without Verona's walls." So whined Romeo to Friar Laurence after the Franciscan had commented that, "Here from Verona art thou banished; be patient for the world is broad and wide." Ah, but what did Larry know about romance? How could the friar understand how moved Romeo was, by love for Juliet and for his home?

Romeo believed there was no world outside of Verona. A rather limited view, but still I venture forth into the narrow confines of this northern Italian city, in search of the romance which so filled young Romeo's heart. I follow his footsteps, thrusting my codpiece towards maidens and wenches alike, my tasselled loafers pounding the aged cobblestones, my tights itching my thighs. Romeo is somewhere within Verona's walls and I am intent on finding him. Perhaps he could explain why this city, and Juliet, made him wax so lyrically. But, as Mercutio mused, "Where the devil should this Romeo be?" I worry that the young romantic may be hard to locate.

The villagers are out in number on this sunny morn, bidding each other a hearty Buongiorno and going about their business, hustling to market or to office. They are dressed in their finery, parading around the Piazza Bra and the Piazza Erbe. And visiting princes, princesses, ladies and lords dismount from their carriages, instruments of photography in hand, and do laps of the first century Roman arena, their jewels glittering in the morning sun, their straight noses thrust into the air. Romeo is not among them and rightly so, for they have come from outside Verona's walls, day-trippers wedged into the unromantic confines of a whirlwind tour, recording romance in digital and not in verse.

Thus, do I steer my codpiece towards the narrow alleys of Verona's old town, away from the bustling hordes crowding around their steel and chrome carriages, and down tight streets immersed in shadow, where orange and pink villas lean against each other and frilly nothings flutter from strings cast out from shuttered windows.

These constricted walkways close one in, but then open into wide courtyards where young maidens dance around wells, their sing-song voices light and lustrous. Alas, maybe they don't exactly dance, but they do gather around tiny screens held in their hands, at what looks to be an old well. The sun shines on their heavenly cheeks. Yes, "arise, fair sun, and kill the envious moon." Amid giggles these maidens scamper away. Perhaps a larger codpiece is required, and tights in a richer and more noble shade of purple. Or I'll have to text them my romantic verse.

At any rate, I need assistance. So, to the house of Montague. Maybe Romeo has some accoutrements befitting a true romantic. But he is not at home; he has even left a message on the door saying that he has lost himself and is "some other where." Lurking below Juliet's balcony no doubt. Alright. On to the villa of Capulet. But it's so crowded, one cannot even pass the front gate. The visiting princes and princesses are jostling while scrawling on the walls, "Deano loves Debbie" or some such, written in pen on a thumb of chewing gum. Others paw at the statue of Juliet, rubbing her right breast, for luck they claim, until that bronze bosom sheens like gold. Romeo would be appalled if he saw this spectacle. I shall return under the cover of night, when all is still, and "with love's light wings…o'er perch these walls, for stony limits cannot hold love out."

Some air, some air, leave these wantons behind and escape. Romeo is surely with his friends Mercutio and Benvolio, funsters who prefer wit and jest to matters of the heart. As the swift tongued Mercutio says of jesting, "Why, is not this better now than groaning for love?" Why, yes. Perhaps these good fellows are trading jibes at the Castel San Pietro, on top of the hill and looking down on the old city. Or are they hamming it up at the ruins of the Teatro Romano? My tasselled loafers take me to these locales, but Romeo is nowhere to be seen. I even venture inside the Duomo to admire the altar and seek a priest's counsel, as Romeo had sought out Friar Laurence, but the church is empty.

Hither and whither I go, criss-crossing Verona's alleys and streets. The colours are striking, the villas and houses in brilliant yellows and warm reds. Balconies jut out from buildings. I look up, hoping to see a young beauty pouring her heart out to the morning sun: "My only love sprung from my only hate!" The balconies are empty, but these romantic houses inspire me. Yes, Romeo was right. The city is enchanting, the old town a vessel of passion. Lovers journey from lands afar to marry or become engaged within Verona's walls. Couples rekindle their lovers' flame, while closet romantics find their true loves sitting in outdoor cafés on the Piazza Erbe or striding along the Via Mazzini.

But it is Romeo I seek, not love. Perhaps young Montague has ventured out into the country, to find peace and solitude on Lake Garda or in the mountains around Lessinia. If he has, then I will never find him, for the nature surrounding Verona is both vast and beautiful.

Hang on. What was it the friar had advised after Romeo was banished from Verona? Of course. "Sojourn in Mantua." I mount my trusty steed. Onward, Trenitalia.

It is rumoured the plague is present in Mantua. I can't believe that. For this is an enchanting city, surrounded by waters of crystal purity and with a labyrinth of historic buildings. "Fearful of infection," no way. The streets and squares are almost as beautiful as Verona's, and my galloping stallion Trenitalia brought me here in under an hour. There is good food and fine local wine; the Lambrusco is chilled and the ham finely smoked. Why, most certainly Romeo and Juliet could have escaped to this city together and had a wonderful life. There are many theatres, the striking Castillo di San Giorgio, some magnificent churches, and no feuding families. Juliet would have been out from under the calloused thumb of Lady Capulet at last.

But my own Balthasar brings me news, a text message that says Juliet "sleeps in Capel's monument, and her immortal part with angels lives." Trenitalia returns me swiftly to Verona. Romeo, from the wealthy Montague family, is richer than me and can afford an express steed, getting him there fifteen minutes faster. I run to Juliet's tomb on the Via del Pontiere, and the crowd there suggests something is amiss. The princes and princesses have gadgets that click and whirr and flash, but the tomb itself is empty. No Juliet, nor her Romeo. In this tomb did "the fearful passage of their death-mark'd love" come to an end. Did romance die here too? I stagger outside with the princes, but do not board their bloated carriage.

My tasselled loafers stumble on the cobblestones. Night is starting to fall. "The sun for sorrow will not show his head." The narrow alleys of the old town seem even more romantic at night. The restaurant windows are illuminated by candles, and old fashioned streetlights burn like fluttering torches from days of yore. Soft light, the stars sparkling in the sky above. I squeeze my codpiece through the gate to the House of Capulet just before the gate closes behind me. The walkway is dark. I am happy I cannot see the graffiti and chewing-gum splattered walls. There's the famed balcony, jutting out from a wall of solid brick. Romeo would have to have been an

44

expert free-climber to mount that wall for a kiss on the balcony. Or he brought a ladder.

I kneel at the statue of Juliet, her face so pensive and pure, so young. Flesh for the taking. An ugly thought wheedles its way into my mind: perhaps Romeo was not in love at all, and only hungry for honeymoon desserts. As the friar commented after Romeo's love had switched so quickly from Rosaline to Juliet: "So soon forsaken? Young men's love then lies, not truly in their hearts but in their eyes." O cynical friar, tucked away in your cell, can you really know what moves men's hearts?

This sad statue of Juliet tugs at the heartstrings, calls forth memories of love lost. This story of woe, whose legacy is locked inside Verona's walls, echoes down the streets and influences and ignites the lives and loves of all those who venture here, be they romantics, lovers, cynics or codpiece-clad fools.

Autobahn

As a hitch-hiker, I figured Germany would be my promised land. The Autobahn, lots of cars, fast rides, maybe a bit of Kraftwerk coming through the stereo.

Fun.

I arrived armed with the usual stereotypes. Everything works and runs on time. The people aren't very friendly. They're punctual, reserved, efficient and a bit uptight. Good-looking and dull and humourless.

But the Germans I knew, and was planning to visit, went against the grain somewhat. They liked very much to laugh, weren't always on time and were a pretty laid-back bunch.

I knew they built great cars in Germany. And that there was no speed limit on the Autobahn. Beer was plentiful. The sausages were supposed to be very good.

My starting point was Munich. On my first hitch-hiking day, I wanted to get to Berlin, some six hundred kilometres away. It was November, cold, grey and dark.

Because I thought it would be easy, and that I'd be travelling at maximum speeds in Porsches and BMWs, I took my time getting started. Which was foolish, as my attempts to make my way to an Autobahn entry ramp with public transport were hampered by a lack of understanding of said public transport's map, which appeared to me as some artistic expression of squigglism.

Finally on a ramp, the only car that stopped in the first hour was a police car, with the officer politely informing me that it was okay for me to stand on the ramp, but that it was illegal to hitch-hike on the Autobahn. His English was very good.

While waiting, I noticed that standing on a ramp made it difficult to get a ride; as the cars entered the ramp, they roared up to high speeds, preparing to join the flow of the Autobahn. No one looked like stopping. The drivers stared straight ahead.

I got my first ride just before noon, in a red car. I couldn't tell what brand it was, but it certainly wasn't anything fancy, or recognisably German.

When the car stopped in front of me, the driver didn't lower his window. He simply sat there, with the engine idling, eyes forward, waiting for me to get in.

As we got underway, he – spectacle-wearing, studious-type, almost junkie-skinny, in pipe jeans and a black skivvy – said something which I didn't understand. I said "Berlin" in reply.

He returned with a substantial volley, from which I picked out the word Nürnberg, which sounded to me like Nuremberg, the next big city north of Munich.

Okay. Not Berlin, but heading north. I was left wondering what else he had said.

He drove fast. Better said: he attempted to drive fast. Because after only twenty minutes or so of driving, it became apparent to me that "no speed limit" on the Autobahn was a superb idea in theory, but it didn't quite work in practice. There was too much traffic, there were sections of the Autobahn under repair, and there were convoys of trucks, often passing each other at snail pace, not to mention the careful and conservative drivers who stayed in the middle lane, regardless of whether the slow lane was clear or not. Whatever high speed we got up to was soon reduced by braking.

This was precisely how it went for the first hour. The red car was all over the road, accelerating and braking, weaving between cars, trucks and vans, with my driver desperately trying to find some open road. He was frustrated, which made me wonder if he was late, and that was what he had explained at the start of the ride.

When he did get some vacant tarmac, he floored it. The car shook a little as we got up towards the 150 km/h mark. I didn't get to find out if the car could go any faster, because he soon had to slow down due to traffic or roadworks, or both.

We drove in silence. We made two stops for him to use the bathroom. The first stop was a little hut at a rest area, surrounded by picnic tables. The second stop, barely an hour later, was a smaller rest area that had three blue and white portaloos.

More weaving, more accelerating, more braking. Closer to Nuremberg, the traffic got even heavier.

For the third time, he stopped at a rest area, but not for a bathroom break. He simply pulled over, stared straight ahead and waited for me to get out. I said "*Danke*," hauled out my gear and he sped off.

This rest area was mostly used by trucks. There were a dozen rigs parked, with curtains drawn behind the windscreens and windows. One truck driver, sitting in the ratty fold-out chair, was grilling sausages on a small portable barbecue and drinking beer from a large can.

One of the trucks came to life, lurched forward and stopped right in front of me. I climbed in with all my gear and off we went, with me not entirely sure where we were headed. It was just good to be moving again, albeit slowly. I figured there would be signs, with all roads leading to the capital.

Like so many hitch-hiking trips before, I kicked myself for not having a decent map, and also rued not having started earlier in the day.

The truck driver was Romanian. He had the radio on because we couldn't communicate. I was finding these wordless rides strange, because I was so used to being a talkative hitch-hiker, keeping the drivers company.

The kilometres ticked over slowly. In the fast lane, cars were accelerating and braking, getting close enough to each other for it to be considered tailgating. There were several near misses.

I wondered what the German word for "braking distance" was. Did they have a word for it?

The driver hummed along to the songs on the radio. He sounded like he had a good voice, and that he knew the songs, but he clearly didn't know the words.

When he put on a CD of what I assumed was Romanian music, he really started to sing along. It was funny at first, but by track six, it was getting a little embarrassing. Had he forgotten I was in the cab with him?

I believe he had, because after he took an exit in the direction of Leipzig, I had to reach over and tap him on the shoulder, in order to say I wanted to get out.

He pulled over and I climbed down from the rig. It was a bit of a walk back to the Autobahn. I passed a telephone box and decided to call Roger and Daniela, my friends in Berlin, to tell them I was running late and might not get to Berlin at all.

I left a message on their machine.

Standing on the entry ramp was just about pointless. As with the ramp in Munich, cars hit the entry here and accelerated. There was also not really anywhere for a car to stop.

But one car did, a sports coupé that had definitely seen better days. A punkish-looking guy got out to open the boot. He was jittery but friendly, and spoke broken English.

I was a little apprehensive, but in amongst the pins, leather and bleached hair, he had an open face with wide, soft eyes.

It would be okay, and he was going all the way to Berlin.

I sat in the back, sitting sideways on a typical coupé rear seat that was designed to accommodate a handbag dog. There were no seatbelts.

Paulo and his purple-haired girlfriend Anna were both social workers. They'd spent the weekend in Leipzig, to attend a demonstration. They both said Leipzig was very nice.

Paulo drove fast and was talkative. He kept looking in the rear-view mirror when he spoke to me. I wanted to tell him to keep his eyes on the road.

As the demonstration was a protest against neo-Nazis, we talked politics all the way to Berlin. These two left-wing punks were smart and knowledgeable. Most surprising, they were open to other ideas and arguments, and weren't simply focused on their own agenda. Paulo himself showed an astute understanding as to why the neo-Nazi movement was on the rise in parts of the former East Germany, explaining how economic factors and lack of opportunities resulted in people reaching for extremes. Anna added that many of the neo-Nazis were young people who were simply angry at the world and used right-ring extremism as an outlet for their anger.

I didn't have much to offer to this intelligent exchange, except my own limited knowledge of social and economic inequality in Australia. But Paulo and Anna were both interested to hear about this and asked plenty of questions, many of which I couldn't answer. In the end, Anna concluded, blithely, like it was all rather straightforward, that the countries in the developed world were facing pretty much the same set of problems, but that citizens of those countries were reacting to the problems in different ways.

All through this conversation, Paulo drove as fast as his old coupé, and the traffic, would allow him.

When we reached the outskirts of Berlin, Paulo asked me where I was staying. It turned out Roger and Daniela's apartment wasn't far out of the way, and Paulo would drop me at the door.

Great. That would save a lot of hassle; namely, trying to figure out another squiggly transport map.

When we arrived, Paulo and Anna both got out, and I managed to untangle my gangly frame from the coupé's rear seat. For closure, we had a kind of weird group-hug. Anna smelled nice. Paulo was a bit too touchy-feely.

They drove off into the Berlin night.

It was great to see Roger and Daniela, but even after a good eight hours on the road, they offered me no respite. Out on the town we went. We had some dinner, took in some experimental jazz that sounded like an orchestra of dying cats, ended at a brewery where trains rattled overhead and got home in the early hours of the morning.

Both of them were students, and both were awake and off to classes before I stirred.

I spent a couple of days exploring Berlin. It was interesting. Worldly and impoverished. Battle-scarred and proud of it. Poor, but sexy, according to the mayor.

After three nights, I headed west to Hamburg. I left some of my stuff at Roger and Daniela's, preferring to travel light and wanting to have further reason to return to Berlin.

It wasn't a long trip, but I was late getting started, again.

It took an hour just to get out of Berlin using public transport.

And it was cold.

The first three cars that stopped were all going to Leipzig.

I eventually got onto the right Autobahn and made it half way to Hamburg in stop-start fashion. But it was time-consuming, and darkness started to fall while I waited for a ride near Wittstock.

The beautiful Mercedes that pulled over promised a speedy, comfortable ride to Hamburg. I got in the back seat and thanked the driver. In the passenger seat was an elderly woman. As we pulled onto the Autobahn, with me buckling my seatbelt tightly and bracing myself for some serious acceleration, the man explained he was driving his grandmother home to Schwerin, and that she didn't like to go fast.

So, slowly down the Autobahn, and not all the way Hamburg. While the man didn't drive at top speed, he certainly talked at it. He spoke English well and wouldn't shut up, telling the story of every town, house, building and farm we passed.

It was agonising.

Finally, he let me out at the turn-off to some place called Parchim.

I stood under a streetlight. The first car turning onto the Autobahn stopped. They were a bookish-looking couple, both in glasses, and their suburban family van gave the impression of nuclear normality. There was even a grill behind the back seat and a blanket on the floor, for the family dog.

The woman explained, again in good English, that they were en route to pick up their two kids from Hamburg, with the younger kid staying with one set of grandparents and other doing some kind of internship in the city.

All very normal and nice. But once we got onto the Autobahn, the man veered into the left lane and floored it. The suburban van responded like a race car.

In such a situation, you'd expect the wife to say something like, "Slow down, darling," or, "I want to arrive in one piece, please." But she didn't even shift in her seat. We were going over 200 km/h and she was making polite conversation with me.

The speed didn't last though, because the traffic was too heavy. Still, we made it to Hamburg pretty quickly.

When asked where I was going, I said they could just drop me wherever. But they insisted and I told them Nadine's address. Out came a battered Hamburg map. The woman located the street, showed the map to her husband and I got door service for a second straight time.

Hamburg was lively and welcoming. I had got lucky and landed a job, so I would be heading back there after picking up my stuff in Berlin.

It has to be said that if you're hitch-hiking east out of Hamburg, there is the ultimate point to start from: the big roundabout where Autobahn 24 begins. The traffic is slow and there's plenty of room for cars to pull over.

The problem being that it's popular.

When I got there at around mid-morning, looking respectable and carrying a small backpack, there were half a dozen others, considerably more dishevelled, with piles of ratty gear and holding up battered cardboard signs. They also occupied the prime positions at the roundabout, perhaps having waited for hours (or days), which meant I was forced to stand over on the other side, where cars were starting to speed up and with drivers already having passed negative judgement on hitch-hikers the world over based on the rag-tag bunch they'd just seen.

While I waited, one hitch-hiker came up to me and started talking. He'd been there since sunrise, he said, and complained that drivers just didn't stop for hitch-hikers any more. I nodded, deciding not to impart the hitch-hiking wisdom that you should at the very least look like someone a driver would want to pick up, and not like someone who lives under a bridge. I wanted to say he'd have more luck if he had a shower and a shave, ditched the hat and sunglasses, stopped holding up a sign, and cut his luggage down to one orderly backpack rather than the pile of possessions of someone between squats. But before I could start my rant, an old van pulled over and I was off.

They were a punkish couple on their way to Leipzig for a wedding. Strange-looking, but friendly. The man's head was shaved into a five-pointed star and the girl had enough piercings to put her in serious trouble near magnets.

They asked how long I had been waiting, qualifying this question by saying that Germans weren't the friendliest people in the world, nor did they want to be made late by picking up hitch-hikers, so it would be understandable if I'd had to wait long.

I replied by saying the waiting times were about normal and that Germans struck me as some of the friendliest people going around. I told them my experiences of getting to-the-door rides in Berlin and Hamburg, with people who had gone out of their way to get me to my final destination.

The punks were very surprised by this.

I then added that they had picked me up as well, and that they were clearly friendly folks.

As the kilometres ticked over, the two punks proved themselves not only friendly, but also funny. They joked about everything, and they both laughed a lot.

The van didn't go very fast, but in the end it didn't matter, because an accident had brought the east-bound side of the Autobahn to a standstill, so the radio said. After some discussion in German, we turned off the Autobahn and started taking country roads. I had no idea where we were going, but I felt no apprehension.

The van rolled through rather pleasant countryside. There were cows in the fields. I saw some deer.

There were yellow and black signs pointing to places I'd never heard of. In the worst case scenario, I figured we'd end up in Leipzig, which I remembered was somewhere south-west of Berlin. From there I could get myself to the capital. Or maybe I'd get invited to a very punkish wedding.

After a couple of hours, we stopped for a break. I asked about our progress and they showed me on the map. We were close to Nauen, the woman said. I saw we were actually near Berlin, and that Leipzig was way south. They'd gone far out of their way. The woman pointed at the map and called the intersecting Autobahns that encircled the city the Berliner Ring. They would drop me just on the other side of the Ring, where I could get easily get a ride into the centre.

I was very grateful, and did my best to express my gratitude. The punks waved me off, thinking nothing of it.

On the other side of the Berliner Ring, I bid them farewell and apologised for making them late. The man replied that it was good, because it meant they would now be crashing the wedding rather than simply attending.

The van drove off, the horn sounding out five times.

I found myself standing near a mall of outlet stores, in a place called Elstal. There was a bus station nearby. I stood there and stuck my thumb out, thinking that if I didn't get a ride, I'd take the next bus.

I waited less than minute. A truck pulled out of a nearby construction site and stopped in front. The driver called out to me. I shouted "Berlin" over the noise of the engine and climbed in.

Being behind the wheel of a truck didn't stop the driver from taking me on a tour of Berlin. He spoke little English. All he could do was point at something and say the name of it. We passed the Olympic Stadium, Schloss Charlottenburg, the Reichstag, Brandenburg Gate, and a bunch of other sights. We even got close to Roger and Daniela's apartment building, the last station before the over-ground U-Bahn crosses the river in Kreuzberg, but I thought it would be impolite to tell him to stop and let me out.

Eventually, he pulled into a waste disposal area and unloaded the truck, dawdling while he spoke with some of the people working there.

Back on the road, with the rush hour traffic getting heavier, I started to get a little nervous.

When he stopped at a kebab shop, I thought I was free, but he got out with me and started talking to the shop owner. They appeared to be friends. I tried to say thank you and walk away, but the driver told me to "Wait, wait. Here, wait, you."

He jumped into the truck and drove away.

The shop owner motioned for me to sit down. Worried, I did so.

A kebab was brought to me, along with a very small glass of tea.

"But I didn't order anything."

"Eat," the shop owner said. "Klaus, he pay for you."

"Oh, okay. Thanks."

"Klaus, he come back. *Bald*."

I thought, bald? Like, with no hair?

The kebab was tasty and the tea strong. I finished both quickly. The shop owner stood near the doorway, perhaps making sure I wouldn't wander off.

I sat back and waited, curious to see how this would play out.

Hitch-hiking can give you a wild imagination. There are plenty of bad stories out there, and I had my share: getting picked up and briefly interrogated by border police in America; being arrested together with a dozen others travelling in a minivan that got pulled over by police in Canada; riding in trucks with strange people in Australia's outback. But through it all, nothing had ever gone wrong. The vast majority of my rides were with regular people who wanted company, took sympathy on me or simply wanted to do a good deed. Quite often, it was all three.

I was pondering this when Klaus returned. He arrived in a two-door hatchback, wearing fresh clothes. His hair was wet, and still there, and combed back from his face.

The shop owner motioned for me to get in the car. I thanked him for the tea and kebab. He smiled.

In the car, Klaus asked, "Address?"

I let out a breath and relaxed into the seat. The street where Roger and Daniela lived was difficult to say; it was a twelve-letter word with only three vowels. I had it written down on a piece of paper, which I showed to Klaus, and off we went, still taking the tourist route and still with Klaus pointing out sights. I couldn't see much in the darkness though.

I realised that not only was I getting to-the-door service for a third straight time, I'd also been bought dinner and given a sightseeing tour of Berlin.

The Germans were proving to be outstanding people.

We went to the door of Roger and Daniela's apartment building. I didn't know what to say. Thank you didn't seem to cut it, didn't seem enough. But it appeared to be all Klaus wanted. So I said *Danke* several times, shook his hand and he drove off.

Upstairs, I regaled Roger with my story. He couldn't believe how lucky I had been. Yet another German convinced that Germans weren't friendly. But I was having the best hitch-hiking days of my life and wouldn't let anyone say a bad word about Germans.

Two days later, I was ready to head back to Hamburg. Roger talked about cheap train tickets and easy bus connections, but I was hitch-hiking.

I started early this time, but it still took a while to get out of Berlin and to a hitch-hiking point near the Berliner Ring.

Within minutes of getting there, a woman picked me up. She was on her way to Leipzig, and I seriously considered going with her, because it seemed Leipzig was the most happening place in Germany. Everyone was going there. But when we reached the turn-off to Hamburg, I asked her to let me out. She checked the mirror and pulled over.

"Quick," she said. "No stop on Autobahn."

I got out and she roared off, leaving me standing in the Autobahn's emergency lane. But if she couldn't stop here, then no other cars could either.

And this wasn't a turn-off to Hamburg, but a continuation of the same Autobahn. So, I shouldered my backpack, climbed over the security rail and started walking. No one would stop here, and I was a little worried about police. I thought my best chance would be to walk to the next rest area or gas station and try from there.

But the Germans did not disappoint.

A small car screeched to a halt and the burly driver beckoned me to get in. As we roared off, he explained in fast German that it's illegal to hitch-hike on the Autobahn. At least, that was what I assumed he said, because he spoke in an authoritarian tone, like he was lecturing me.

I responded with the one thing I knew how to say in German: "*Ich komme aus Australien und spreche kein Deutsch.*"

He didn't say anything after that, but I had the feeling he was annoyed. Maybe he had wanted some company on the drive, someone to chat with, but without a common language, we sat in silence.

He drove like a maniac, honking the horn and flashing the lights. But he seemed bored by it all, like it was just an afternoon drive through the countryside.

We stopped once so he could buy black coffee, and a second time so he could fill up his car.

It's always a bit awkward when you're hitch-hiking and the driver pulls into a petrol station. You feel somewhat obliged to kick in some money. My strategy in such a situation is to buy the driver a drink or a snack. In this case, I bought my driver another black coffee. He was surprised and grateful, yet he remained somewhat annoyed and distant.

The second shot of caffeine spurred him on, and his risk-taking behind the wheel went up a notch. I quietly hoped I wouldn't become an Autobahn statistic.

But still he didn't speak, and he didn't have the radio on either. The silence was weird, almost uncomfortable.

When we reached the turn-off to Lübeck, he said, pointing at himself, "I, Lübeck."

He pulled over and let me out. I barely had the door shut, before the car took off again.

The next ride was in a truck, en route to somewhere in Hamburg's harbour. While that broke my streak of to-the-door rides, I wasn't disappointed.

I settled into life in Hamburg. I worked at an Irish bar, as you do when you're an expat in Germany. November became December and the days got even shorter. I didn't really notice, because I got to work at around three in the afternoon, when it was still light, and came out of the bar after midnight.

Truth be told, I hated the work and looked for something else. Teaching English was a possibility, but I didn't have any qualifications or a visa for working in Germany.

Nadine invited me to join her family down near Stuttgart for what she promised would be a typical German Christmas and New Year. She gave me the address and flew down.

I pulled beers all night on the twenty-second and was late getting up the next morning. I took a train to the south-bound Autobahn, but couldn't find anywhere to stand. No entry ramps, rest areas or petrol stations.

After a bit of walking, a man pulled over and took me further south to the first petrol station. It was an amazing act of generosity; he explained, once we got there, that he wasn't going in that direction.

Very nice of him.

I waited about an hour in the freezing cold. Plenty of cars stopped, but none of them were going south down Autobahn 7. I was holding out for a first ride that would take me a fair chunk of the way. Every second car that pulled over was going to Leipzig, and I rued that Nadine didn't live in what was shaping in my mind as the greatest city on the planet.

In the end, I was too cold to stand anymore and got in the next car that stopped.

It was a brand new Audi. Black, with leather seats. It even smelled new. Best of all, it had seat heating.

The driver was small, wearing a dark suit and sporting a thick moustache.

"You are cold, yes?" he asked.

I nodded and said I was trying to get to Stuttgart.

He said he was going to Bremen. "I turn, soon. Maybe twenty kilometres. Or do you say miles?"

"I'm Australian. We deal in kilometres, and twenty's not a lot."

"Yes," he said. "Is a very large country."

"But thanks anyway for stopping."

"Moment."

He pressed a button on the steering wheel and the sound of a phone ringing came through the car's audio speakers.

The phone was answered, and there followed an animated conversation, with quite a lot of laughing.

"Okay," he said, pressing the button again and flooring it.

The Audi was like a racehorse out of the gates. We'd been cruising along at around 130 km/h and were quickly up to over 200 km/h.

"My friend," he said calmly. "He also driving. He take you to Stuttgart."

"Oh, really? Wow. Thanks."

I wasn't really buying it, as it sounded too good to be true. But we pulled into the next rest area and stopped alongside a white station wagon, which had two occupants and was crammed with stuff. The car required repacking to get my backpack inside and to make room on the back seat for a passenger.

I shook the Audi driver's hand, thanked him again, and got in the back of the station wagon.

Off we went, going fast down the Autobahn when the traffic allowed.

The driver said nothing, but the guy in the passenger seat, who was the Audi driver's friend, wouldn't shut up.

"It's so great you come from Australia," he said. "I made my best holiday there. Best ever."

"Awesome."

"I'm Rudy." He turned to the driver and asked, "What is your name again?"

"Rolf." The driver sounded annoyed.

"Ah, yes, how do I forget that? Like a dog. Rolf, rolf, rolf." Rudy turned around in the passenger seat to talk to me. "The Muppet dog. He play the piano. You know?"

"I know." And I sang, "'It's time to put on make-up.'"

Rudy laughed very loudly. He even slapped Rolf on the shoulder.

"That's good," Rudy said. "Don't mind this Rolf. He have no humour. We leave him in Hannover, and is okay because no one in Hannover have humour. Ha. Maybe we just slow down and let him jump."

Rudy laughed some more.

What a freaking weirdo, I thought.

But Rudy talking, laughing, making pop-culture references and ribbing Rolf made the time pass quickly. We soon got to Hannover. With Rolf gone, Rudy got behind the wheel, I sat up front and the chatter continued. He drove much faster than conservative Rolf.

Of all things, Rudy was a nurse. He was as tall as me, but sturdier built. Mid-forties, blonde hair fading to grey, big hands. Not exactly the type you could imagine administering care in a hospital.

He said he never picked up hitch-hikers.

"Why?"

"There aren't any in Konstanz," he explained. "People don't do it."

"Where's Konstanz?"

"Down in the south, near Switzerland. Is very, very beautiful. You shall visit."

"Sounds good, but let me survive Stuttgart first."

"Ach, is not very beautiful. Konstanz," he said, taking his hands off the wheel and steering with his knees, "has the lake. There is water. So much water."

Wow. Water.

"Stuttgart. Tja, only shopping. And everyone with a tan from the machine. Sun studio. You know?"

"Yeah." Suddenly I missed Australia very much. It was summer there, and I was running seriously low on vitamin D.

"Where you go in Stuttgart?" Rudy asked.

I showed him the address. He was still steering with his knees, changing lanes to pass cars as well, and took the piece of paper in both hands.

"Eberdingen. I don't know this place. But we find it. I take you to the door."

"Rudy, that's really nice of you, but you don't have to go out of your way."

I said this as sincerely as I could, but I didn't mean it. Because it was already starting to get dark and we were still a long way from Stuttgart. I'd also come to just about expect to-the-door service in Germany.

"I take you. We invade Eberdingen. Ha."

"That's great, Rudy. Thanks."

As we continued to talk, I started to understand why Rudy would make a great nurse. He had an easy, jovial manner, which I transported to a hospital, envisioning him comforting and amusing patients while also caring for them. And while he was talkative and informed, he also listened.

He'd been to Australia, and while the trip was great, he also confessed that there had been bad moments.

"The country is beautiful," he said. "So very, very beautiful. But the people. Tja, I never know where I am with them. What do they really think? You know? Do they like me? Do they want to be my friend? It's all, g'day, how are you, can I help you and have a nice day. But I never know what is real. The Germans, they say what they feel. Like Rolf. We get out of the car in Hannover and he tells me, 'Rudy, I don't like you.' This is fine. I say to him, 'I also don't like you, Rolf.' *Auf nie wiedersehen.*"

Rudy laughed.

"What does that mean?"

"The Germans are straight. They are honest."

"Yeah, I'm learning that. I mean that last sentence."

"Ha. Goodbye and I never see you again. Something like this."

We both laughed.

I wanted to get off the topic of Australia and asked Rudy about his work. He said he cared mostly for old people, suffering from dementia and Alzheimer's.

"Is difficult," he said. "But also can be fun. I make the same jokes every day. They always find them funny. I tell them one day, and the next day, joke is forgotten, so I tell again. You know?"

"What about new material? New jokes?"

"Yes, sure, I test this too. See what works and try again next day. And if I tell a bad joke, the people can't say the next day, 'Rudy, you are not funny,' because bad joke also forgotten."

This made me smile; this big lovable oaf entertaining people suffering from awful illnesses. It also made me like him more.

He went on to explain that all the stuff in the car wasn't his. It belonged to his parents, and to friends of his parents. They lived in Travemünde, he said, at the Baltic Sea.

"The sea air is good for them," he said. "Lots of water. Good for health. They are retired. You know?"

"What's the stuff for?"

"A friend of mine, he start a social project. It's a big apartment for teenagers. They don't want to live at home, maybe not safe there, so they go to his apartment."

"I get it. The apartment needs to be furnished."

"No, not furniture. He have all that. More small things, lamps and kitchen machines."

"Appliances."

"Yes. So, I go to Travemünde and get all this good stuff from the rich old people living there. Bring all back."

"That's really good of you."

Rudy nodded. "Is good of me. But Michi is my friend, and I do this for my friends."

He told me about some of his other friends, what they do and how he helps them sometimes.

We talked all the way to Stuttgart. Rudy never seemed to tire from all the driving. When we stopped for a break, he had a hot chocolate and an ice cream. I offered to buy it for him, but he insisted on paying. He said I was his guest, and he even bought my cup of tea.

It was dark and late when we got to Eberdingen. Some of the streetlights had already been turned off. We drove around the small village, trying to find the street where Nadine's parents lived. Rudy stopped to ask some locals, but they didn't know. They suggested trying the nearby village of Neudorf. It was only a few kilometres away and Rudy drove us over. This village was even smaller, but we couldn't locate the street.

"I have hope," Rudy said. He pulled into a supermarket and went inside.

When he came back, I said, "Look, you can just leave me. I'll call Nadine and tell her to come get me."

"No, no. I have the way. The people, they say this street is in Altdorf. Very, very small village. But all villages here part of big village of Eberdingen."

Off we went to Altdorf. It was amazing how determined Rudy was to deliver me at the door. So generous, that it was also just slightly suspicious.

As we circled Altdorf's dark streets, Rudy reeled off sentences in German that I should say to Nadine's parents in order to charm and impress them. He spoke so fast, I couldn't tell where the gaps in the words were, or even if there were any.

We found the street and pulled into the driveway of number ten. The outside lights came on. An oldish man stood in the doorway. Rudy jumped out of the car and went straight to him, talking in rapid German and pumping the old man's hand up and down in greeting. Then, he threw the passenger door open and hauled me out, pulling me towards the front door and making the introductions. He kept on taking, even while I was shaking the man's hand. It appeared he was explaining who he was, who I was and the journey we'd taken together. I took a moment to get my backpack out of the car.

Rudy, satisfied he'd brought me right to the door, left me there with the bemused old man. He jumped in his car and drove away, without giving me the chance to say thank you.

The man said something to me.

"Uh, sorry. I don't speak German. Is Nadine here?"

"Nadine? No. Nadine not here."

He went inside, closed the door and turned the light off.

I stood there, stunned, wondering what the hell I would do next.

The front light came back on and the door was opened again. The old man stood there smiling.

"I only make joke," he said. "Nadine, she here. Come in. The beer is cold."

If I

In Padua, Italy, around two and a half years after we met, my thoughts turn to I. She has been mostly absent since I settled in Germany, but after a day spent wandering around Venice on my own, surrounded by couples – I somehow managed to witness three separate marriage proposals – I sit in the Duomo di Padova and recall my time in Montreal, romancing I, and the fall-out of having her break my heart.

A church is an appropriate setting to contemplate an angel. She was the kind of girl who seemed to have fallen from the sky.

In my memory, what was a short time together stretches into a long, troubled relationship. Yet, we didn't sleep together, and I can't even remember her last name.

Even now, I'm not able to say her first name without feeling a sharp pain somewhere inside. It also hurts to see it written down, and if I meet someone with that name, I take an instant disliking to her.

It started in Seattle, where I met Caroline from Montreal. We spent an enjoyable day together, knowing we would go our separate ways at the end of it. The day was capped by forgettable sex in a youth hostel bathroom and a promise that I would visit; a promise I didn't intend to keep. I felt the situation demanded such a promise, and for me to be the one to make it and who would break it.

We stayed loosely in touch.

After a few months in New Orleans, I was keen to be on the move. Montreal seemed like a good destination, possibly to spend the summer and earn some money. My work visa for Canada still had five months on it. Maybe Caroline would be useful in helping find a job and somewhere to live.

I flew to Boston, then took my time hitch-hiking through New England to Montreal, staying a couple of days each in Peterborough, Conway and Burlington.

On arriving in Montreal, I knew it was a mistake. Caroline seemed surprised to see me, despite knowing I was coming, and was less than welcoming. A nurse, she worked nights and slept for much of the day. She had no interest in showing me around or spending any time with me. Whatever connection we had forged in Seattle had dissipated.

After one night on her sofa, I moved to the city's big youth hostel.

I could only get two nights there, as the place was booked out for the weekend.

I wandered around Montreal, pondering my next move. I liked the city, and had the sense I could make things happen, if given the right circumstances. While walking, I also searched for a new hostel. Most were pretty awful. One in the Vieux Port was passable. It had a nice communal area and large dormitories. I booked myself in for five nights. That would be my deadline to find work and somewhere temporary to live.

The hostel had some recent newspapers. I availed myself of the complimentary tea, sat down and looked through the classifieds, starting with the employment section. There were a couple of good leads, including for movers and garden labourers. While I didn't want to do either of those jobs, it was the kind of temporary work that was easy to get and offered decent money, and I'd done it before.

I made a jobs list, writing down phone numbers. In a second list, I put down some promising sublets. My timing was right, with summer about to start; students who were going away, or home, were looking to rent out their rooms. Finally, I checked the entertainment section, to find the bars where live music was played in the hope I might land a few gigs. Working through the three lists would keep me busy for a few days.

At some point, the previous hostel receptionist had left and been replaced by a colleague. She was small, wearing a floral dress and flat-soled sandals. Her glasses were almost horn-rimmed and a bit old-fashioned. She had a round face, pretty, but with a slight overbite that was less pronounced when she smiled, which she did a lot. Her mass of long, reddish-blonde hair was centre-parted, combed back and tucked behind her ears.

I went up to her and asked if she would like a cup of tea.

"*Oh, oui, monsieur*," she said, smiling broadly.

I made her a tea, and a second cup for myself, and served it to her. "*Merci.*"

We swapped names. She was friendly and chatty; she smiled a lot, and it was a fabulous smile. A pair of tired-looking new arrivals meant she had work to do. I drifted back to my lists.

During that limited exchange, I'd fallen for her.

It was my first time falling in love and I knew it straight away. It wasn't like being hit by a ten-tonne truck. It was more like being slapped ever so gently in the face, and wanting that hand to stay there.

In Padua, I leave the Duomo and wander back to the hostel. Memory can sometimes be harsh, especially when dealing with hurt and trying to cope with it, but with this girl in Montreal, this is not the case. In my mind, she has grown and improved, to be even better looking, friendlier and more receptive. She lingers, beautiful, glowing and smiling, surrounded by question marks.

What if?

What did I do wrong?

What happened to her?

Is she still in Montreal?

During those first few days, once I escaped from Caroline, Montreal opened its arms to me. All the stars aligned. I found temporary work, lined up a sublet in an apartment on Avenue des Pins, near the Parc du Mont-Royal, met a semi-professional tennis player and started hitting with him, and even managed to organise a couple of low-paying, mid-week gigs. By the time I moved into the hostel in the Vieux Port, I was entrenching myself in for a three-month stay, which was the duration of my sublet.

She did the afternoon-evening shift at the hostel. The first night I stayed there, knowing already the Vieux Port could be a tad dangerous at night, I offered to walk her to the next Metro station, which was Square-Victoria. She accepted immediately, seeming very glad about it.

I played my guitar while she cleaned up the communal area and did all the necessary things to finish her shift. When ready, she led the way to the station, walking quickly with bouncy steps, sometimes looking behind her. She carried a large backpack, hooking her thumbs under the shoulder straps as she walked. It wasn't far, but we had a nice chat. There was definitely something happening between us, and I felt that she could sense it as well. We hardly knew each other, yet we seemed very comfortable together. Conversation flowed. We both laughed, though she was more of a giggler, which was very sweet. There was none of that awkwardness of two people feeling each other out and wondering if it's worth to try to get close.

Though fully smitten and keen to spend time with her, I was reluctant to push things. I assumed guys staying at the hostel hit on her all the time and that she must have been fed up with it. So, for my five days at her hostel, my focus was on getting settled in Montreal. I did my first moving job, played tennis at the McGill University courts and found an outside basketball court in Westmount that had decent pick-up games in the afternoons. Through tennis and basketball, I met some people and started making friends. But the days felt like me killing time until I could see her again.

Every evening, I walked her to the Square-Victoria station, and she was very thankful that I did so. On my last night in the hostel, I tentatively asked her if she would like to meet the next day for a coffee.

"*Oui, monsieur,*" she said.

She had the morning free. We met at the Gare Centrale. The weather was bad, so she took me to a large gallery which had exhibitions from up-and-coming artists. While going from room to room, she told me that she was also attempting to pursue a career in art and design. The hostel job was a necessary evil, a bill-payer while she got things together and decided which direction to go in. She said she was living at home, but didn't say where that was.

One of the exhibitions included Polaroid photographs of intricate figures made in mud, sand and snow. She found this interesting, and she stared at the photos for a long time. She also talked with the artist, who was sitting at a desk in the room. They spoke in French. When they were finished, she put the artist's business card in her pocket and we left the room.

"What did you talk about?"

She flashed that stunning smile of hers. "I asked how she could make such beautiful art that would disappear."

"She's got photos of it."

"Yes, but what she created is gone. It's lost."

"What did she say?"

She let out a sigh. "That beauty doesn't last."

"What do you think about that?"

The shrug of her shoulders made me think she was confused or annoyed. I didn't know her well enough to tell which it was. Maybe both; or maybe she was feeling something else entirely.

In the next room, the artist wasn't present and we were alone. I went up to her and tried to kiss her. It was a fumbled attempt, the wrong moment and poorly executed. Taken by surprise, she stepped back and giggled.

"I'm sorry," I said. "I thought that maybe it might make you feel better."

"I'm fine. Really. Shall we continue?

"Yeah."

You idiot, I thought to myself, believing I'd just blown whatever chance I had.

The gallery seemed to have an endless number of rooms, and we went into a lot of them, not saying much. Outside, the rain continued to fall. Eventually, it was time for her to go work. We walked down to the hostel in the Vieux Port, both of us under her umbrella, which I held.

I was expecting her to say that she didn't want to see me anymore, but instead she asked me what I was doing on the weekend. I was playing tennis on Saturday morning, but was free after that. We agreed to meet for a picnic in Mont-Royal. While very glad to be still in with a chance, I feared I was entering dangerous "friend" territory. I was already at that point when being around her but not together with her would be far worse than having no contact at all.

I thought about her all the time. I went back over our exchanges, made notes, tried to recall any particular body language that might offer a hint or two, and plotted ways I might get her to drop whatever barrier she had to getting close. Because it felt like there was something there, something restrictive, keeping her at a distance.

I'd fallen for this girl, but I was also falling for the city. Montreal was great. After just a week, I was starting to feel like a local. The sublet was working out well. The two girls I was sharing the apartment with were nice. They were both McGill students and invited me to parties and social events. There was always something happening.

I was playing the best tennis of my life.

Making a relationship with her work would make this new Montreal life complete. Foolishly, I got way ahead of myself, contemplating a permanent move that would involve finding a real job and us possibly getting married.

That was way wrong.

I'm the only one staying at the hostel in Padua. It should be comfortable, having the place to myself, but I'm finding it rather scary and lonely.

The common area has a large map of the world on the wall.

Previous guests have marked their hometowns with crosses, writing the town or city in pen when it's not already on the map. A lot of Americans have stayed here, perhaps unable to get a bed in crowded Venice and using Padua as a base instead. That's what I've done, and I'm glad about it, as Venice was busy, beautiful and not enjoyable on my own.

There are several crosses crowded around Montreal. I stare at them, tilting my head slightly so the city looks more like a cemetery.

Just seeing the name of the city makes me feel sad. It makes me wonder, makes me regret.

There's a computer in the common area, and a pay phone.

I decide I have to know. If anything, to get some kind of closure.

I use the computer to find the Montreal hostel's phone number and dial it on the pay phone. As I can't remember her last name, the hostel is my only shot. I'm so nervous, I drag a chair over and sit down.

A man answers. When asked, he says that she still works there and will start in a couple of hours. I say I'll call back, and hang up.

I check my watch and do a loose calculation of the time difference. She's still doing the afternoon-evening shift. Two and a half years later, nothing much has changed, which is disappointing and sad. I assumed she would be well into her chosen art career by now. I wonder if she's living at home as well.

Her work schedule and living situation made it very difficult for us to spend time together. We couldn't really date, or get in an intimate situation. This was also my fault, as all the tennis and basketball, and the occasional moving jobs, had me exhausted. I was also practicing on the guitar for two hours each day, to get myself gig-ready. As a result, I often fell asleep before ten, which was when her shift finished. There was also the hassle of walking half an hour from my apartment to the hostel, from where I would escort her to the Square-Victoria station, before walking all the way back home. I still did it, just about every evening. I'd ache all day for that seven-minute walk together.

But while nothing physical was happening between us and each chaste day made me feel more like a friend, I still wanted to believe there were sparks, which was why I kept trying.

She didn't come to my first gig. That was all right, because I played to an empty bar on a Tuesday evening. She was working anyway. I did succeed in getting her to come to a party at my apartment building, being held by those who were leaving for the summer, which included

Stephen, the guy whose room I was in and who was bunking with his girlfriend in the meantime.

My building on Avenue des Pins had a courtyard in the middle. The party was held there, with just a handful of people at the start. When she arrived, I was speechless. It was the first time I'd seen her out of her usual casual hostel clothes and really dressed up, in tight pants and heels. Gone was the heavy backpack she normally carried. She looked fantastic, and I was really hoping she'd made this effort for me.

She was all smiles, giggles and sweetness.

For the first hour, we drank and were social. More people arrived. At one point, Stephen asked me to grab my guitar and play some songs.

I headed up the stairs, stopped and turned. Back in the courtyard, she was already surrounded by guys. I asked her if she'd like to see the apartment.

"*Oui, monsieur.*"

She took the stairs two at a time.

The fourth-floor apartment was L-shaped, with two long hallways and all the rooms on one side. There were two small bedrooms and the bathroom along the first hallway, a lounge room at the corner, then my bedroom, and a kitchen and dining area at the end.

She was complimentary. She asked about my housemates, and I explained they were students, both a bit younger than me and both due to arrive at the party later.

She sat on the bed while I tuned my guitar.

"Play me something," she said.

I did.

At the end of the song, I put the guitar aside and we started kissing on the bed. There was nothing forced about it, nothing fumbled. It seemed like a very natural progression of events. Very right.

It got intense quickly. She was more physical than I'd imagined her to be, and more aggressive.

We rolled around, bodies entwined, slowly undressing.

It was glorious.

At one point, her hair got tangled in the Velcro closing tag of my sleeping bag. She giggled as I freed her hair. But once freed and the sleeping bag tossed to the floor, she sat back from me, looked like she was going to cry, then ran from the room.

It was so sudden and unexpected, the front door was closed before I'd managed to call after her.

In my room, I stared at the floor, wondering what had just happened and what exactly I'd done wrong.

Someone has arrived at the hostel. I can hear talking: the receptionist with his Italian-accented English and a guy who sounds Irish. As the accents collide, there's quite a bit of repeating required, from both of them. It's funny to listen to.

The Irish guy says hi as he passes through the common area on the way to the dorms, sheets in his arms and a big backpack on his back. He looks as if he doesn't eat enough.

In Montreal, the girl taught me some French, but we spoke English mostly. A native Quebecois, she spoke with a lovely accent. The words sometimes got stuck inside her mouth, from whence they'd all fall out at once, in a sweet jumble that needed a few seconds to be deciphered, ordered and comprehended. It meant that talking with her on the phone was difficult.

After she fled the party, I let things sit for two very long days. Then I called her. The phone wasn't the right medium, but we had a few chats, with me sensing that she wanted to get off the phone quickly. Each of those chats killed me a little bit, as I feared she was drifting further out of reach.

We met one more time in the city, about a week later, during which I'd done a lot of thinking and pining. I'd also written her a letter, trying to explain my feelings. I was twenty-three years old, in love for the first time, and didn't know how to put any of that into words. I was honest, too, explaining that I wasn't sure if I was ready to settle down and get married, or even if I wanted to get married.

We met in the Vieux Port. She kept her distance. She sat down on a bench and read the letter, with a very concentrated look on her face. At the end, she cried, sneaking fingers in from the sides of her glasses to wipe away the tears.

I told her that I couldn't imagine not seeing her.

She said I'd be gone in a few months, so what did it matter.

I said I'd stay, make a life in Montreal and see what happens. I told her that I was in the running to get a travel writing job, putting together a guidebook about Montreal, which would mean at least another year, possibly two.

"You won't survive the winter," she said.

"Probably not."

She had to go to the hostel to start her shift. She took the letter with her, saying she would read it again.

"Can I walk you to the station tonight?"

She considered this, then said flatly, "*Oui, monsieur.*"

It was a difficult day. I played tennis, but my game was way off. I tried to sleep in the afternoon, in order to be awake by ten, but stared at the ceiling. I turned down offers from both housemates to go out.

In the end, I got to the hostel early and helped her clean up. Finished, we headed down the stairs.

"Your letter was wonderful," she said.

I felt the energetic buzz of hope.

On the street, a car was parked right in front of the door. It was a two-door coupé, blue, with a young man behind the wheel. He had rather long hair, was smiling and waving eagerly.

She dropped her backpack and ran up the stairs.

The car drove away.

Confused, I carried her backpack up the stairs, but the door to the hostel was locked.

I knocked a few times.

"Go away," she shouted, "or I'll call the police."

"It's me. The car's gone."

The door slowly opened, with her beautiful face shadowed in the crack. She looked past me and down the stairs, at the empty space where the car had been parked.

She stepped through the crack and hugged me very hard, crying as she did so. But it wasn't the crying of sadness; it was fear and anguish.

"It's all right, I got you," I said. "Who was that?"

She didn't reply. She kept hugging me. In my selfishness, I wanted the hug to last for as long as possible.

When she let me go, she said, "Please walk me to the station."

"Sure."

This time, while walking, she did a lot more looking behind her than usual. We took a different route, to Bonaventure station, as the guy in the car knew she went to Square-Victoria.

He was an ex-boyfriend, and had been stalking her. She told me some of the story as we walked. It was dreadful, and worse, it was all very recent; a long relationship that had turned bad at the end. It was why she was living at home, why she appreciated the escort to the station, and why she didn't want to get close to me.

"I really want you to be my friend," she said. "I need friends at the moment."

That felt like a really hard slap in the face.

"I don't know if I can do that," I said. "I'm crazy about you. Being just your friend would kill me."

Angry, she said something in French that didn't sound very nice.

"I'm sorry," I said, not so much that she'd been stalked, but that the stalking would prevent us from being together.

"I'm also sorry," she said, walking away.

"Wait. That's it?"

"*Oui, monsieur.*"

She headed into the station and that was indeed it.

The Irish guy, who has introduced himself as Liam, is staring at the map and trying to make conversation with me. He gives me a summary of his trip so far and, when prompted, I do the same. We both agree that Bergamo is a find. After doing a swing through northern Italy, Liam is on his way back to Milan to fly home. I tell him I don't really have a plan.

"How about we go for a pint?" Liam asks.

I don't want to.

"Sounds good, but I have to make a really important call to Canada. Sorry."

"No matter."

He adds a cross to the few around Galway and heads out.

With the girl having removed herself from my life, I lost my way. I drank, partied and slept with lots of women, including one of my housemates. I sometimes woke up in places I didn't remember getting to. I began a relationship with a girl who worked in the sports store where I got my rackets restrung, even though she spoke only French, and I cheated on her as well. I played tennis sometimes for five hours a day, throwing myself around the court and sweating through several shirts each time. My tennis partner said we should enter a few satellite tournaments, to play doubles and singles. I declined, thinking I wasn't nearly good enough. I got into fights during pick-up basketball games in Westmount.

I became sadder and more pathetic the longer the summer went on, and I seemed to become more attractive to women in the process, like a wounded dog that needed to be cared for.

Countless times, I picked up the phone to dial her number, but never got to the end.

She lingered, and I kind of mentally stalked her. In my mind, I followed her around the city, from her job at the hostel to the Square-Victoria station, to various art galleries and cafés. I thought of all those guys in the hostel hitting on her, making her cups of tea, playing songs on their guitars and offering to escort her to the station. Maybe they were more gentlemanly and carried her backpack. Maybe she'd let one of them in.

It was a relief when my sublet came to an end and I could leave Montreal.

Unfortunately, she followed me, boomeranging in and out of my thoughts for the next few years. I couldn't shake her. Falling in love a second time helped, but it didn't heal the wound or make me forget.

In Padua, I dial the hostel's number again.

She answers. She remembers me, is friendly and chatty, and I envision her smiling. She manages to say early on in the conversation that she has someone in her life; she uses the word "lover", which for some reason hurts much more than "boyfriend" and is more physical and graphic. From there, I lose interest, not because I want to get together with her again, but because I'm satisfied to hear that she's got her life back on track, even if she's still working the same shift at the hostel and not pursuing her artistic dreams. She has let someone get close. A lover. That lover wasn't me, and I tell myself to be glad about it.

After about ten minutes, I wind up the call. I want to get off the phone, as the sound of her voice, her sweetly accented English and giggling, is really starting to cause some pain.

I hang up and sit back. I'm feeling a certain kind of relief, but I think the most disappointing thing of all is that she is still working at the hostel. I expected more from her.

Looking at the map, I imagine that one of those crosses is her, and that I've mentally buried her in a Montreal cemetery. Wishful thinking. I have the feeling that she will linger forever.

Not for the first time, I wonder what if? What if it had all worked out? Montreal, love, possibly fighting off a stalker or two, guidebook writing, a bleak winter, moving in together, a bill-paying job, another bleak winter, getting married. Her talking about an art career, but continuing to work at the hostel. Getting old and drifting apart. Decades of bleak winters. Me thinking about all the places I had wanted to get to, but didn't.

Stuck in Montreal.

But whenever I ponder what if, I think about myself, not her. And I tell myself that Montreal would have been a concession when greater challenges and experiences awaited. Perhaps she would have been more than worth settling for and we could have had a good life together, but I wasn't ready for it. And neither was I.

The Prussian Peasant

Was it really good to be the king?

Standing in the glittering and glamorous Marmorgalerie (Marble Gallery) of the Neue Palais, with its shiny chessboard floor, weighty chandeliers, massive arch windows and lavishly decorated ceiling, I think, no, it wouldn't have been good to be the king. Too many responsibilities and obligations. Too much work. Friedrich III, burdened by the pressures of the throne, died in this very room after ruling for a mere ninety-nine days.

I might have preferred to be a hapless count or lowly duke. Some kindly landlord presiding over a farming county, enjoying an existence of quiet drudgery, with my hunts and dinner parties and visiting aristocrats, my mistress tucked away and bored in some lonely tower on a lake. On special occasions I would strap on my corset, pin on a collection of medals never earned in battle, and troop off to the palace for some reception or party, honouring the presence of a visiting royal of importance. We would gather in the Grottensaal (Grotto Hall), with its embedded gems, sea shells and fossils making the room seem like a giant upside-down bath tub, drink champagne and discuss whatever scandalous affair was sweeping such and such a court.

"And the girl is just a commoner."

"It's an outrage."

"Shocking."

"A disgrace."

No. That also sounds a bit boring, and comes with too many obligations. I don't want to wear corsets, and I don't believe in aristocracies; that someone can receive such an exalted position simply by birth.

I think being a peasant would have been more my thing. Someone who looked at the palaces with respect and knew his place. And yes, someone who would join the revolution and slice off the king's head if things got very bad.

This is why I come to Potsdam, to let my historical fancy take hold. The palaces in and around the city are very well preserved, having survived two world wars and the attempts of highly misguided communist architects and town planners to Sovietise the city. With the beautifully landscaped parks, the palaces offer an experience both individual and peaceful for visitors, rivalling the Loire Valley in France for magnitude and magnificence.

The palaces and gardens retain their royal feel, allowing the luxury of imaginary travel. Depending on my mood, I might be an unpleasant peasant, sneaking around the parks, plotting regicide; or a young worker, keeping the gardens in order while carrying on an illicit affair with an aristocratic girl; or a conscript, returning from battle, minus a limb or two, to receive a medal. Whatever I imagine, it normally includes placing myself low on the Prussian food chain. The royals aren't for me.

This area gets over two million visitors a year. The palace of Sanssouci draws the vast majority of the tour bus traffic, while Neuer Garten, Park Glienicke, Pfaueninsel (Peacock Island) and Park Babelsberg (altogether comprising the largest landscaped park in Europe and a UNESCO world heritage site) are less popular, but equally rewarding. The palaces and parks offer a glimpse to the former glory and power of the Kingdom of Prussia.

Built between 1745 and 1747, the small palace of Sanssouci was established as a summer residence for Friedrich the Great, who named it as the place "without cares". With only twelve rooms, it's hardly a palace of grandeur, but taken together with the sloping vineyard spread out below, and flanked by the Picture Gallery (the first purpose-built museum in Germany) and the New Chambers guesthouse, it is an excellent example of *Kulturlandschaft* – the palace and buildings constructed in harmony with the landscape. The only thing that looks out of place is the historic windmill, rebuilt in 1993 for Potsdam's millennium celebration.

Sanssouci Park is quite large, being formerly a hunting ground, and requires a bit of walking. It feels like a giant maze, except one with many exits. Other buildings of note in the park include the Orangerie, styled like the Medici villa in Rome and the Uffizi in Florence, and the richly-gilded Chinese House, once a summer dining room. The Roman Baths and Charlottenhof Palace are also worth a look, but all paths in the park eventually lead to the enormous Neue Palais.

After suffering from heavy losses in the Seven Years War, the palace was built as a showpiece of the kingdom's remaining power. With two hundred opulent rooms, festive halls, galleries and theatres, it is just how we peasants imagine castles to be. There are also over five hundred statues on the roof, causing one Prussian general to reportedly quip that there were "more people on the roof than in the streets." Unfortunately, very little of the original furniture remains, with Kaiser Wilhelm II having packed everything into wagons and transported it with him to the Netherlands when he went into exile in 1918.

Walking distance from Sanssouci, and much less visited, is Neuer Garten. It was laid out in 1787 under Friedrich Wilhelm II, known as Fat William, as a getaway from Sanssouci. Why he needed a place to escape the place "without cares" remains a mystery. The garden is home to the Marmorpalais, Belvedere on the Pfingstberg and Schloss Cecilienhof, the last castle built by the Hohenzollern Kings, constructed during World World I for Crown Prince Wilhelm. Cecilienhof was the location for the Potsdam Conference in 1945, where the post-war fate of Germany was decided.

Among the royal sights are some rather bizarre buildings, including the Eiskeller, an ice cellar shaped like an Egyptian pyramid, the Küchenhaus, a kitchen designed like a sunken and ruined Roman temple, and a second Orangerie, which has an Egyptian portal and sphinx.

Fat William's court was famous for its debauchery and willingness to engage in vices. He maintained a lifelong relationship with his mistress, a commoner he elevated to Countess Lichtenau, and built the romantic castle on Pfaueninsel as a residence for her and the five children she bore him. It's a beautiful castle, with fairytale towers, but in garish white, making it stand out like a theatre prop. It's hardly discreet.

There is something fantastic and mysterious about this island, landscaped as an extension of the Neuer Garten and only a short boat ride away. Even before the castle was built, the island was shrouded in legend after alchemist Johannes Kunkel tried to make gold there in the seventeenth century, producing ruby glass instead. The island is reached by regular ferry from nearby Park Glienicke.

It's a nice walk from the ferry stop along the lake to Schloss Glienicke. The palace and grounds were laid out by Schinkel and Lenné in the nineteenth century for Prince Carl of Prussia, whose passion for Italy is evident in the style of the buildings. Nearby is Glienicke Brücke, the famous east-west bridge where spies were traded and exchanged during the Cold War.

Across Königstrasse, in the direction of Park Babelsberg, is a hunting lodge from 1653. At various times, the lodge was used as a hospital, a wallpaper factory and an orphanage. Renovations in 1859 gave it the baroque appearance it has today.

Laid out by Lenné and Prince Pückler, Park Babelsberg is more rugged and wild than the other landscaped gardens. Schloss Babelsberg was used as a summer residence for fifty years by Prince Wilhelm, later Kaiser Wilhelm I. The main tower rises out from the trees and looks over the wide expanse of the Tiefersee, looking west over the water towards Sanssouci.

In the park, the rolling hills are peppered with statues and stone benches, and the remains of a small theatre. A victory column is perched on one hill while the Flatowturm is a residential tower made in the style of a medieval city gate.

The days of Prussia are long gone, but the royals left some very nice remnants behind. While I would have been excluded from these areas two hundred or so years ago, as a modern day peasant, I'm able to walk these parks, explore the palaces and quietly rejoice that the king is dead.

Dream Job USA

When a friend was working as an editor for a company that published travel guides, I asked him to put in several good words for me in an open display of it's-not-what-you-know-it's-who-you-know. As a result, I landed the undeserved chance to work on the USA guidebook, ahead of a multitude of people who were surely far more qualified and experienced. But as the rookie in this book's writer-researcher-updater team, I was saddled with the assignment no one wanted: the Great Plains, including North Dakota, South Dakota, Nebraska, Kansas, Oklahoma, Iowa and Missouri. I was convinced, though, that this could be the dream job for a traveller, and so set off with a printout of the guidebook's section under my arm and a grin on my face. It turned into a nightmare, fast.

Day 1

Montreal, Canada, to St. Louis, Missouri

The year is 1999, and this is how the trip began. Hairy flight from Montreal to Newark, then an even hairier one from Newark to St. Louis. The windy autumn weather makes it seriously white-knuckle stuff. They have tornadoes out here, don't they?

I arrive in one piece, but my backpack doesn't arrive at all. I'm told it will follow me, delivered to my digs at the Embassy Suites the following day, or the next, or the next.

Not a good start.

Off to the rental car company to pick up my ride. It turns out the big-name guidebooks company has reserved me the cheapest car possible, in dull white, with a radio. Gone are my visions of cruising the interstates of the Great Plains with the top down of some whale of an American car, something with steer horns on the front. Instead, it's all aboard the Chevrolet Lawnmower.

I muscle the car out onto the freeway to join the grizzled fray heading towards downtown St. Louis, the skyline of which is tinged a hazy yellow.

Every exit says "St. Louis."

I have no idea which exit to take and rue my lack of preparation. No, strike that. I'm actually very prepared, but all the necessary documents, information and maps are in my backpack, which is probably still spinning around the carousel at Newark, or God knows where.

But it's Sunday, and downtown St. Louis, which like most American cities functions primarily as a place to work, is deserted. I negotiate the vacant streets, cutting across lanes and executing a couple of ambitious u-turns and asking a homeless man for directions, until I pull into the Embassy Suites car park.

A confession: I'm not being shy about throwing around the big-name guidebooks company's big name. This is because said company pays a pittance for several months of work, leaving the writer-researcher to get enterprising and try to save money by scoring stuff for free. As much stuff as possible, starting with a couple of free nights at the swanky Embassy Suites.

The receptionists are all smiles. I'm introduced to everyone in the back offices and get a bundle of marketing-type papers. I'm advised to partake of happy hour in the lobby bar, from 5-7pm, with snacks.

Upstairs, there's a big welcome basket in my suite, full of fruit, chocolates and wine. There's also a bag with some Cardinals merchandise, including a t-shirt, cap, key-ring and several pens. No Cardinals underwear, but at least I've got a clean shirt to wear tomorrow, one that might even help me blend in.

I'm keen to get started and to do a good job. I had a full afternoon planned, visiting several museums and hotels, but all the documents and printouts are in my backpack.

Unable to start the work, I wander St. Louis, taking in the Gateway Arch and meandering along the pooh-brown Mississippi River. There are several floating casinos, awash in flashing lights, despite it being mid-afternoon.

Not many people about, save a few tourists at the Arch.

I give up exploring in favour of the pursuit of happiness in the lobby bar. Happy hour turns out to be seriously happy, with free cocktails and beer, and chips, nuts and pretzels by the bucket-load.

The lobby bar is in an atrium, replete with fake trees and bubbling pond. Every voice echoes. I'm surrounded by businessmen who have dressed down for Sunday (no ties, collars open). It appears the hotel is hosting some kind of conference, as these guys are all wearing name tags and congregating in groups. There's something greasy about their exchanges, and something nasty about the way they gesture with their glasses in the general direction of the lone waitress.

I'm not really much better, a transient drinking free booze, in town for business reasons, a salesman of sorts. Just without a coterie of similar writer-researchers in tow.

I put away three bourbon and cokes, two tequila and grapefruits, and one vodka and cranberry. I toast my lost backpack and scarf down more chips and nuts. There's not a lot of alcohol in the drinks, but that gives more reason to have another and to not feel bad about it.

Close to 7pm, I get talking with some of the conference guys, dodging their questions about what work I'm in St. Louis for and turning down their invitations to head out on the town and find some real fun. I really don't like the sound of that and what it might involve. Greasy, nasty fun is not my kind of fun.

It's better to go upstairs and sleep off the bourbon, tequila and vodka, as tomorrow looms as a long day. I've got just one day to cover the whole section on St. Louis.

Day 2

St. Louis, Missouri

At 7:30am, I'm woken by a knock on the door. My backpack, hand-delivered by a porter who refuses any tip.

A half-hour later, I'm walking the streets of St. Louis. I start at the visitors centre, where I nab every brochure and pamphlet on offer.

Then it's a blur of museums, galleries, bars, restaurants, hotels and cafés. I also spend an hour on the phone at the Embassy Suites, chasing information and updates.

I miss happy hour. I miss dinner.

I eat all the fruit from the welcome basket and fall asleep just before 9pm.

It has begun.

Day 3

St. Louis, Missouri, to Iowa City, Iowa

Long drive, with half a dozen stops along the way at towns and sights listed in the book. I have lunch in Hannibal, the birthplace of Mark Twain, but I'm in no mood to contemplate his writings or to savour the apple pie I order for dessert and wax lyrical about how it tastes of everything that's right about America. Because I've got listings to go through, phone numbers to check, motel prices to update, opening hours to confirm. A single page of the guidebook is utterly overwhelming in terms of the amount of information to change, confirm or remove.

And I've still got about a hundred and fifty miles to go, to reach

Iowa City, and ahead of me are a couple of weeks filled with days exactly like this one.

Pages and pages and pages of information.

What the hell have I got myself into?

There's not much to look at in Iowa, from the interstate at least. Cornfields and trucks and more cornfields. Oh look, a cornfield.

I spend six hours behind the wheel of the Chevrolet Lawnmower. My back is very sore, as if I'd spent those six hours ploughing the myriad cornfields of Iowa by hand, or maybe building a baseball field in one.

But Iowa City turns out to be quite a happening little college town, one with a relaxed mid-west vibe. I find a nice bar that serves soup in giant bowls made of sourdough bread.

I hang around to watch a baseball game with a few college students. They give me tips of things to do in town, bars and clubs and such. I make notes, stupidly adding these places to my list of things to check tomorrow.

Day 4

Iowa City, Iowa, to Des Moines, Iowa

My suite has three bathrooms. Three! Now what could a man possibly need three bathrooms for? What could a man possibly be doing in Des Moines? The manager of the Hotel Fort Des Moines has put me in the presidential suite, and I'm feeling right at home.

I meet with the hotel manager, to thank him for his generosity and hospitality. He explains he's a fan of the big-name guidebooks company. He reels off some of the books he has used on past trips and points out what was wrong with them.

If only every hotel manager was a critic and a fan. Then I could be lectured about books I didn't work on and enjoy suites with three bathrooms each night. The latter is how I'd imagined this gig to be. It hasn't been that way so far, given the tragic motel room I had last night in Iowa City. Still, I'm presidential for this night.

On the way to Des Moines, I passed the Iowa State Fair. A lot of pick-up trucks and animal transportation trailers. A very barnyard smell as well, when I lowered the window of the Lawnmower. So I kept on driving.

The chapter on Des Moines is short, thankfully. The main attraction is the Skywalk, a three-mile enclosed walkway that joins many of the buildings downtown. Once inside, it feels like being on board the Starship Enterprise. Not a new Enterprise from a recent *Star Trek* movie or TV show reboot; the old Enterprise, with its seriously dated version of how the future might look.

The Skywalk seems a little unsteady underfoot. The windows vibrate with each step.

I wonder if the city of Des Moines employs people to open all the Skywalk's doors by hand to give the impression of automatic doors, because there's something static and inconsistent about how the doors open, as on the old Enterprise.

I give up on the Skywalk in fear we might just lift off, and retreat to my presidential suite, where there is a pile of pamphlets and brochures for me to go through, gathered from tourist offices and chambers of commerce between Iowa City and Des Moines. For an hour, I sit and stare at it all, feeling like I might just start weeping.

Day 5

Des Moines, Iowa, to Lincoln, Nebraska

The day's long drive includes a miserable hour circling Omaha, trying to find the visitors centre. This came after I availed myself of the Hotel Fort Des Moines free telephone calls the night before, using the phone in bathroom number two to call my editor-friend at the big-name guidebooks company in London to tell him I couldn't go on. His advice to the quivering wreck cowering on the granite tile floor: stop going to every single place.

"Fudge as much as you can," he said. "You'll go crazy otherwise."

A veteran of several updates, he talked me through the art of fudging. It includes skipping places and getting others to do the work. It means enlisting the help of people at every visitors centre and chamber of commerce. And not simply gathering brochures and pamphlets – the Lawnmower was full of them, impacting the car's already bad fuel economy – but putting the current guidebook in front of these people and getting them to check everything. Getting them to make the calls and utilising their local knowledge without having to go to every place listed in the book to check if it's still there, and that they have lobster on the menu, and that it's closed on Mondays, and that children under twelve are free, and that there are rotating exhibitions so ask at the office for what's on, and that entry costs $15 for adults and $12 for students and seniors with valid ID cards, and so on and so on. To be completely thorough meant the research would never end, and I barely had time to spend a day in each major city.

Which is why I drive up and down Omaha's grid of streets to locate the visitors centre; to fudge that section and avoid spending a night in the city. But the visitors centre had moved, and moved again. Exasperated, I ask for directions and receive bad advice.

But once at the centre, it's worth the effort. When I say who I am and what I'm doing, and ask very politely for assistance, three women get to work checking, updating and double-checking. I'm offered tea and home-made cookies. They work the phones. It's all done in half an hour, far better than my update on St. Louis, which I realise I'll have to do again at the end of the trip.

Back in the Lawnmower, I'm a little less jittery on the drive to Lincoln. I know the rest of the update still won't be much fun, but at least I've got a way to cut some corners and make it easier.

Lincoln is another college town, but college-rowdy rather than college-relaxed. I drive past many fraternity houses. There are signs outside liquor stores saying, "Welcome back students" and "Students receive discounts." There are a lot of liquor stores.

Out of the Lawnmower, I start exploring on foot, encountering many young men roaming in packs; they drink beer and yell obscenities at young girls roaming in packs. It's all very juvenile, very high-school, but it appears to amount to a good time for all involved.

Guess that says a lot about Lincoln, Nebraska.

Day 6

Lincoln, Nebraska, to Mitchell, South Dakota

Barely a week in, I know I'm failing at this. And I don't care.

This is due to a startling realisation I have on Interstate 29, on the way from Sioux City to Sioux Falls. The Sioux connection, and a frustrating morning, prompts me to lower all the windows of the Lawnmower and shout, "I am Wind In His Hair!"

I pump a fist out the window as I say it again and again.

And I'm almost crying too, because the tourist office in Sioux City had been closed, forcing me to speed all over town trying to update false information and encountering numerous instances where the guidebook was so wrong that the whole section on Sioux City would have to be rewritten. But that would take days, so I updated as best I could, jumped in the Lawnmower and fled north.

"I am Wind In His Hair! Do you see that I'm shit at this job?"

Yes, very shit. But I've got to keep moving. There's Sioux Falls up ahead, and I need to get to Mitchell before the Corn Palace closes. And tomorrow I have to somehow do the whole of North Dakota in a day.

"I am ... not going to North Dakota."

And it hits me. My predecessor clearly skipped Sioux City, not mention a lot of other places. So I don't see a problem with me also skipping lots of places, including an entire state.

I rationalise this by working backwards: the guidebook won't be published until well into next year, as the book is Bible-thick and requires a long time to go through the final editing process. Which means that people won't buy it for at least another year or so, and by that time, everything that has been updated will be a good twelve months out-of-date, or more. Which kind of makes what I'm doing out here a pointless endeavour. I'm killing myself to update information that will no longer be current by the time people hold the guidebook in their hands. No matter how exact and thorough I am, no matter how many cities and towns I visit, the reader will still end up complaining that the guidebook is out-of-date, and with good reason.

Because there is no way to update this guidebook.

So why bother?

I decide to take guidebook-update-fudging to a whole new level, starting with crossing North Dakota off the itinerary. Who visits North Dakota anyway?

It feels very good to be Wind In His Hair, and I don't care if I'm bad at this job. Even if I'm brilliant at it, the result twelve months down the road will still be bad.

When I reach Sioux Falls, my first stop is a large paper recycling bin. In it, I dump all the brochures, pamphlets, flyers, corporate magazines, folders and business cards collected over the first week. The car feels much lighter as result, and it feels good to get rid of all that clutter.

The tourist office is open. I hand them the short paragraphs on Sioux Falls and get them to check everything. It takes fifteen minutes. One employee tries to get me to add more to the section, eagerly pushing pamphlets and brochures on me that I refuse. I babble some lie about the book having a restricted number of pages, because of printing costs and market forces and consumer habits, or whatever. My charter is simply to update what's already there.

Yep, update a guidebook that will be out-of-date when it goes to print.

"Screw it," says Wind In His Hair.

In Mitchell, I find the monstrosity that is the Corn Palace, which is a bizarre, camel-coloured, Arabian-looking place, with minarets, and decorated with designs made of corn. But I don't go inside. I go straight to the Motel 6, where the Mitchell tourism people have put me up for the night. It's awful, the kind of place where criminals lay low when on the run. Still, my single room has a phone that works, even if the receiver's a bit sticky to touch. It takes a few calls, and waiting on hold, but I manage to get the key person responsible for North Dakota tourism on the line. Curiously, she doesn't ask me why I'm not visiting North Dakota, which makes me wonder if she also thinks there's not much reason to do so. The section in the guidebook comprises just four pages. The guidebook itself is well over a thousand pages long.

She agrees to have me fax those four pages to her. She will then update the section and fax it back to me tomorrow morning.

Brilliant.

I celebrate with take-out pizza, a couple of beers and a pint of Ben & Jerry's ice cream, all consumed on the lumpy bed in my Motel 6 room while watching *The Bridges of Madison County*. I'd passed through that area just a few days ago. It looks more attractive and romantic on film than in real life. I remember there being many more cornfields than bridges. Still, *The Cornfields of Madison County* doesn't sound quite as romantic. More like a horror film.

I don't venture outside to see what Mitchell is like by night.

I put the chain on the door and sleep restlessly on the lumpy bed.

Day 7

Mitchell, South Dakota, to Rapid City, South Dakota

Dull drive. Long and straight. I have trouble staying awake.

It's all very boring until I reach Badlands National Park, where I park the Lawnmower and attempt to take a short hike.

The Badlands is an eerie landscape of sharply-contoured ridges and multi-coloured hills. A bit like the ruined skyline of a city abandoned long ago, with the windows filled in.

It's anything but abandoned, though, because the parking areas are jammed full with campervans, pick-up trucks and rental cars. Plenty of people are milling about, taking photos and shouting at each other from a distance. Their voices echo between the high-rising ridges.

So much for a peaceful hike.

The campervan people are cooking lunch on small outdoor barbecues in front of their large vehicles. They sit in foldout chairs, next to coolers full of ice and beer. All the people, including the children, are a bit larger than necessary. A bit louder, too.

It's all distracting from the strange natural beauty of this place.

The Badlands is hell?

A tad harsh.

How does that line from Shakespeare go? Something like, "Hell is empty, and all the devils are here."

Very large devils.

Badlands National Park: beautiful. The visitors: hellish.

Back in the Lawnmower.

A quick stop in Wall to check the motels there, as Wall is an entry point to Badlands National Park and described as a convenient place for visitors to stay.

I do the rounds. Behind the counter at the Best Western Motel is an absolutely stop-traffic beautiful girl. It's as if she's stepped straight out of some mid-west farm-girls calendar. Her hair is lush and chestnut-coloured, and it looks like that's the hair's natural colour. I have visions of barns filled with hay bales and early morning cow-milking. I see this girl out of her Best Western garb and in blue overalls with a red-and-white checked shirt, the sleeves rolled up, a few strands of straw in her hair.

She's so gorgeous, and working at a motel in a town with a population of less than a thousand, that the situation seems sinister, almost unreal. Or surreal, in a *Twin Peaks* kind of way. Incredible beauty in a place of isolation, loneliness and weirdness. It just doesn't fit.

Her name is Heidi Jo. She speaks in full sentences and has a bright smile with perfect teeth. She seems rather smart, and is more than happy to help. She even corrects a couple of spelling errors in the text.

While we update the blurb on the Best Western, she tells me she was born and raised in Wall.

It's hard to believe. She's an anomaly?

A part of me wants to take her away from all this, to rescue her from Wall and from all the devils visiting the Badlands. Instead, I thank her for her help and drive out of town.

I should be feeling uplifted by the experience, that even in desolate Wall, such beauty can be born and bred. But I'm actually feeling scared. Heidi Jo, at the Best Western Motel in Wall, South Dakota, potential Miss USA.

Can't be true.

It was a trap, of some kind.

Had to be.

Heidi Jo really was some kind of monster.

Surely.

As I drive to Rapid City, I check the rear-view mirror every now and then, to be sure I'm not being followed.

Day 8

Rapid City, South Dakota, to Deadwood, South Dakota

Things have changed. Rapid City was never on the itinerary. I stopped here last night because it looked interesting and I'd spent enough time in the Lawnmower for one day.

It felt great to make such a spontaneous decision. I even bunked at the local youth hostel and mixed in with the few travellers staying there. The hostel owner put on a barbecue for everyone, for $2 each.

I'm up early in the morning and take a run through the hills near town. It's a beautiful day.

I'm enjoying this little corner of South Dakota, and the guidebook tells me there's something interesting stuff ahead, including the Black Hills, Custer State Park, Mount Rushmore and some place called the Crazy Horse Monument.

It's leisurely today. Sunday speed. As I drive to Sturgis, I think that all the update days should be like this: slow, relaxed, and with the possibility for diversions and detours.

There are some great town names out here: Black Hawk, Crook City and Spearfish. I see a sign pointing to a place called Mud Butte.

With the required towns covered, I take the winding Spearfish Canyon Byway towards Deadwood. It's a beautiful drive. Rivers, lakes, tree-covered hills, a dramatic vista around every corner. I drive slowly, enjoying the views, and get passed by a logging truck and half a dozen mobile homes along the way.

When there's space enough, I pull the Lawnmower to the side of the road, get out and lie on the bonnet.

No clouds. Some birds circling. The forest alive with noises.

I'd like to set up camp, but I don't have any gear, and I'm not sleeping in the Lawnmower.

So, it's on to Deadwood. The former cowboy town lives up to its name. "Frontier western" is the pervading theme, while gambling is the main pastime and attraction. There are plenty of casinos; even the laundromats and supermarkets have slot machines, which is both funny and depressing.

The buses are parked along Upper and Lower Main Street. Rows of them, with the doors open and the drivers gathered in a group. Though they represent different bus companies, every driver is wearing a short-sleeved shirt with a tie.

My first stop is the tourist office. It's a bit of a shame to be told they've booked me a room in some cheap motel on the outskirts of town, and not in a suite at one of the casinos. Other freebies I'd expected but which weren't forthcoming include a pile of complimentary chips, tickets to a show and a ten-gallon hat. Instead, I'm given a single voucher for the buffet at the Silverado Casino. In exchange, I hand them the section on Deadwood and ask them to correct and update it. Rather than waiting, I hike up to Mount Moriah Cemetery, where Wild Bill Hickok and Calamity Jane are buried.

The cemetery is interesting.

You get a sense of the town's colourful history by looking at the graves, headstones and signs. Who the heck was Potato Creek Johnny and how did he get his nickname? About a third of the graves are unmarked, a sign says, and I wonder who those people were and what lives they lived. And what about all those children who died during the smallpox and scarlet fever epidemics? Something tells me those stories may be more interesting than Wild Bill's and Calamity Jane's.

The cemetery offers a nice view over Deadwood. From here, I can see the convoy of buses on the move. Where are they headed? Is there another gambling hot-spot three hours down the road?

Back in town, the update work done, blessedly by someone else, there's really not much to do. I don't have any intention of feeding quarters into a slot machine or putting all my update earnings on red.

The motel is miserable. I think I'm the only guest.

It's tempting to leave.

Day 9
Deadwood, South Dakota, to Alliance, Nebraska

Like many vagabonds before me, I depart Deadwood at dawn.

It's another beautiful drive through Black Hills National Forest, and another cloudless day.

I'm rather chuffed that this update has brought me out to this part of America. It's not such a bad trip after all, and fantastic driving country.

My first stop is Mount Rushmore, which is much smaller than I expected. I'd thought the Shrine to Democracy would be as tall as a skyscraper. I'm actually left a little nonplussed, more so by the fact that it costs $8 to park at the visitors centre, while it's free a little further down the road, with both car parks about the same walking distance from the monument. The free car park was empty and the $8 car park was close to full.

There are far too many people to enjoy this small monument, forcing me to look between heads to see the four presidential heads, and Rushmore disappoints anyway. I update the section in the guidebook and get back in the Lawnmower.

The next stop is Crazy Horse.

As I drive away from Rushmore, there's a continuous stream of traffic heading towards the monument. I'm hoping Crazy Horse will be a bit quieter.

It turns out to be very quiet, and a lot more impressive.

Talk about ambition.

The visitors centre is a full mile from the monument itself, which will have Crazy Horse on horseback, pointing at the lands where "his dead are buried." I learn this at the visitors centre, which also has a sublime scale model of how the finished monument will look. They've been carving Crazy Horse out of the side of a mountain since 1947, and the only defining feature so far is his face, inside of which all four Rushmore heads could fit. The outline of the horse is painted on the mountain in six-foot wide white paint. As the story goes, the original sculptor, Korczak Ziolkowski, was enlisted by Henry Standing Bear, in reaction to the Rushmore unveiling, to create a comparable monument. The Sioux chief wanted to show that the Sioux and other Native American tribes had great heroes as well. Ziolkowski started on his own with a chisel, a jackhammer, a 700-step ladder and a vision. His children, and his children's children, continue the legacy.

It's mindboggling how big this thing is, and that it's decades from being finished.

Back in the Lawnmower, driving south for Nebraska, I think that there is nothing I'll see today that can top Crazy Horse.

A couple of things get close.

The first is reaching the Nebraska border. There's a large green sign, welcoming you, and behind the sign, the interstate undulates towards the horizon, a string of telephone poles following alongside. There's nothing but parched-brown fields. I can't see any houses or animals or people. There aren't even any cars. Rubbish is piled up on both sides of the road.

The sign says: "Nebraska ... the good life."

Indeed. It looks pretty good from here.

Further down the road, things get better, or weirder, as I come across Carhenge.

It's exactly as it sounds: a collection of old cars, painted grey and buried upright in a very accurate replica of Stonehenge.

Bizarre.

So this is how Nebraskans enjoy their good life. They turn wreckage into art. It's impressive and head-scratching.

The nearest town is Alliance. I decide I've seen enough for one day and take a room there.

Rushmore, Crazy Horse, the good life, Carhenge: only in America.

Day 10-12

Alliance, Nebraska, to Steamboat Springs, Colorado

I secretly get off the grid, detouring to Steamboat to visit some friends. I spend most of the time in the hot tub.

Day 13

Steamboat Springs, Colorado, to Dodge City, Kansas

The Lawnmower strikes back. On my way to rejoin the update route, the car struggles on even the slightest rise, and eventually overheats on the outskirts of Denver.

I wait for everything to cool down, fill the bare radiator with the water I have and manage to limp to the rental car company's lot at the Denver Airport.

While hardly apologetic for my car troubles, and with the service clerk eying me suspiciously, like it was all my fault, I do get upgraded to a better car: a Kia Sephia, and I'm not kidding.

Is it possible to look cool in a Kia Sephia?

Hey, girl, you wanna ride with me in my Sephia?

No way.

Sephia, the goddess of good mileage and turtleneck sweaters.

I'm calling the car's colour "mountain river green."

It runs much better than the Lawnmower, and even has a tape deck. So, name aside, I'm feeling pretty good about things as I dig in for the long drive to Dodge City.

About ten miles from the airport, I approach the first toll station of the day, but can't find my wallet. I pull over just short of the toll station and rifle through the Sephia, even looking under the seats.

I realise I must have left it in the Lawnmower. Of all things: my wallet.

Back in the car, I drive up to the toll booth and explain my situation. I'm given a bill that must be paid within twenty-four hours.

Through the toll, I make an illegal u-turn across the highway, dirtying the Sephia and adding mud to the mountain river green. I get another bill on the other side, then speed towards the airport, cursing my idiocy.

The Sephia's got quite a bit of zip.

At the car rental lot, I go straight to the Lawnmower. It's still parked where I left it and unlocked. I search the entire car, watched by several rental company employees, but can't find my wallet.

I'm panicking now, thinking some enterprising car cleaner nabbed my wallet while I was switching cars.

In the office, I report the incident, leaving my contact details and generally making a tourist scene. I drop the big-name guidebooks company's big name, to no avail. Through the window, I see some of the employees searching the car. I go outside and tell them it's a lost cause. Then, a guy pulls my wallet out from between the driver's seat and the floor, and smiles at me like I'm a complete idiot.

Hmmm.

I'd really combed the car, even moving that seat backwards and forwards, and looking underneath and on the sides. Had I really missed it?

I decide not to think the worst of people, as all my money and cards are still there.

I thank all the employees present, and admit that I must have somehow missed it.

Back in the Sephia, and back to the toll station, where I pay the two outstanding tolls and a new one.

Still a bit rattled, I tell the toll booth lady that the next time I come back to Denver, I expect the roads to be in prime condition. She sneers at me, shrugs and goes back to her magazine.

It takes six hours to get to Dodge City.

While better to drive, the Sephia really guzzles the gas. So, not really the goddess of good mileage.

Storm clouds make for a stunning sunset.

It's late when I pull into the Thunderbird Motel, but not late enough for a rep from the motel to want to meet me and tell me all about the motel's recent renovations and improvements. He follows this by launching into a detailed history of Dodge City. As I'm being spotted a night in this esteemed establishment, I'm forced to smile politely and listen.

He craps on and on about Wyatt Earp.

Oh gawd, will you just tell me what a room costs, double and single, and let me go to sleep? I've driven nearly ten hours today.

Day 14

Dodge City, Kansas, to Wichita, Kansas

There's no time to spend here. No time to visit Boot Hill Cemetery, where cowboys were buried with their boots on. No time to explore this former cowboy town that's become a long strip mall of souvenir shops and tacky western-themed attractions. No time to eat ribs for breakfast.

All there's time for is a quick stop at the tourist office.

From Dodge City, it's a pretty boring drive across the flatlands to Wichita, aside from passing through the town of Pratt, home of the 1997 Miss America, according to several signs. Is she here, still living in Pratt, maybe working at the counter of a local motel?

I can't help thinking about Heidi Jo, that stunner at the Best Western in Wall, South Dakota. And again, I'm checking the mirrors as I drive out of town.

No locals with pitchforks, thankfully.

Wichita doesn't exactly disappoint, as I had pretty low expectations coming in.

It's the home of Pizza Hut.

Wow. Pizza.

The nice people at the visitors centre update the section and recommend that I include something about the aeronautical industry, with Boeing, Cessna, Lear Jet and such. When she says this, I start hearing the planes flying overhead. She boasts that Wichita has half a dozen airports, plus an air force base.

Wow. Airports.

"Wichita is the air capital of the world," she says with a smile.

"Is that right?"

"You should definitely check out the Aviation Museum."

I nod.

She says quite a bit more about Wichita, but I'm not really listening. I'm trying to map a route to the hotel they've got me staying at, which appears to be out in the suburbs and near a couple of airports.

Once there, I'm given a nice room on the top floor. Planes fly over the building all night. I don't eat any pizza.

Day 15

Wichita, Kansas, to Oklahoma City, Oklahoma

I've upped the ante with cajoling the city marketing people to do most of the update work, by faxing sections a couple of days ahead so all I need to do is pick them up on the way through. This saves me not only from going to all the hotels, restaurants and sights, but also from spending an hour or more in the visitors centre, waiting for them to update and having to listen to them talk about airports and pizzas, or whatever their fair city has to offer. However, it has the negative effect of presaging my arrival, which might result in a dreaded "personal tour" or, worse, a lunch or dinner with key city personnel.

Such is the case in Oklahoma City. At the tourist office, Marketing Man is waiting for me.

A head shorter than me, he's got just about the right combination of politeness and smarm befitting a person who pushes a city for a living. A bit like a used car salesman for upmarket brands, or the guest services manager on a four-star cruise ship. Cheerfully slimy, seeming to both love and hate his job, and the people he has to deal with.

So, it's with a mixture of zeal, suffering and animosity that Marketing Man takes me around Oklahoma City. We go to the stockyards, to take in the enthralling spectacle of cattle being bought and sold. We stop for breakfast at the Cattlemen's Steakhouse. Marketing Man says the famous restaurant was won in a craps game in 1945, and suggests I try the brains and scrambled eggs. I have a cup of tea and try not to stare at my watch.

We go to the Cowboy Hall of Fame and the site of the Oklahoma City bombing. We hit some other places in between; they're a blur and nothing remotely memorable.

Throughout, Marketing Man is an endless stream of chatter. I'm not terribly impressed with what he says, but I am impressed that one person knows so much about Oklahoma City. Still, there's something in his delivery and manner that bespeaks memorised information rather than local knowledge and civic pride.

The personal tour ends at some massive arena. We have lunch in an empty sports bar and restaurant, looking down on all the empty seats and the empty field. I don't recall Oklahoma City having a major league baseball team. Marketing Man mentions something about the city pushing for a sports franchise of some sort. They've got the sponsors and a fan base, but he can't understand why the city isn't appealing enough for a sports team to move here.

I shrug.

Blessedly, after lunch, the personal tour is over. Marketing Man drives me back to the tourist office. Once there, he tells me the Marriott is "hosting my visit for the evening." He offers to escort me to the hotel, but I assure him I will be able to find it. He attempts ingratiating humour, remarking that guidebook updaters must be such experienced travellers, they could find their ways out of the jungle of Borneo.

"Yeah, that's about right," I say, refraining from adding that such travellers usually find personal tours a complete waste of time and find getting a version of a city filtered fully through someone else as the worse way to experience a place.

The Marriott is easy to find. The receptionist informs me that my room is on the restricted floor, and so it should be, given what I've endure today. In the elevator, there's a special slot to slide in my card to get to the restricted floor.

Superb digs.

I relax in the Concierge Lounge, eating fruit and drinking tea, trying to get Marketing Man out of my system.

It takes a while.

By late afternoon, I decide to do some exploring of my own, starting at the site of the Oklahoma City bombing. When we'd come here earlier, a tourist bus had just disgorged its occupants. Their presence had distracted somewhat from taking in this scene, and Marketing Man had talked constantly.

It's deserted now: more stark, more real, more hitting. A lone tree stands firm on the site. Marketing Man said it took the full brunt of the blast and survived. He also said that the flowers and tributes that line the construction fences are cleared away every month, because it gets so full, and taken to a special place where they are stored. And he also said they're building a memorial, a museum and an Institute for the Prevention of Terrorism.

Marketing Man should've just shut up and let me take in this place. I'm glad that I get to do it now, alone, without the prattle of accompanying information, and without the tourists posing and prancing.

The tree is beautiful.

The bombing seems senseless.

I start to like Oklahoma City.

Day 16

Oklahoma City, Oklahoma, to Tulsa, Oklahoma

The restricted floor is where I want to be every night. You can keep your three bathrooms and your presidential suites and your happy hours. I want a floor that only a selected few can be on. I want a Concierge Lounge with a sublime breakfast. I want orange juice squeezed at my table. I want eggs Benedict. I want a bed that doesn't feel like it's been slept in by thousands of others.

Looking back on the last two weeks, I think the whole trip would have been so much easier if every night I'd been able to go up to the restricted floor.

In Tulsa, it's back to motel living; to lumpy mattresses, thin walls and dripping faucets. To carpet stains and doors with sliding chains. To sticky phones. The motel is downtown, which is deserted not long after the working day ends. I'm actually a little scared to venture outside. There's no one. It's a ghost town.

Speaking of which, Marketing Man told me yesterday about a flooded city not far from Tulsa, which was apparently now a diving site. That sounded interesting. On the drive to Tulsa, I tried to locate this place, even stopping for directions at several petrol stations. None of the locals had heard of it. The one old station attendant who did know about it was cagey when questioned.

"There used ta be divin thar," he said. "But no one talks bout that round here no more."

"Where is it?" I asked.

"Well, yeah, don't know exactly. Best to leave it, son. There be lots to do in Tulsa."

Yes, there sure be. The guidebook tells me one of the sights is the prayer tower at Oral Roberts University.

Pass.

I do venture outside, but in the safety of the Sephia. I find a Sonic Drive-in, which are these retro burger joints where you drive up and order. But my dinner is ordinary, as I'm alone, eating in a Kia Sephia and not quite the coolest kid in town. Not even in Tulsa.

Day 17

Tulsa, Oklahoma, to Lawrence, Kansas

Driving. Driving. Driving.

I feel like I'm in a daze. When I finally reach Lawrence, nothing is quite in focus.

It's another college town. Liquor stores and "Welcome back students" signs.

Wait, am I actually in Lincoln? Or Iowa City?

Where the hell am I?

Day 18

Lawrence, Kansas, to Kansas City, Missouri

Keen to escape Lawrence, I get to Kansas City early enough to beat the rush hour traffic, and well before my walking tour date with Marketing Woman.

I take the chance to do some exploring of my own.

Kansas City is kind of two cities really, divided by the state line. Most of the suburbs are on the Kansas side of the city, while most of the interesting stuff is on the Missouri side.

There's a lot to do, and it's a beautiful day. The time runs quickly. I nearly miss my appointment with Marketing Woman, which would have been a disaster, because she's already updated the section on K.C., far better than I ever could have, and she's taking me to dinner at some fancy joint tomorrow night, and I'm staying in five-star accommodation on the Missouri side, where waiting for me in my suite were free passes to basically every sight in town, plus a ticket to something called the Kansas City Spirit Festival, happening tonight, and a six pack of Boulevard Pale Ale, which I think is a really nice touch and in line with the city's relaxed vibe.

I'm also glad I make the appointment on time because Marketing Woman turns out to be far more pleasant than Oklahoma City's Marketing Man, and all the other Marketing People I have encountered. She's a local, and her civic pride seems genuine. As we walk around K.C., she tells me about her plans to become a walking guide when she retires in a few years.

She doesn't try to sell me the city, and she only talks when I ask her a question. As a result, it's enjoyable to do the walking tour with her. Marketing Woman becomes Cheryl.

Cheryl knows just about everything there is to know about Kansas City, and she seems to know everyone as well.

We go to the Negro Leagues Baseball Museum, where Cheryl introduces me to Buck O'Neill, the first African-American manager in major league baseball. And we hit the Jazz Museum next door. Cheryl's a music buff. She even sings a few lines of the Fats Domino song *Kansas City*.

We take a cab to the Nelson-Atkins Museum of Art and spend an hour in there, with a few turns around the sculpture garden as well, which has these giant shuttlecocks.

All through the tour, Cheryl plies me with local goodies like root beer and gourmet chocolate, and buying me a few souvenirs as well, jokingly saying she has "an expense account for people like you."

"Like me?"

"We'll burn a hole in it tomorrow night as well," she adds.

And with that, she takes her leave, at just about the right time too.

I go back to my suite and relax, knocking back a couple of Boulevard Pale Ales on the balcony before heading to the Spirit Festival.

It turns out, much to my delight, that the festival is actually a live music event, and not some strange religious gathering. Men at Work are headlining. I also catch sets by the Violent Femmes and Rick Springfield, who gets the whole crowd singing along to *Jesse's Girl*.

And I'm just lovin' Kansas City.

Day 19

Kansas City

I sleep in.

Better said: I'm awake early and lie around in bed, thinking about the trip so far. While it was incredibly stressful at the start, to the point I crumbled into a quivering heap on the floor of bathroom number two in the presidential suite of the Hotel Fort Des Moines, dialling the big-name guidebooks company's suicide hotline, I now find myself quite snug in the rhythm of the update. "Delegate" and "fudge" have become my two favourite verbs in the English language. The update is made simple when others do it – ideally locals who know much more about the place than I ever will – and when I accept that no matter what I do, the guidebook won't be up-to-date when it goes to print. And this is a nice little safety net, too, because if, down the line, I get asked why X and Y are wrong in the book, I can claim that it was right when I was there, one year ago, and that won't be an outright lie. More like a false truth.

As I head down for a five-star, continental breakfast, I'm feeling pretty good about the world. A lazy day in Kansas City stretches out before me. I'm not even sure how to spend it. All that's on the schedule is dinner with Cheryl.

I spend the morning reading newspapers while consuming the world's slowest breakfast.

But it's another nice day, and just before noon, I decide to venture outside. As it's nearby, I take a look at the River Market and also go through the Steamboat Arabia Museum, which Cheryl had recommended and organised a free ticket for. The museum has artefacts from the *Arabia*, which sank in the Missouri in 1856, and is like a time capsule, documenting life from the mid-nineteenth century. I'm fascinated by all the keys on display in the Hardware section, and by all the boots. I also get a sense of how important the river was for transportation, supply and trade.

Nice tip, Cheryl.

Outside, I buy a root beer and take a seat on a bench. I'm thinking: this update business would be a total breeze if I had a Cheryl in every town and city. A knowledgeable and helpful local with an inflated expense account for people like me.

At dinner, Cheryl's not interested in talking about Kansas City. She wants to know about my trip, the highlights and the places that left an impression, good or bad.

So I take her through it, telling her about Crazy Horse and Carhenge and the Badlands. The story about Heidi Jo in Wall makes Cheryl laugh, as does my description of Marketing Man.

"I think I might have met him," Cheryl says, "at a convention, maybe. Well, I've certainly met a lot of people like him."

We both have two desserts.

When it comes to paying the bill, Cheryl leaves a pile of cash on the table, with what looks like a very generous tip, and pockets the receipt.

We part with a handshake outside before Cheryl drives off, heading for the suburbs on the Kansas side. I walk all the way back to my hotel, trying to burn off what was far and away the best meal of the trip.

And I'm sad to be leavin' Kansas City.

Day 20

Kansas City, Missouri, to St. Louis, Missouri

Back to where it all began: drunk in the lobby bar of the Embassy Suites, but feeling far happier during happy hour than three weeks ago.

I got here early, in order to fix all the mistakes I'd made when first updating St. Louis. Some nice folks in the visitors centre helped me out. They weren't quite Cheryl-calibre, who will forever be the benchmark for city marketing people, but helpful nonetheless.

Afterwards, the update pretty much finished, except for keying all the garnered information into the final master document, I checked out the City Museum, a new attraction that was closed when I was last here. It's a wild place, made almost entirely of junk. When you go in, they stop you and say, "Have fun, and don't lose your adult." There are all these tunnels and caves to explore, and some really bizarre exhibits, such as the world's largest pair of y-fronts. Just a whole lot of good fun, and a nice way to end the trip.

It's over, and it's a relief. I spent around five hours a day, on average, behind the wheel, and covered nearly 3,000 miles in total. I don't want to drive a Chevrolet Lawnmower or a Kia Sephia ever again.

As for updating another guidebook, I'm not sure. I think I figured out how to do it with the least amount of stress and pain. But there's still all the travelling involved: the mad rush to get from place to place, the lack of time to enjoy the interesting things which appear on the path, and no chance to take detours. There's also the conundrum of updating something that will end up out-of-date when it's produced.

Nightmare Job France

The big-name guidebooks company hauled me in again a few months later, to do the France chapter of the whopping Europe guidebook. Seriously, who can carry around these tomes? I was given a rail pass, a large bag of pennies and four weeks to cover the whole country, and that included spending a week in Paris. In the days leading up to my departure, I did my best to learn as much French as I could, in order to back up my claim to the big-name guidebooks company that I was fluent. So, I mastered important sentences such as, Where is the tourist office? and Can you update this section for me? and Do you have a fax machine? and All the other hotels give me free nights so you should too. It was winter, cold and wet. Not the best travelling weather. But I figured because I'd managed so well in the States, I could knock off this update with ease. Wrong, or rather, faux.

Day 1

   Hamburg, Germany, to Paris, France

   This is how it began. I'm at the Hamburg central station at dawn. I spend much of the ten-hour train trip to Paris staring out the window, as the northern lowlands turn into hills, the hills lead to rivers, and Germany meets with France. It's very pleasant to sit on the train, much more so than behind the wheel of some ghastly rental car. A comfortable German train (the seats recline, the toilets work, the floor looks quite clean), running almost on time. I swap to a French train in Saarbrücken. This is also comfortable, but not running on time.

   It's not long after we pull out of Metz that I conclude that I hate travel guidebooks. And I kind of fume the rest of the way to Paris, wondering why the hell I'm doing this again, slaving away to improve something I despise while also opening up travel to a broader range of people; yet when I'm really honest, travelling with a guidebook takes a lot of the adventure and fun out of it, and I'd selfishly prefer all those tourists stay home.

   To justify my actions, I decide that updating a guidebook is far more of an adventure and challenge than simply travelling with one, which makes me feel both smug and sad.

   It is February, 2000, a date that looks more science fiction than reality.

In the five months since finishing the USA guidebook, I've forced myself to become an internet expert; to make what I'd stupidly thought to be a passing sci-fi fad my reality. Before that, I wasn't really sure what this internet thingy could do, beyond sending digital telegrams and helping me get sports scores from the other side of the world. I discovered that you can update a fair chunk of a guidebook just from information found online, and contact people ahead of time to do the updating for you. So, gone is the updater who faxed and fudged. Enter the updater who emails and surfs the web.

Which is why, as the train pulls into Gare de l'Est, I feel ready for the France update, even if I hate guidebooks in general. I was given the chapter a few weeks before departure, and in that time got as much of it updated as I could, thanks to the information superhighway.

It was clandestine work, though. I have no intention of telling the big-name guidebooks company that I've fudged a big chunk using the internet, as it would probably cost me, and all the other updaters, this awful job.

It's my first time in France, and I'm excited. Paris, museums galore, the Loire (once I learn how to pronounce it correctly), wine, croissants, the Alps, the Riviera, more wine, more croissants, and maybe a few rude Frenchmen thrown in.

In my first half an hour, I step twice in dog shit, see a man pull a knife on two others and rob them, and watch a woman get accosted in the street.

I'm scared.

Day 2

Paris

I'm staying at a youth hostel in Montmartre. It was my last resort after I contacted the tourist office and got no joy, and all the hotels I emailed only offered lean discounts. I wanted a free bed; the one I had to settle for was in a room with seven others. Arriving late last night meant I had to take a top bunk, with the snores and odours rising to the ceiling.

So, the big-name guidebooks company is not as big in France as it is in the States. There will be no presidential suites, no three bathrooms, no restricted floors, no marketing people. I'm in a crummy hostel surrounded by young backpackers sporting hefty guidebooks.

I'm trying to fly under the radar here. I don't want anyone to know

I'm updating a travel guidebook, which would result in repeated claims that I have the best job in the world, followed by a list of personal recommendations they'd like to see added to the book, followed by a list of personal gripes about the previous book, and about other books, followed by a demand for me to give them a leg-up in order to obtain such an updating job, and ending with the claim that guidebooks are useless because they're always out-of-date.

I want to avoid all those potential conversations.

Over a breakfast of baguette, jam and tea, I read the paper, fan away the cigarette smoke, and keep any chats firmly superficial.

"Yeah, I'm just travelling around France a bit. You?"

My conversation partner reels off a list of all the places he's been up to now, then asks about my plans for the day.

"I'll probably check out one of the museums. You?"

He now lists all the important sights of Paris, aiming to see them all today.

"What about the lines?" I ask.

He shrugs.

"I read in my, er, in the guidebook I have for France that there are lines in front of all the museums."

He shrugs again. "I don't travel with one of those things."

And suddenly, I quite like him. But I've got work to do and not surly friends to make. I wish him a good day and head out into the sunny Paris morning. My first stop: the tourist office on Avenue des Champs Elysées.

I'm feeling confident, a seasoned veteran, honed by that trek through America's mid-west. I know what I'm doing, and this internet thingy has me ahead of the game.

It's actually great to be in Paris.

It takes all of ten minutes in the tourist office for me to realise that using the internet to update the book was a colossal waste of time. Despite my awful French, I manage to get a couple of friendly helpers to assist with checking the Paris chapter. Helper one asks about the corrections already made to my printouts, while helper two explains that it's been quite a while since their website was updated. As in, not since it went live several years ago.

So, what was supposed to be a short morning double-checking a few things before hitting the Louvre turns into a full day spent in the tourist office.

Not only do I hate guidebooks. I now also hate the internet.

By the end of the day, both helper one and helper two hate me and my guidebook.

As I trudge back to the hostel, I'm fully aware of the task that lies ahead. It's America all over again, only this time I don't speak the language and the big-name guidebooks company's name isn't big, which will make it that much harder to persuade tourism and marketing people to update for me and to get any free beds.

Day 3

Paris

I'm up early, take a packed breakfast and get on the first train to Rouen. Not much chance to see the city, beyond passing the cathedral that Monet painted en route to the tourist office. Once there, I'm assigned an intern to help me with the section on Rouen and the surrounds, as he's the only one in the office who speaks English. It also turns out he's the only one in the office not from Rouen. Every single point has to be checked with someone in the office, and they all get annoyed with his questioning. Several times, the intern is forced to make phone calls to get the right information.

I greatly appreciate his efforts, as the hours pass. He even manages to joke that he's learning a lot about Rouen, which will be helpful for him in dealing with other tourists.

Finally done, I thank him and walk back to the station.

I reach Paris by mid-afternoon, in time to visit the Musée Marmottan before it closes. There, I get to see the Rouen Cathedral in several fuzzy shades, part of what amounts to the largest collection of Monet's works in the world. The museum is quiet enough to enjoy in relative solitude, and small enough to save me from trying to see thousands of artworks in an hour. I go slowly from one painting to the next, in a blissful daze. Water lillies, haystacks, blurry stuff that can only really be made into shapes and things from a distance or by looking slightly from the corners of my eyes.

When I emerge, it's late afternoon and drizzling. The work day is over and the streets are full. I buy a sandwich and eat this as I walk down Rue de Passy, towards the Jardins du Trocadéro and the Eiffel Tower. Even with the update, I'm still seeing the sights, and that makes me feel good. Though I wonder how I will find the time to get through the Musée d'Orsay and the massive Louvre.

Along the Seine, past the palaces, through the maze of streets of the ninth arrondissement, feeling like I've been here for weeks already. Getting deep into a guidebook means I end up knowing a lot of place names and things to see, without ever seeing them. So, I know the city, but fleetingly, from afar, without really experiencing it.

I decide to see as much of Paris as I can in my remaining days.

Day 4
Paris
Sleeping is tough in a room with seven other guys.

I'm awake at dawn and take a run through Montmartre, up to the Sacré Coeur, which is an off-cream colour in the dull morning light; almost smog yellow. Homeless people sleep on benches, hugging their possessions, while hawkers are already setting up to sell their wares, getting out early to occupy what I assume to be the prime hawking real estate.

Touring the eighteenth arrondissement, I take whatever street looks interesting, and it's a joy to lope around like this without any real destination or schedule. I get happily lost, but eventually find my way back to Sacré Coeur, where the tourists are already milling, the homeless people are gone, and the hawkers are mobile, darting through the crowd and trying to tie decorative bands on tourists' wrists.

I get back to the hostel early enough to beat the morning shower rush, and to get first crack at the fresh baguettes and croissants. The hostel's global mix of occupants share the common characteristic of not being morning people. When I headed out for my run, I crossed paths with a large group of guys coming back to the hostel to sleep.

I've got another day trip planned, this time north-east to Reims and the regional tourist office there, which promises to be another long morning, perhaps with another unsuspecting intern. My hope is to get back early enough to visit the Picasso Museum, part of my lofty goal to mix work with pleasure.

It has to be said: the rail-pass is an absolutely beauty. It allows me to get on any train, at any time, without having to bother with seat reservations or having to figure out those exceedingly complex-looking ticket machines, which seem like they might consume you if the wrong button is pressed. The rail-pass also saves me from having to deal with Paris traffic, which is mad, and oscillates between going nowhere and going everywhere very fast. I'm very glad to not be jamming a Lawnmower or Sephia through that mess. Paris is best explored on foot anyway.

Reims turns out to be a time-consuming success, though as in Rouen, I see little of the city. On the train back, I get some more work done.

I declare the day productive and over. It's around 3pm when I make it to the Picasso Museum, where the line is staggering in its size and organisation. It's a zigzag of dividers, like the ones leading towards airport security. The people stand very close together, and have the slouched-shoulders and fatigue of people who have been standing for quite a long time in line.

I join the end and do a quick head count. There are roughly three hundred people in front of me, and now also a dozen behind. For fifteen minutes, the line doesn't move.

"Screw this."

I buy a bottle of water and drink this as I weave through Marais. Over the Ile de la Cité, past Notre Dame, then following the Seine to the Musée d'Orsay, walking to forget: about guidebooks and tourists and lines and hostel-dwellers.

I'm me, in Paris, savouring. Lucky to be here.

The line at d'Orsay is no less staggering than at Picasso, but this one actually moves. It takes about half an hour to get in, and it's a pleasant wait, as I wind up in line with some chatty, knowledgeable people. As serious art buffs, they're not quite in my big-name guidebooks company's demographic. But they offer some good tips, for some of the works people might pass by in favour of seeing all the famous stuff in a hurry, which is how I end up entranced in front of Rodin's Porte de l'Enfer. This very large and very graphic sculpture portrays the gates to hell as seriously hellish, and I find myself relating.

The struggle, the pain, the descent.

I have already journeyed to America guidebook hell, and somehow survived. Four days into this trip, I stand at the gates to France guidebook hell.

The Thinker encourages me to think.

Just quit. That's what I think. All this effort and stress is not worth the measly money I'm getting.

No. Stay strong. I'll find a way through, just as I did in the States. And if it all turns out bad, the worst that can happen is my career as a guidebook updater will be over.

I mosey around d'Orsay until it closes. My favourite piece is

Monet's *The Rue Montorgueil in Paris*, which is a mess of French flags waving from windows, in a scene that is utterly joyous.

Vive la France indeed.

I wander back to the hostel, where I arrive as the evening's pub crawl group is assembling. They allow me five minutes to dump my bag and change.

As we head out for some drunken fun, a moveable feast for the gap-year crowd, I'm keen to be adding "drinking problem" to my list of failures as an updater. Well hey, the book has a list of bars, and I'm obliged to check some of them out.

Day 5

Paris

My last day here, and I'm slow to get started. I miss breakfast, and also miss the train to Evreux, which has the last regional tourist office I needed to visit.

Pass.

I decide to have faith in the internet-aided updating I did for Evreux and its surrounds. And if it turns out all to be wrong, then to hell with it.

I'm hungover this morning. Remorseful. I can't really face the prospect of another big museum, more art and more introspection. If anything, I'd like to take the day off from myself.

So I walk, without my printouts, without lugging around my bag full of pamphlets and brochures, without a map or destination. I let Paris guide me.

It's Saturday. The city is busy. There are a lot of tourists. And they get me wondering about the evolution of travel, because there was certainly a time when Paris wasn't like this.

Which came first, the tourists or the guidebooks?

Did the guidebooks open up travel to more people, or were those people already here and in need of local guidance?

Don't know. Don't care.

But it's not that simple. Because I'm in Paris, one the world's great cities, and I like it, but I'm not able to enjoy it. My head is swimming with facts and place names and opening hours and prices. All of that isn't so bad in places like Des Moines or Wichita, but here, it's keeping me from soaking in this glorious city. Better would be to enjoy Paris without a care in the world. *Sans souci.*

I walk all day, through the course of which I drink six cups of tea in six different cafés. At café number four, sitting outside and keen to blend in, I ask a man at the table next to me for a cigarette. It's French and vile, but I smoke it to the end, hoping it might snap some synapses in my brain and get me thinking more lucidly.

As the bluish smoke clears, I think: this will be my last guidebook update, and one day I will come back to Paris, and to France, and experience it unfettered.

Day 6

Paris to Tours

The day includes stops in Chartres (one hour in the tourist office) and Orléans (two hours), before arriving in Tours (two hours and seven minutes, at which point the tourist office people kicked me out to close up and go home). Sadly, there's no time to visit any of the castles in the Loire, or to even learn how to say Loire properly.

An utterly exhausting day. This is the job I agreed to do, and I'm determined to complete it, even if I'm not as thorough as I should be. It doesn't matter. While updating the USA guide, I was aiming for more possible guidebook work. Now, I know I'm done and have no reason to impress.

I've managed to score a free hotel room in Tours. It doesn't have many stars and the walls are rather thin, but my room's most redeeming feature is that it has just one bed.

Day 7

Tours to Bordeaux

A major difference between this update and the last: there's a lot more to see. Every village the train passes through urges me to get out and explore. The names alone are tempting: Rochefort, Cognac, Mirambeau, La Rochelle, all these places named after saints. Each village and small city has an old town and a couple of churches. History going back over a thousand years. Cobblestone streets and cafés. Maybe a square where some famous person had his head sliced off.

As the train pulls out of another station, leaving yet one more stroll-worthy village behind, I ponder all that I'm missing. It's only the places listed in the guidebook that I have to cover, and I'm already skipping most of them. My one lengthy stop of the day is in Poitiers.

With the help of the tourist office, I manage to cover a vast swathe of western France. But it takes hours.

I reach Bordeaux in the evening. My neon-buzzing hotel, comped by the local tourism people, is in the old town, which I have just enough energy left to explore, but not quite the attentiveness to take it all in.

In my hotel room, there's a complimentary half-bottle of local red wine, courtesy of the tourist office. No wine opener, no glass, and I decide I really don't want to be that guy, alone in his single hotel room, drinking wine in the last hour before midnight. It's bad enough I'm in this one-star fleabag, on this whirlwind Tour de France, with over a hundred pages of facts filling all my available head space. I should at least try to not become the drowner of sorrows who wakes with wine-stained teeth.

Day 8
Bordeaux

I've now been in France for over a week, and I confess I'm on a steady diet of croissants, sandwiches, yoghurt and tea. This is more necessity and circumstance than choice. I don't really have the time to sit in restaurants.

I nibble at a croissant on the train to Périgueux. It's Saturday, and the train is just about empty. We pass through some very nice countryside, with Périgueux turning out to be an attractive place. The guidebook calls it a "busy and prosperous market town," which sounds like a description from the Middle Ages.

I waste an hour wandering the old town and take in the Roman sites. Some clever Frenchmen have turned the old amphitheatre into a park, replete with water fountain and pond. I sit on a bench in the sun, in just about the centre of the amphitheatre, and envision a gladiator being killed on this very spot, for the amusement of locals. What was Périgueux like back then? A busy and prosperous market town?

The one person working in the tourist office looks a few weeks from retirement, but he's very friendly. For the next few hours, we work through the section on Périgueux and the surrounds. Grand-père has a wealth of local knowledge, yet much of it is more out of date than the guidebook. He's not terribly adept at using a computer, and allows me to sit down at the office PC to access their database. Anything I can't find there, grand-père makes a call to check. He's chatty on the phone, in a way that makes me think he knows everyone in town.

As the time passes, not a single person comes into the tourist office. The only visitor is grand-mère, who shows up with a pot of goulash in her hands and a baguette under her arm. Grand-père produces glasses, bowls, spoons and a bottle of wine, and the three of us have lunch together.

It's extremely tasty, the first hot meal I've had all week. I'm also touched by how grand-père and grand-mère are with each other, sitting close, smiling, sharing glances; the kind of natural intimacy of two people who have spent a long time together and are still very much in love.

I envy their happiness.

At the end of the meal, I try to ease myself out, saying I want to visit the Lascaux Caves and see the Palaeolithic paintings. Grand-père says it's not worth the trip, as there are far too many tourists to enjoy it and you only see a replica, as the original paintings were damaged by the steamy breath of visitors. He also says he saw the originals, before they closed the cave in 1963, and that it was the most incredible thing he had ever seen.

"To think, these Stone Age people, they painted with such emotion and feeling," he says. "It shows they were much more than, how do say, savages?"

"That's right. Savages."

"But to look at a copy, is not the same. *Non. Non.* Not the same at all."

His wife talks to him in French. I assume she wants a translation, which he gives, saying considerably more than he said to me. When finished, she smiles at him, strokes his left cheek and kisses his right.

I skip Lascaux and take the train back to Bordeaux, feeling rather lost and lonely, and also that I'm wasting myself on this guidebook. I'd rather be writing stories and novels.

Twenty thousand years ago, painting with emotion and feeling turned savages into artists. Now, updating a guidebook has turned an artist into a savage.

Day 9
Bordeaux to Bayonne
At some point on the train this morning, the season changed. A

day that started cold and grim in Bordeaux has ended with me on the beach in Biarritz and, incredibly, in the water. It's knackering, the kind of cold that makes you feel like your skin is shrinking, but I'm in anyway, because the sun is out and the air temperature just about qualifies as warm.

Lord, my skin is so white.

I'm not alone in spending this glorious Sunday afternoon at the beach, but I am the only one in the water. I'd also wager I'm the only one who ran here, having pounded the pavement for six kilometres from my hotel in Bayonne just to get in some beach time.

I walk back barefoot, shoes in hand, feeling a whole lot better about the world. I feel cleansed.

Bayonne strikes me as seriously sporting, with rugby fields, tennis courts, jai alai walls and bull-fighting arenas. I'd like to get involved with all of it – especially to have a go at jai alai – but I've only got one day, and I need to cover all of the French Basque region.

After a shower and a change into respectable attire, I get to the tourist office an hour before it closes. The friendly staff help me get everything done, but say repeatedly that I'm missing out; that I should spend more time in the Pays Basque, even go across the Spanish border to visit places like San Sebastian, Bilbao and the coastal villages. I make a promise to them, and myself, that I will come back again one day.

By evening, I'm too tired to do any more exploring, beyond a short walk through the old town, sandwich in hand, and end up at my hotel watching television. In keeping with the day's sporting theme, there's football on just about every channel. The French commentary adds high drama to this dull sport, but not nearly enough to keep me awake. I'm out by 9pm.

Day 10

Bayonne to Tarbes

Into the Pyrenees, with a couple of hours in Pau before reaching Lourdes in the early afternoon. The weather is glorious, the scenery impressive and the kitsch piled high. Just an extraordinary array of religious souvenirs on sale in Lourdes. Oh, and I think the local tourist office has put me in the town's worst hotel. That's really saying something, because Paris is the only city in France with more hotels. A tourist office employee even bragged that there are over three hundred of them. That being said, I would like to ask why I've been put in the one that's right at the bottom of the list, but I hold my tongue. Not only are there hundreds of hotels, they are also very expensive. My half-star prison cell, with its fold-out cot, wafer-thin pillow and grimy sink, apparently costs over a hundred Francs a night, without breakfast.

It's mind-boggling to wander around this little mountain village, as it's practically all hotels. Any building that's not a hotel is a restaurant or souvenir shop. The most enterprising locals have one establishment combining all three. The footpaths are covered with signs, calling tourists into shops selling "genuine" items. The hotels have names like Saviour and Sacrilege.

If you're not familiar with Lourdes, the story goes something like this: in 1858, Bernadette Subrious, at the tender age of fourteen, had visions of the Virgin Mary at a grotto near the Gave de Pau, and everyone believed that her visions were real, which meant the town quickly became a popular place for pilgrimage, with numbers running upwards of five million visitors a year these days, according to the tourist office, hence all the hotels, restaurants and souvenir shops.

The cynic in me thinks Mademoiselle Subrious, perhaps unintentionally or under the influence of a local entrepreneur, had carried out an early form of tourism marketing, as her Marian vision catapulted Lourdes to the top of France's tourist tree. From the price of things to the number of people wandering around, you can only wonder what kind of money this town pulls in thanks to Bernadette and what she "saw".

The locals aren't shy about exploiting the visitors. You can get a tweenish-looking Bernadette in every size, adorning key rings, barometers, candles, bottles and more. There's nary a visitor not toting some kind of plastic bag from a souvenir shop, straining with its contents. You have to pay to do anything, and I'm pretty sure the local government has added an "air tax" to every hotel tariff, to charge people for breathing the blessed local air.

Sure, sure, there are the reported healings, some of which have been recognised as miracles by the Vatican. Faith is a powerful thing. But at the grotto, and inside the massive basilica, I don't feel anything overwhelming. I'm not sensing any magic, which is probably my own fault. I can't help thinking there's something contrived about this place; that it's all made up, a giant ruse. I mean, come on, a girl has visions that no one can see or verify, so now five million people come here every year to drink the water and part with their hard-earned?

The visitors are not just your average tourists on typical trips through Europe. These are people who have come a long way specifically to visit this place, to drink the water and light a candle at the grotto for the waxwork Virgin nestled in a cranny, and they probably won't see much else. I admire their commitment, and a part of me even envies the strength of their beliefs, but this town and these people are not for me. Most of the town's attractions and museums revolve around Bernadette and her legacy: the Musée Bernadette, Cinema Bernadette, and even the Wax Museum, which portrays the life of Bernadette and tells the story of Christ, including an impressive wax replica of Da Vinci's *The Last Supper*.

But I've seen enough, and I have no intention of sleeping in that cell I've been comped.

The work done, and all my aches and pains surprisingly still remaining, I retrieve my backpack from the hotel and head back up the hill to the station.

The next train is going to Tarbes and I get on it. The guidebook tells me there's a youth hostel there. I've no doubt it will be considerably better than any cheap hotel in Lourdes.

Day 12

Tarbes to Toulouse

I'm still getting Lourdes out of my system. A lot of my thoughts are about money: the economics of ecclesiasticism and the profits of pilgrimage. I'm tempted to add the greed of God, but I can't help thinking that God doesn't really have much to do with Lourdes, which I conclude to be a wholly ungodly place.

Toulouse seems to belong in a completely different country to Lourdes. It's laid-back, youthful, vibrant and inviting. Colourful too, with many of the buildings made of peach-pink bricks. A lot of students, plenty of bars, and a decent hotel for the night. The cheery, helpful workers in the tourist office leave me wondering why the stereotypical French person is considered rude. I haven't encountered any rudeness beyond what I've experienced in other countries. If anything, I've found the French very friendly and warm, and the fact I can't really speak French hasn't resulted in emergency calls to the language police.

Not only does Toulouse tourism place me in a nice hotel, they also update the guidebook section and give me a pass that covers all the city's sights and museums. So I take in the sculptures of the Musée des Augustins, fly through the town hall and visit two churches, though I'm a little fed up with religion.

By evening, I'm exhausted, and end up in the bath of my swanky hotel, drinking complimentary red wine and working my way through the mini-bar's snacks.

I like Toulouse.

Day 13

Toulouse to Montpellier

I wake late with wine-stained teeth. As I wash my face, I realise I have become that guy: lonely, on the road, in another hotel, drowning my sorrows.

But I plough on, running well behind today. I miss the train. I spend too much time in Carcassonne and Narbonne, where all the people I deal with are rude.

I eat nothing.

I arrive in Montpellier in the early evening, just as the tourist office is closing. They explain, rudely, that they cancelled my hotel booking, as they weren't sure I was coming. I implore them to contact the hotel and help me out, as I'm weary and dirty and I've just had enough of the day. A phone call confirms that the room has been given to someone else. The tourist office woman, annoyed that she is now working past her usual hours and who tells me exactly that, makes one final call, where she books me into the local youth hostel. She orders me to pay, keep the receipt, and they'll reimburse me tomorrow.

At the hostel, the owner, aware I'm on tour for the big-name guidebooks company because the tourist office woman dropped the name, lets me stay for free. But word quickly spreads. As I have a cup of tea in the hostel's communal area, a crowd starts to form, triggered by two hostel workers who sit down at my table uninvited and inform me that I have the best job in the world.

"You get paid to travel," one says.

"That's brilliant," says the other.

"You can have it," I say. "Seriously. I'll pay you to update the rest of my chapter in the book. You've got about a week to cover half of France. Think you can do that?"

"Sure."

"Easy."

"And all the hotels, restaurants, bars, cafés, museums, churches and town halls. And all phone numbers, addresses, opening hours and prices. And then you arrive in a city and realise that everything is marked on the map in the wrong place, and that the map itself has been drawn by a blind monkey, and you've got about ten minutes before the train leaves to take you to the next place, which is full of things to check and probably has another map that's completely wrong."

The two hostel workers share a glance.

"Yeah, I guess it would be a bit tough."

"A lot of work, I'm sure."

That's when more people start to gather.

"Are you the guidebook writer?" a girl asks. "That's awesome. You get paid to travel?"

"Can you give me a tip where to stay in Paris?"

"My sister runs a café in Lille. Can you put it in the book?"

"I always thought that guidebook writers were old, experienced travellers."

"Yeah, you look more like a backpacker."

"Are you qualified for this job?"

"How did you get it anyway?"

"The guidebooks are always wrong."

"I want this job."

Surrounded, I try to smile.

Day 14

Montpellier to Marseille

I escape the hostel at dawn, to avoid another inquisition, which is smart because there is a lot to cover.

I'm a train warrior today, riding the rails first to Nimes, then Avignon, Arles and Aix-en-Provence, all on different trains, getting off at each city to hike to the tourist office, struggle through the update work, then walk back to the station to wait for the next train.

Over the course of this miserable day, things start to unravel. I get lost several times. Every train is late. I can't eat any more sandwiches or croissants. And while it doesn't rain, the sun shines in what I deem highly mocking fashion.

On the last train leg, I have to get off in some place called Septèmes-les-Vallons, as I'm on the verge of having a full on panic attack. It's something I haven't had since university, when I was trying to balance studying with basketball and part-time work, while living on my own, and all the time feeling like an eleven year-old boy trapped inside a nineteen year-old's body. I just wasn't ready for all that commitment and responsibility; all those things that had to be done in one day. My panic then was centred on the fear I'd let people down. The pressure to succeed was immense, and the energy-sapping lifestyle I was living, which included showering at least three times a day and sleeping about five hours each night, ran me down until I couldn't cope.

I find a bench near the Septèmes station, sit down and try to calm my breathing.

I tell myself that the panic is just violent chemistry, a demonic internal reaction that feeds on itself, if I let it.

The sun is going down, hidden by the scattered clouds that are close to the horizon, but sometimes breaking through. It's something nice for me to look at, a focal point, a distraction.

I realise that the source of my anxiety remains the same. I've been telling myself since Paris that I don't care about the guidebook, but I'm also determined not to let anyone down: the editor, the big-name guidebooks company, the readers. A bit like having coaches or players or fans saying the basketball game was lost because I missed some shots or made mistakes. It's not a quest for perfection, but an avoidance of being the scapegoat, or worse, the villain.

Calmer, I walk back to the station in time to catch the next train to Marseille. It's too late for me to visit the tourist office, so I decide to go straight to the youth hostel in Bonneveine, where I've been given a bed for the night, and do the city update first thing in the morning, before beginning another day as a train warrior. Thinking about all that, I can feel the panic starting to rise again. I try to distract myself by talking with the guy next to me. I ask him where Bonneveine is in relation to the main station. I show him the guidebook's map of Marseille, which he laughs at. He says it's too far to walk, and that I should take the Métro to Point du Prado and try to get a bus from there.

This is what I do, though I forgo the bus in favour of walking. I'm not feeling particularly safe, as I head down Boulevard Michelet, then negotiate a dark narrow alley to get onto Avenue Alexandre Dumas, but the fear of getting beaten and robbed seems more internally manageable than the fear of letting people down.

I get to the hostel just before the reception closes for the night. As luck would have it, my six-bed room only has one other occupant: a Canadian who isn't very talkative.

In the communal kitchen, I make a cup of tea. While the water slowly comes to a boil, I ponder whether it's worth heading out to find something to eat. It's already late, I'm tired, and another long day looms.

There's some kind of sports team staying here; big burly men who look and sound Russian. They're all wearing the same dark blue tracksuits, the coaches too, and sitting in a tight group in the dining area. They move between boisterous conversation and loud singing.

When a girl enters, they let out a cheer. Beyond the hint of a smile on her face, she ignores them, and they go back to singing.

The girl, blonde-haired, round-faced, bespectacled and short, comes up to me and says hi. I offer her a cup of green tea. She produces a packet of Oreos. We sit down and get chatting. She's from St. Louis, and is surprised to learn that I've been there.

She dunks the Oreos in her tea.

When asked, I explain I'm travelling through France at light speed, trying to see as much as I can because I'm so short on time. But I deflect the questions and get her talking about herself.

This girl from Missouri is twenty years old, but looks younger. She's travelling on her own through Europe, without any real plan, and without a guidebook. She says she has pepper spray, but that she hasn't had to use it yet.

As we talk, I wonder if I'm looking at a relic from the past or the traveller of the future. Either way, she doesn't seem quite of this time.

Day 15

Marseille to Cannes

I'm up early and walk down to the beach. Sleeping was difficult, as the quiet Canadian found his voice during the night, snoring with impressive volume.

Despite it being seven in the morning, there's a lot of traffic on the main drag that follows the coastline, going in both directions. The collective sense of urgency doesn't quite befit this pleasant beach-side setting.

The beach itself is developed, with a promenade, small stores, restaurants and cafés, and even a skateboard park. The narrow stretch of sand is gritty and hard, the water flat. Old guys are fishing from both points of this small crescent bay, with really long rods, like those used by surfcasters on the beaches back home in Perth.

The water, while a nice shade of blue, looks uninviting, and is very, very cold. I go in anyway, enough to get fully wet and feel something attune to electric shock therapy. As I towel myself down, I think that, with my history of anxiety, I might have been subjected to actual shock therapy, had I been born about fifty years ago. Locked inside a padded room, considered unstable.

Things are different now. People with anxiety and fears are out in the real world, trying to cope. Until they run themselves down to the point that all the demons surface; rush from city to city and work ridiculously hard through difficult situations, fruitlessly attempting to please everyone.

As I slowly wander back up to the youth hostel, where breakfast with the blue track-suited Russians awaits, I consider the day ahead. It's planned like this: Marseille tourist office, train to Toulon, tourist office, train to St. Tropez, tourist office, train to St Raphael, tourist office, train to Cannes, tourist office, hostel.

I'm kind of missing America. That update was considerably easier than this one, and I got a lot more help along the way. While it was certainly tough, at least that trip felt a bit like travel, and I had some time in between to digest what I was seeing and to take it slow.

France is all work.

Day 16

Cannes to Nice

Yesterday was awful, but I got through it. A key change was to think of this as work rather than travel, and badly paid work at that. Basically, it's volunteer work.

Today has been better. A stop in Antibes on the way to Nice, where the local tourism people have put me in a two-star hotel. After all the youth hostels and fleabag hotels, this actually feels like luxury.

I get the work done and take the afternoon off. At the harbour, I check ferry times to Corsica, wondering if I can make it to Ajaccio and back in a day. Unlikely, given the trip is about six hours, one way.

The fact that I don't do well on boats means Corsica is quickly removed from my to-see list. I'll have to do it over the phone.

Nice is full of English people. Much of the city's old town is given over to serving, feeding and amusing them. There's an Irish pub on just about every corner, and many restaurants claim to serve "full English breakfast".

I'm not finding the city terribly appealing, so I walk over the hill of Parc du Mont Boron to explore Villefranche-sur-Mer. This hilly village is more my speed, quieter, without the English breakfasts.

When I get down to Villefranche's main beach, which is a long, curving bay dotted with yachts large and small, it's tempting to keep on walking: around Cap Ferrat, to Monaco, then Menton and Italy.

Walk clear off the guidebook's map and disappear.

Day 17
Nice

In order to avoid spending twelve hours on ferries, I've spent the morning on the telephone, updating Corsica. At one point, the Calvi tourist office puts me on hold for almost half an hour while someone who speaks English is found.

But by lunchtime it's done. I head out for a bite.

It's another beautiful day.

Nice is quite large, and there are a couple of museums, but there doesn't seem to be that much to do. The tourists are at the beach or in the restaurants, or en route from one to the other.

I find a place serving takeaway salads and eat one sitting on a bench near the water. It's a pebble beach. Nearly all the beachgoers lie on rented sun-chairs, and when they go into the water, they wear these strange slip-on shoes so they can negotiate the rocks.

It's fascinating watching these people trying to walk on this rocky beach, to have what might amount to a regular beach day.

Eventually I head back to the hotel room for what promises to be another lengthy session working the telephone, this time updating the Alps section.

Day 18
Nice to Lyon

The train to Lyon turned out to be a real milk-and-post run, which pulled into stations so small that the train had to shuffle forward a few metres and then stop so people could get off on the short platforms.

This was completely okay.

I stared out the window, slept a few hours, did some work and arrived in Lyon in darkness.

A much needed day off.

Day 19

Lyon to Dijon

I've left the warmth and sun behind. Walking around Lyon this morning, I'm back in my winter jacket, even needing to wear a wool hat. I'm good with the weather, because Lyon is worth exploring. I'd thought it might be something of an industrial wasteland of a city, but it's got quite a bit going for it; no less the bevy of Roman sites that are close to the youth hostel.

I eventually find my way to the tourist office, get the work done, which includes fixing yet another awful map, then head for the station to take the train to Dijon. One night there, then one in Strasbourg and it's over. I actually find it strange, that this trip is about to end, because I think I've finally found the right rhythm. It's work. I'm not getting paid to travel. I'm getting paid to work, and that work includes a lot of travel.

It's a fast train to Dijon, and I get there early enough to hit the tourist office, knock off the section and explore some of the old town. The guidebook, seriously short on adjectives, also describes Dijon as prosperous. There's money in mustard, I guess. Sadly, the Musée de la Moutarde is closed, leaving me to walk the prosperous streets without much else to do.

Dijon was the capital for the dukes of Burgundy, yet the Palais des Ducs is not terribly fancy on the outside. I assume its interior is more opulent; at least, that is what the leader of a walking tour says to her group of senior citizens, who look American. I inch closer to the group, to listen in. The tour guide talks about some of the dukes, name-calling Philippe the Bold, Jean the Fearless and Charles the Rash. You wouldn't have wanted to share a bed with that last duke.

The tourist office has put me in a four-star B&B for the night. The best so far.

Day 20

Dijon to Strasbourg

Into another French city described as "prosperous" by this infuriating guidebook. The whole thing needs to be rewritten, or recycled.

I'm now a punch-clock Joe updater. I go through the required motions: a few hours in the tourist office, correct the map, explore the old town, eat a sandwich. There's not much to say about Strasbourg. It's attractive, if not a little dull. Maybe it's me. I'm done. Finished. Killing the time until I'm on the early train tomorrow back to Hamburg. I can't even muster any conclusive thoughts, some clever way to pull all the loose French ends together and weave a nice little memorial quilt. Screw that. It was work. France is a blur. I'll have to come back one day and see it all properly, at my leisure.

The tourist office gives me a hotel right by the cathedral. The bells ring every fifteen minutes, and each time it sounds like the war has come to an end.

Day 22

Strasbourg to Hamburg

For about an hour, between Stuttgart and Frankfurt, my seat partner is a website designer from Freiburg named Christoph. We talk about the internet. I complain about how all the websites I used to update the guidebook were out-of-date and useless.

"The companies have no IT departments," Christoph explains. "They outsource the work, or they get an agency to do it. Make the website once and never update it. This will change, at some point. The internet is going to become the main source of all our information."

By the time Christoph gets off the train in Frankfurt, I realise that even if I wanted to do more updating work, the big-name guidebook company soon won't have a need for people like me. Some poor person will sit in the head office and update the whole thing using the internet, email and a telephone. Or, the guidebook is kept constantly up-to-date, without the twelve-month lag between updating, editing and publishing. But, if all the travel information is available on the internet, why would a person even need a guidebook?

Silver Harz

From 1949 to 1990, there were two Germanys. The border between East and West not only split Berlin in two, it also carved a broad expanse right through the land.

Which is why, when you jaunt around the Harz Mountains in the middle of Germany, you come across some interesting remnants of that Cold War division. Here, it wasn't so much that an Iron Curtain descended. It was more that green drapes were pulled.

I visit in winter, and my base is Goslar. From there, I use local buses and cross-country skis to go deep into the Harz National Park, to the top of the Brocken mountain, to the scattering of small villages, and down a long stretch in the heart of the park that was cleared in around 1961, when the Berlin Wall went up and East Germany sought to protect its borders.

This cleared stretch is the old borderline, a good thirty metres wide. The trees were removed to make way for observation towers, patrol roads and tank traps. Some of the concrete bases of those towers remain. They jut out of the snow, like huge oatmeal pancakes sprinkled with icing sugar. Young fir trees, some poking through the snow and others with their skinny tips about head high, are starting to cover this once razed area. In a few more years, the divide will no longer be visible.

There's just enough snow for cross-country skiing. It's too early in winter for the branches of the fir trees to be crusted with snow and hanging almost vertical under the weight, and too early for the groomed tracks to be lined with luminous, steam-puffing skiers. A few squirrels are darting about, and there are tracks in the snow that I hope are lynx prints, but are more likely foxes. The snow is slushy and the going is slow; more walking than shushing.

I continue along the old borderline, unsure what to make of it, as this isn't my history.

When researching for a book about East Germany, I learned that the Brocken's peak was surrounded by a nearly four-metre high concrete wall and used as a centre to spy on communication signals from the West. The railway station served as quarters for East German border troops and the Soviet Union's Red Army. The Brocken was right at the frontline of the Cold War, secure behind the curtain, and only metaphorically accessible for westerners through performances of Goethe's *Faust* and the writings of Heinrich Heine. Stuck behind the border, this devilish, mist-enshrouded mountain was thought to have been lost forever. Perhaps Goethe had foreseen the future, that the only way to get to the peak was to ride there on a wine barrel in league with the (red) devil.

Interestingly, it was during this time, with the Brocken and surrounding areas no longer a tourist destination, that much needed regeneration occurred. Many species of animals that had been hunted almost to extinction and rare plants that had been trampled on were allowed to thrive again. Moors deepened, trees grew with raw abandon and the forest became a mysterious wilderness again.

Now, the Harz is a wild place. Dangerous animals lurk deep in the forest. The only damage forty years of communism inflicted was to create the broad expanse I'm skiing down, which one day will grow over and disappear, perhaps with just a skinny path remaining.

A squirrel is following me. This miniature, furry Mephistopheles cocks his head, inquiring if I might want to make a pact; to sell my soul for another ten centimetres of snow. Or maybe he thinks I have a nut or two to offer. I don't, but the way the squirrel stands there on his hind legs, so fearlessly, makes me think other visitors might.

Did the border guards feed the squirrels? Did they stand on top of the tower taking pot shots at innocent deer? Did they dream of skiing to the west, like some dramatic James Bond style escape, ducking under the barricade, jumping over the tank traps and shushing away to freedom as bullets dug into the snow behind them?

Probably not. But they presided over this stretch, sitting for hours in observation towers. How did they deal with the boredom? From up so high, they probably didn't even see the squirrels or take note of what animals had left tracks in the snow.

The toot of a steam train scares the squirrel and he ducks between the trees. Towards the Brocken, a puff of black smoke is snaking over the tips of the firs. I head towards it, skiing up a long rise, still following the old border, but not chancing on any more concrete slabs. Higher up, the snow is deeper, covering the trees. At Dreieckiger Pfahl, which once marked the border between the Kingdom of Hanover and the Duchy of Brunswick, groomed trails lead invitingly in all directions: to the creek-side Rote Bruch trail; the hilly Achtermann loop; the lengthy and exceedingly pretty trail that ends at the hamlet of

Schierke; the straight downhill run to Oderbrück and to a restaurant serving sublime apple cake; the winding trails around Oderteich that twist towards Sonnenberg and Altenau; and the steep run up to the Brocken. The toot of the train sounds again.

The tempting, witchy peak draws me upwards. I hope the view is worth the climb.

The smooth, straight tracks groomed by other skiers have been trampled on by walkers. A red-faced woman, spindly and sinewy even in a thick down jacket, and driving her Nordic walking sticks into the snow with possessive intent, comes from the opposite direction and says, "*Das ist ein' Wanderweg.*" Her walking partner, following a few paces behind, perhaps feigning distance, gives me a don't-mind-her smile, making me feel I have as much right to this walking trail as anyone. The sight of a few other skiers – okay, one skier – further ahead spurs me on.

The trail, Goetheweg, follows the train tracks, and it's not long before a black steam engine curls around the bend and chugs into view. I stop to watch it pass. The coal shoveller is doing most of the work, sweating in his blackened undershirt, while the driver, all silly hat and cheesy grin, is having most of the fun, his arm cradled on the window, one hand yanking the whistle. One would hope that in these egalitarian, unified times, shoveller and driver would change positions for the trip down. The train to the Brocken leaves from Drei Annen Hohne station and is part of a broader narrow gauge network that runs from Wernigerode to Nordhausen, where a V-2 rocket factory from World War II was located in the mines of nearby Kohnstein.

The passengers crowding around the windows and leaning over the railings at the back of the wagons are enjoying the ride, but I'm glad to be on skis. There's no reward in being shuttled up a mountain, quaint train or not, especially when that peak, at just over a thousand metres, is an easy two to three hour climb, on foot or on skinny planks. Most are on foot today, brandishing walking sticks, defying their age and giving us skiers a hard time.

The sky is bright blue and the crisp air enters the chest so sharply you could rip out one of your lungs and fold it into an origami crane. Fog normally enshrouds the peak, sometimes creating the eerie phenomenon called the Brocken Spectre, and this rare clear day has walkers scurrying to the top to take in the view that extends in all directions.

When I finally reach the peak, it's crowded, and not just with people who have taken the train. Many parked their cars at Torfhaus and walked the five kilometres from there. This purist clicked, shuffled and slid, and fell a few times, the fourteen kilometres from Braunlage, the region's most popular base for winter sports and reachable by bus from Goslar. Braunlage's drawing power is its proximity to numerous cross-country trails and to the Wurmberg ski hill, which has an almost three kilometre long gondola, but snowfall is irregular.

While Braunlage exhibits a very dated version of West German cool, Goslar is exceedingly more attractive. It's on the north-western rim of the Harz, meaning you get the benefit of enjoying a mediaeval city while using it as an entry point for the national park. And it saves you from having to stay in a place like Braunlage. When there's enough snow, it's possible to ski from Goslar to some very nice areas, such as Schulenberg im Oberharz and the nearby lakes; the only time I saw any people during that day was when I stopped for lunch in Schulenberg. Or you take the bus to a town and ski from there back to Goslar, as I did using the old borderline, scaling the Brocken, taking a wrong turn and ending in Bad Harzburg (exhausted), and then taking the train back to Goslar.

Though about twenty kilometres west of the old border, there are no remnants in Goslar of this once being near the fault-line of East and West. The same can be said of Quedlinburg, which was in East Germany. The old towns of both cities are UNESCO listed heritage sites. Quedlinburg gets more visitors. Goslar, with its hilly backdrop, is quieter and more picturesque. It also has a fascinating history, straight out of a children's book.

Once upon a time, Ramm, a knight, was hunting on a hillside and tied his horse to a tree. The horse dug at the dirt and exposed a large tract of silver. And so Goslar was founded, in 922, from the chance meeting of hoof and hill. The hill was named after the knight and the town and river after his wife, Gosa. The believability of the story is debatable, but the impact of the discovery of silver is not. With the silver mine on the Rammelsberg, Goslar grew quickly into an economic and commercial centre. In the eleventh century, Heinrich II, of the Salian dynasty of Holy Roman Emperors, moved the Imperial Palace from Werla to Goslar, and many of the town's most impressive sights were built during this period, including the foreboding Kaiserpfalz, the expansive Breites Tor, the Market Church, with its mismatching towers, the St. Jacob Church, and numerous other churches and monasteries.

By the Middle Ages, Goslar was a wealthy town boasting almost fifty church towers.

Thankfully, many of these sights remain and are in excellent condition, having been spared from the bombs of war. Every gilded house and shuttered window, every shadowy nook and dusty cranny are links to what was: a thousand years of history, Imperial and Hanseatic, the silver-veined Rome of the North, where Hans Christian Andersen stood on the Market Square and felt "as if I were standing on charmed city earth, of which I had heard so much as a child in many fairy tales."

On this "charmed city earth", it is very easy to pass a pleasant few days, regardless of the season. Look south from the Market Square (the eagle on the fountain is looking in that direction) and there are gentle hills covered in fir trees. Breathe in the air and there's not even a tinge of vehicle exhaust. The days take on an easy rhythm: cross-country skiing in the park, lunch at a village inn, and then enjoying the old town in the evening. While Goslar is relatively popular, for the most part the visitors are day-trippers, unloaded from buses for a quick tour of the Imperial Palace and a piece of cake at the Historisches Café on the Market Square. That means Goslar at night is for locals, once described by a chronicler of a twelfth century pope as "quarrelsome, obstinate and restless fellows."

These days, that couldn't be further from the truth. While Goslar has hit on hard times in recent years, especially since the closing of the Rammelsberg Mine in 1988 (it is now a museum and a UNESCO listed heritage site), the locals remain friendly and accommodating. They like to sit shoulder to shoulder, quaffing brews at the Brauhaus Goslar and the Worthmühle, and are completely welcoming to strangers who come in pink-cheeked from spending the day in the national park.

The old town is most beautiful at night, when the tourists have left and the locals amble simply for the sake of ambling, greeting each other as they pass. It's at night that Goslar shows itself to be a village, with the locals constantly running into people they know, gathering in impromptu groups on cobblestoned corners or pausing on a short wooden bridge over the Gose River to recount the gossip of the day. Such plain, usual street life makes Goslar even more appealing. You don't have to share the old town's charms with thousands of other click-happy visitors, as you would in Bernkastel-Kues, Cochem, Heidelberg and Rothenburg. Goslar is yours to enjoy.

The one part of the old town that really lends itself to a fairytale setting is the path that follows the Gose River, from where it enters the old town at the base of the Rammelsberg to the point it leaves near the Breites Tor. The river is barely three metres wide, and you can imagine young lovers leaning over the railings on both sides, making eternal promises despite their families' disapproval.

Along the river, the houses are crooked and bent, curving with the narrow road. They seem to lean against each other for support or are still jostling for position after sharing space for over five hundred years. The wooden beams are the colour of dark chocolate and are waiting to be bitten into, while the white-washed walls are glazed icing sugar you want to attack with a spoon. The cobbelstones have been made smooth by time, and the museum's old water wheel creaks and groans as the river trickles north.

In one of those gilded houses, Albert Niemann, who discovered cocaine and is perhaps Goslar's most famous son, died during an experiment, possibly from sulphur mustard poisoning. Another house, on Berg Strasse and one of the most splendid in the town, belonged to ancestors of the Siemens family, the famous German industrialists. A few steps from Siemenshaus, on the corner of Berg Strasse and the Market Square, is the Brusttuch house, a gilded wonder with a slanted slate roof like a massive witch's hat. Inside, carved into the supporting woodwork, is the *Butterhanne*, depicting a girl churning butter with one hand and lifting her skirt with the other.

The Market Square itself is surrounded by striking buildings, including the orange Kaiserworth, the arches and stained glass of the town hall, and the Kaiserringhaus, which has a carillon of figures that act out mining scenes on the balcony four times a day. The afternoon and evening chimes are the call to bring you back from the mountains to enjoy the pleasures of an evening in the old town.

This is one fairytale town that lends itself wholly to imagination. The mine has closed, but the clouds over Goslar most certainly still have their silver lining.

Abandoned Water Park

It's hard to believe that Portugal once ruled the world. It was the Portuguese who kicked off the Age of Discovery in the mid fifteenth century, who had Vasco de Gama and Bartolomeu Dias sailing into uncharted territory, who boasted the world's most powerful naval fleet, who got into globalisation and world trade before anyone else, and who ruled the seas with the first ever global empire. It lasted for a few centuries, with Portugal even dividing the world in half with Spain at one point, but the Portuguese Empire was soon superseded by the empires of other rising nations, including France, England and Holland.

These days, Portugal is one of western Europe's more impoverished nations. It's a bit like the country peaked in high school, lost its way and has gone steadily backwards since. Meanwhile, it has also been overtaken by other countries which have developed and grown.

The resort town of Costa da Caparica, south of Lisbon and just over the Tagus River, captures the country's demise and current status rather well, without having to go all the way back to the fifteenth century. The results of the last twenty-five years are proof enough.

Caparica is a popular spot for locals and tourists wanting to escape the heat and crowds of Lisbon. There are cliffs to the east of the town, where bell-wearing sheep graze on top, and a large flat section runs down to a long stretch of sandy beach. Such a geographic location bodes well for a sunset-facing resort town of beauty and splendour.

Caparica is not quite that.

The flat expanse from cliffs to water is dominated by ugly high-rise apartment buildings that are in such disrepair as to be almost decomposing, while the newer, hastily constructed buildings to the north of the town have already lost their sheen and appear half empty. Some of the streets barely look safe to walk down, at any time of day, and there are numerous people just sitting around, talking or staring into space. Despite the beach and sunshine, the locals – those over thirty, at least – look sad and unhealthy. The young look fresh and lively, but I wonder if they are aware that they are at their peak and that they will slowly start to shrivel like their elders.

There are many restaurants along the water serving seafood, and the smell of oil lingers. The beach, meanwhile, is seriously ill-cared for. Trash gathers at the water line, including water bottles, plastic bags and cigarette butts, while the sand feels gritty between your toes. It's not unusual in the morning, when locals fish from the beach, to see a man drop his pants, crouch down between the rocks and take a dump. Owners also let their dogs shit all over beach. It's a game athlete who decides to run barefoot in this sand.

It's disappointing to see that the locals take such little care of their beach, as if they expect the government to do it for them or for the tide to take all their crap away. The sand doesn't look to have been cleaned or ploughed in years, and the trash and shit piles up. It makes me think the locals are completely okay with letting Caparica rot.

At the bottom of the cliffs, south of the main entry road, behind the eye-sore high-rises and barely hidden, there's a shanty town of shacks and tents. Heading up that main road, towards the highway, is perhaps the most fascinating sight of all.

Hidden behind a green fence and not quite visible from the road is an abandoned water park.

I stumble onto it by chance, trying to get on top of the cliffs and enjoy the view over Caparica. I'd thought that this dismal place might look better from afar. From the road, my attention is drawn towards what look like large pieces of coloured pipes. I see graffiti too, painted on a faded light blue background. The mesh fence that leads to the green metal fence, which obscures the park from view, has been partly pulled back where the fences meet, enough for me to squeeze through.

The pools have a variety of sizes and depths. There are also large sections of pipes and half-pipes scattered around. The concrete is cracked and overgrown with weeds. That was the kids' pool, and that was the pool for splashing into after coming down the water slide; the blue covering on the four-lane slide has peeled away, exposing the concrete underneath. Those coloured pipes look to be part of what was an elaborate tube system, leading into a deeper section of the main pool. The spiral staircase and ledge was for the lifeguard. A building half-way up the hill looks like it was a restaurant. Up there, I think I might chance upon a homeless community camped under the shelter, but there's no one. The whole place is deserted. It hasn't even been commandeered, like other abandoned pools, for skateboarding purposes. Some of the pools still hold water, which is murky green and has pieces of pipe and metal lying in it.

I'm finding there's something monumental about this place,

something historical; the way it's been left like this, so swiftly abandoned and not cleaned up or replaced with something else. Just left, for everyone to see, if they bother to peek behind the green fence. As it's on the main road, locals drive past it every day on the way from Caparica to Lisbon.

Around twenty years ago, this would have been a thriving place of fun, with slides and tubes, packed with kids, teenagers and families. Back then, Caparica was perhaps a very cool place indeed, with the water park and the beach, and those now ugly high-rises sporting their first coats of paint. But the water park is shrivelled and old, left to rust and decay.

The remnants are eerie. A centre of enjoyment made ghostly and sad by time. As the wind blows, I think that it carries the shouts of kids, the splashes of bodies hitting the water, the calls of parents ordering their children to the restaurant for something to eat, and the demands of lifeguards to play safely and not run near the pool's edge.

How many teenagers shared first kisses here? How many kids learned to swim? Did any kids break bones on the slides and tubes? Why did it stop being popular? Did the owners go bankrupt?

I can't really leave Caparica without knowing what happened and how this water park got to be like this: an outdoor art exhibition making a statement about urban decay.

So, I head back down the hill into town and find the tourist office on the Avenida da República. This pedestrian street, joining Praça da Liberdade, is a popular gathering place for locals, who smoke, chat, drink and stare into space. One old woman is sitting on a bench, with her shopping trolley next to her. She has her hands in her lap and is slowly looking around her. I wonder if she's been sitting there all day, just looking, ageing on the spot, and perhaps trying to muster the energy to do her shopping.

At the tourist office, the man is friendly and welcoming. I ask about the water park and he tells me it's closed.

Then he points and says, "Go to beach. Caparica, it has best beach in all of Portugal."

"What about the water park? When did it close?"

"I don't know," he says, his friendliness fading. "Long time. Ninety-something. Is a relic. Should be removed. Enjoy beach here instead."

He turns his attention to his computer screen.

"What was it called?"

"It is Caparica Beach. What else could it be? Best beach in Portugal."

"No, the park. What was the name of the water park?

"Ondaparque," he says flatly. "But forget this and go to beach. Have a nice day, sir."

So, I've got the name, but not the story. The way the man spoke, I have the feeling that a tragedy might be involved. A drowning perhaps. Something the locals don't want to talk about.

Unsure what to do next, I wander towards the water, passing the Polícia Marítima de Almada. The maritime police have a lot to do with water. Maybe they can help.

I head inside and get chatting with a woman working at the front desk. Her English is good. I take a different approach than at the tourist office, talking first about the beach and boating, and then asking her about pools, potentially for lane swimming.

"Or perhaps a water park? With slides and what not."

"There was one," she says. "But it is closed for as long as I remember."

"Yeah, I think I saw it on the way into town. What happened to it?"

"Oh, it is not a very good story. There was another water park, in Restelo near Lisbon, that had something wrong. Two children died there. Was very sad. The government did inspections of other parks, you know, to be sure they are safe. Many of the water parks, they closed. The Ondaparque, too. People, they were also scared and stopped going."

"And it's just been left there? Why hasn't something else been built?"

She shrugs. "No money, maybe."

"Wow. Thanks. Er, *obrigado*."

Outside, I buy an ice cream and sit down in the shade. A country which dominated the world five hundred years ago and triggered the Age of Discovery, couldn't build a water park correctly and now doesn't know what to do the ruins left behind. So, it becomes part of the urban jungle: overgrown, rusted and unwanted. A cemetery of sorts, on the hill, on the outskirts of this decaying town.

Paradox Island

Shaped like a giant anchor laid flat, Sylt (pronounced "Zoolt") is Germany's glamour island getaway of choice. Here, the sky is huge, the beach long, the North Sea extends to the horizon and the Porsches are brought in by train.

Three hours from Hamburg and the largest of the North Frisian Islands, it's a place of contrasts: stylish and dated, wild and over-developed, low-budget and top-shelf.

It's where the German middle class rubs tanned shoulders with the very wealthy. There are blocks of ordinary apartments available for week-long rental and acreages of swampy campgrounds, along with five-star hotels and stately, thatched-roofed holiday homes. Expensive restaurants and popular fast-food eateries. Forty kilometres of pristine coastline, with many of the beaches littered with these unsightly, boxy, baskety things (*Strandkörbe*) that people rent and sit in.

Sylt has been a tourist destination since the nineteenth century. The railroad causeway, completed in 1927, opened up the island to more visitors, but the spate of celebrities buying holiday homes is a more recent phenomenon.

The island is best accessed by train. Driving involves putting your car on the train in nearby Niebüll, or taking the passenger and vehicle ferry from the Danish island of Rømø to List, the town at Sylt's northern tip. The difficulty of getting a car to Sylt doesn't stop people from doing it; driving around the island in a Porsche, Mercedes or BMW seems essential to the Sylt experience. There's also an airport boasting international connections, with direct flights from half a dozen German cities as well as Zurich.

The largest town is Westerland, which somehow manages all at once to be garish and quaint, enjoyable and embarrassing, partying-all-night and early-to-bed, and swinging singles and conservative families.

The main pedestrian street of Friedrich Strasse leads pretty much from the train station directly to the beach. It's up and down Friedrich Strasse, and on the Kurpromenade running alongside the beach, that the holiday-makers parade in all their holiday finery. The designer labels mix with off-the-shelf stuff; the very daggy sharing the streets with the very chic. People sit in cafés and judge those strolling past, with the street value of certain outfits and accessories loudly estimated over half-drunk cups of coffee. Everybody name-drops, whether it's a brand, a designer, or a possible celebrity sighting.

Lined with shops and eateries, Friedrich Strasse is busy all day and well into the night. Seafood is popular, ranging from servings in expensive gourmet restaurants to affordable, over-the-counter fare from Gosch and Blum's.

Gosch has been a Sylt institution since the seventies, and is one of those unique places that transcend wealth. It started first as a snack shop in List, before expanding to Westerland and Wenningstedt, and then to the mainland, with franchises popping up in Berlin, Hamburg and other German cities. Visitors to Sylt, regardless of annual incomes, belly up to the bar at Gosch. At midday and in the evening, it's hard to find an empty seat. The beachside restaurant in Wenningstedt, just north of Westerland, is especially popular.

If Gosch gives a utilitarian impression of Sylt, it's an aberration. It's one of the few examples on the island of value for money and lack of pretention. You have to pay to use the beach, and pay even more to sit in a *Strandkorb*. In smaller towns such as Kampen and Rantum, wealth is fully on show, and it's rather disgustingly shown as well, with airs of superiority and exclusivity: long-sleeved pink shirts with the collars turned up and cashmere sweaters draped over shoulders; big sunglasses, designer handbags with dogs inside and very high heels; people driving convertibles with the tops down even though it's fifteen degrees and windy; and places like Sansibar, which is almost impossible to get into at a reasonable hour without being moneyed, famous or knowing the staff. Ideally, you need all three.

Like many visitors to Sylt, I attempted to have a drink at Sansibar.

My first mistake was arriving by bicycle. I'd taken the bus to Hornum, at the island's southern tip. The public buses have bike racks on the back, which means you can avoid riding into some stiff head winds, especially when going from north to south.

Hornum is an attractive village, with small thatched houses scattered among the dunes, like a settlement of Hobbits. The island narrows down here, sometimes to barely four hundred metres wide. Sylt is eroding naturally, and a stretch of this narrow finger of land may soon be permanently under water. The road sometimes floods when the tide is high, and sand is constantly transported out to sea and pumped back towards the beach all along the coast. But as many visitors don't go further south than the Sansibar, Hornum might just as well be an island already.

From Hornum, I rode with the wind at my back. I'd chosen the Sansibar as a stop-off on the way to Westerland. The very full car park was like an auto show: sports cars, large SUVs and old-timers. I locked my bike to a fence.

My second mistake was not sticking to the required "pretentious nautical" dress code. Every single patron looked like they'd just stepped out of a photo shooting for a luxury yacht magazine. There were men in sock-less deck shoes that had never seen a ship's deck, and in windproof sweaters, again with the collars turned up, that had never seen a yacht. Tans were mandatory, whether earned from the sun, bought in the sun studio or applied as a cream.

Every table was full. The patrons looked at each other, judging, commenting, talking behind their hands. It made it a very unwelcoming place. And I wasn't welcome anyway, because I didn't have a reservation, and I wasn't moneyed, famous or in with the staff.

The Sansibar is best described as famous for being famous. Everyone tries to go there because this is where everyone tries to go. There's nothing special about the place. It's tucked behind a dune and doesn't have a view of the water. There are far nicer places on the island, such as Wonnemeyer, Sturmhaube and La Grande Plage, all with beach views and more welcoming atmospheres, but the Sansibar is where everyone goes. Or at least, they try to.

I prefer the quiet of Keitum, which is east of Westerland and away from the main stretch of beach. It was once the capital of Sylt, when the harbour was the main connection to the mainland. There are many historic thatched houses here, built during those prosperous days, giving the village an almost mediaeval feel. Keitum makes an excellent place to stroll around without the posing tourists, and to drink a cup of tea in peace.

While coffee is the most popular hot drink in Germany, save for *Glühwein* in December, the Frisian islands have a surprisingly robust tea-drinking culture. They favour a strong black tea, taken with cream and candied sugar.

In the Kleine Teestube, in downtown Keitum, I asked the waitress why tea is so popular on Sylt and the other North Sea islands. First, she rather tersely told me to stop stirring the tea, as that wasn't done.

The cream shall "mushroom" (her word) to the top. She then launched into a brief history of local tea drinking, from which I garnered that the islanders leaned more to the English and Dutch influences than to those of the mainland. Something about passing ships and tea traders. Captains, merchants, pirates and such. I listened with half an ear, nodded when necessary and enjoyed the tea.

I like Keitum. It seems here that Sylt relaxes, takes a load off and has a cuppa. There's a bit of ceremony involved in the tea drinking, but for the most part, no one's putting on any airs, pretending to be posh, boasting of being posh or desperate to be seen. And there's none of that nautical-inspired fashion, which looks just ridiculous unless you're sailing solo around the world. The luxury cars are absent here as well, with most people getting around on bikes.

From Keitum, you can ride up the east side of the island, along the Wadden Sea, past Munkmarsch and Braderup, to Kampen. The village is not terribly fascinating, unless you like branded boutiques, expensive cocktail bars and the smell of petrol, but it's worth a look for the flash houses, as this is where many celebrities and wealthy Germans have holiday residences. They beat the worn path between Kampen, the Gosch in Wenningstedt and the Sansibar in Rantum, maybe pausing long enough to rent a *Strandkorb* at the beach and play a round at Golf-Club Sylt. It's all very fashionable and upmarket, but there's also a quiet sense that most of the people are trying too hard. Kampen was the place to be in the seventies and eighties, and is now living on old fame, attracting those who accessorise with the intent to impress and who come only to be seen. It's rather lame to dress stylishly just to see stylish people.

The less wealthy stick to Westerland.

The island is visited all year round, but is really popular in the summer months, especially during school holidays. When the sun is out and the weather is warm, the beaches are packed. The North Sea is more grey than blue, and in many places, swimsuits are optional. Finding an empty *Strandkorb* can be a fruitless search, as the best ones are taken at dawn. The long beach promenade is also full, walked by white-legged visitors with socks and sandals, and those couples who wear matching jackets and look strangely alike.

So, where does all that leave Sylt? For some, it's the German Riviera. For others, it's a family campground. For still more, it's a tacky beach resort. But then there are the Hobbit houses of Hornum, the tea-cosies of Keitum, the heathers full with sheep, and oddities that take you by surprise. Like the Cemetery for the Homeless in Westerland, close to the beach and busy Friedrich Strasse. This very small cemetery, built in 1855, is for people who washed up on Sylt's beaches. Each grave has a simple wooden cross, a date and a location. Moving.

And I really don't know what to make of Sylt.

Nullarbor Plain

Australia is huge. When you look at the country on a globe or world map, it kind of hides down the bottom, tucked under the earth, lost in blue and not appearing very large.

But it's massive.

If you want to know just how big it is, cross the Nullarbor Plain by land. You'll enjoy endless kilometres of endless nothing, for several days.

Before no-frills airlines drove flight prices down, the cheapest way across this great southern land was a second-class ticket on the Indian Pacific train. And cheap meant just a seat; not a bed in one of the sleeper cars. A seat, and not a very comfortable one.

It was in such a seat that I once wedged myself for two days and tried to stay sane.

In 1995, the Indian Pacific was twenty-five years old. This was when I boarded the train, in Perth, to cross the country from west to east. A one-way ticket was Au$100, for students. I went with Simon, the one friend I had to show for twelve years of school. By the end of the train trip, we were well on the way to not being friends any more, a rift that would tear for good a few weeks later.

Being on the train felt more than a little like travelling back in time. It was surely the same train as twenty-five years ago, a rolling rectangular cuboid of orange-tinged steel and limited facilities (at least in the area I was sitting). What might have been modern in the early 1970s was looking severely dated a quarter of a century later. The train was also slow.

The second-class wagon had one shower and one toilet, both at the front of the wagon, so you could always see who was going in and out of each facility, and how they looked before and after, and smell the accompanying odours. There was no visible air conditioning or ventilation, and no heating. The same tape of classical music played over and over, coming through speakers placed above the shower and toilet. Some passengers hummed along.

The seats were dark green, with the reclining mechanisms rusty and stiff. The footrest in front of my seat barely moved. I had to kick it down, at which point it went all the way to the floor, where it got stuck in a dent.

I had a window seat, but the window didn't open. Simon had the aisle.

We departed Perth in the early afternoon, and the journey started with promise. The beginning of a cross-country adventure. I wanted to see what my country looked like and was determined to spend the whole trip looking out the window, watching the outback roll past.

That feeling of excitement and wonder lasted barely an hour.

Because once we got outside of Perth and started chugging east, there was nothing to look at. The landscape was flat, dull and unchanging all the way to Kalgoorlie. In fact, it was pretty much the same all the way to Adelaide. If you looked out the window, then looked again two hours later, you might have thought the train hadn't moved at all.

With nothing to look at outside, I focused on my fellow passengers in the second-class wagon. But looking at them wasn't terribly different to looking out the window. The people had a collective plainness. They were dull to the point of colourless. While their sameness – of appearance, manner, type and behaviour – was disconcerting for me, it might well have been comforting for them. They were among known company, and probably felt good about it.

While I didn't want to be lumped into that bracket, Simon was blending in well, slouching in his seat, seemingly at ease with the arduous two days that lay ahead. It made me see him in a new light.

Through a difficult last year of high school, where I'd cut plenty of classes and watched my grades plummet, Simon had been a constant. He was funny, clever and loyal. About my height, he was athletic, in a rubbery way, but wasn't as interested in ball sports as I was. He liked to go fishing and wave-skiing, and was a huge fan of Midnight Oil and U2, often singing lyrics when he thought them appropriate to a certain situation.

On the train, he was proving himself far more adaptable than me; at home with the kind of traveller the cheap ticket attracted.

When boarding the train in Perth, I'd noticed that the passengers in second class had an inordinate amount of luggage, much of it in large plastic bags. Luggage is the wrong word; they had belongings. They also got on the train with pillows, sleeping bags and lots of food, carrying these items with an assurance that bespoke experience. They wore baggy tracksuit pants and pullovers in dark colours; many had ugg boots on. They slept most of the way, with what appeared to me as a sense of resignation. They knew the journey, knew the stops, knew how arduous it was, and so they wisely pulled their sleeping bags over their heads and tried to sleep through it.

There was something nomadic about them; that they perhaps made this journey often, with all of their stuff, following seasonal work or endeavouring to visit family and friends dispersed around this huge country. Or perhaps trying several times a year to make a new start somewhere else.

They struck me as being equally at home on long-distance buses, and would know the ins and outs of those trips as well, and would pack accordingly.

They were cross-country commuters. It was fascinating how quickly Simon started to look like one.

The passengers who were on board for the experience and to see the country – and who could pay the same amount to fly – were up front, enjoying the restaurant, lounges and sleeper cars. Those who were trying to get from A to B (again) were in here.

Bored out of my brain, I got to wondering if the collective plainness of my fellow passengers meant they were the kind of people who might be considered interchangeable; that each day, a few dozen of them boarded the train in Perth, with all their worldly possessions and their smelly sleeping bags and their bacteria-infested ugg boots, and those people weren't much different from the same few dozen who got on the day before or from the same few dozen who would board the next day, or even from the same few dozen making the trip from east to west. And that if all of them gathered together, they would blend into a oneness of dark-coloured tracksuits and large plastic bags. Their faces would disappear, as would their stories, personalities and characters.

This was a nasty thought and it made me sad.

It also made me sad to look out the window at the Nullarbor Plain and see nothing. I'd expected vast beauty, and saw nothing but sand.

Why didn't the landscape interest me?

Why did the second-class passengers all look so similar?

I turned to Simon. He was asleep. I shook him awake, as friends do, and tried to put my thoughts into words. He looked at me like I was a bit off, and said none of it mattered because it was almost dark now and the lights in the wagon had been turned off, and that I should stop over-analysing and just try to sleep like everyone else.

Resourceful Simon had taken his sleeping bag from his backpack and was now huddled inside it.

I didn't want to sit here and sleep like everyone else.

I climbed over the top of Simon and looked up and down the wagon. It seemed like the passengers were cryogenically frozen, enclosed in sleeping-bag pods, to be revived once we reached our destination in two days time.

Like cloning, I thought. Or robots. The Borg. A sci-fi nightmare. All these people, all exactly the same. Nullarbor cyborgs, fashioned from one strand of DNA. And my best friend had revealed himself as one of them.

I had to get out.

The next wagon had a small shop where the unprepared could buy food and drinks. Next to the shop, which was shuttered for the night, was a locked door that led to the wagons at the front of the train. The first class cars. The restaurants and lounges. I knocked on the door. After a while, a conductor appeared. I explained I wasn't feeling well, which wasn't a lie, because I'd consumed an awful concoction of reheated stew and sticky rice from the shop while the other passengers had munched on the crap they'd brought with them. It took a fair bit of acting, but he let me in, saying I could stay for a few hours.

Up front, it was blissful. There was colour. There was light. There was space. It was clean. There were benches, chairs and tables. There were no sleeping bags covered with biscuit crumbs and food stains. No tracksuit pants. People were having conversations. Some were gathered around a television, watching a film and laughing together.

This was where I should be. I found a bench sofa in the corner of the lounge and lay down on it.

I slept until the conductor woke me up.

"Time to go back now, mate," he said. "You're looking a bit better."

"Okay. Thanks for letting me lie down." As I reluctantly got up, I could feel the train slowing down. "Are we stopping?"

"We're at Kalgoorlie."

"What? Do you mean we're still in WA?"

The conductor nodded. He seemed proud of the fact.

"Reckon we're about halfway to the border," he said. "Better get back to your seat before we stop. Someone might run off with your bag."

I passed through the door to the shop. It closed behind me with a resounding click. In the second-class wagon, the stuffiness hit me like a sickening wave. The air was so thick, it was wafting.

I felt dizzy.

The train stopped. No one from my wagon got off. No one moved. The stillness was fascinating and frightening.

I took the chance to stand in the open train door and breathe in some fresh air. From here, Kalgoorlie didn't appear terribly inviting. The air was dusty and hot. I recalled a school trip, when I was nine or ten. On a bus without air-conditioning, where the best thing we did the whole week was visit an old gold mine, because it was cold and damp underground. While I pretended to marvel at tiny specks of gold in the rock-face, I thought that the people of Kalgoorlie would have been better off living far below the ground, or in caves, or somewhere else. On the bus ride there, which began at dawn and ended long after sunset, with all of us asleep, we were so utterly bored that each teacher and tag-along parent had tried, unsuccessfully, to entertain us. One parent, thankfully not mine, handed out squares of paper and challenged us to tear the paper in order to make it one long, unbroken piece, and to see who could make it the longest. Exciting.

As with all the school trips I can recall, we were really keen for it at the start, then half the kids got sick, the other half were glad they didn't, and everyone wanted to go home.

A whistle blew. The door slowly closed and sealed itself shut, sucking all the stuffy air back inside. The train chugged forward.

Twelve hours had passed since we left Perth.

I returned to my seat. In my absence, Simon had made himself comfortable, taking up both seats. His angular limbs made him look like a mutant larva trying to break free from a cocoon. When I nudged him awake and got him to move, he eyed me with something very close to resentment. Maybe it was because I was looking at him the same way; taking the train had, after all, been his idea.

Simon repositioned himself, turning his back slightly to me and stretching out into the aisle. He went immediately back to sleep, snoring loudly, his mouth open.

I was cold. I could have, like Simon, retrieved my sleeping bag from my backpack, wedged in the rack above, but I didn't. I took some extra clothes out of my pack and put these on.

Everyone slept. There was a choir of snorers, led by Simon. Each sleeping bag had its own peculiar odour.

Unable to sleep, and trying to keep myself from having an all-out panic attack, I closed my eyes and thought about where I was: me, nineteen years old, no girlfriend, not much in the way of direction or prospects, out in the middle of nowhere at someone else's behest.

Poor me, sufferer of motion sickness and hater of closed-in spaces, encaged in a rolling nightmare and heading further into the desert from where there could be no escape and no turning back.

Passive me, always letting other people make decisions and going along with what other people wanted in fear of being labelled contrary and difficult and losing what very few friends I had.

Pathetic me, a history major, lucky to even get into university and just scraping through, not terribly bright, wanting to drop out, and vaguely trying to earn a degree that would be all but useless.

What did I want to be? Not a bloody historian, that was for sure.

Did I want to take control of my own life? Yes, but I didn't know how.

Could I spend two days on this train? No way.

What the hell am I doing out here? No idea.

The night slowly dragged on, as did the train. When I pressed my face to the windows and cupped my hands around my eyes, I saw black nothingness. But if I looked up, craning my neck, I could see an inordinate number of stars. The night sky was epic and beautiful. It made me feel like a seriously insignificant speck.

I thought that driving across the Nullarbor Plain would be better, more of an adventure and more of an experience; an expedition requiring bottles of water, canisters of fuel, a box of spare parts, a tool box and maybe two spare tires. It would offer the chance to stop and look up at all those stars. The opportunity to go at my own speed and control my own journey.

I wanted to be out on the Eyre Highway, windows down, desert air blowing through the car. But I was on this train, sealed inside and suffocating.

I wondered: do these people ever look at the stars? Or are the crumbly bits at the bottom of a chips bag more compelling?

At some point during that long night, the train stopped. There was no announcement, no station. The train simply stopped, and stayed put for well over an hour, at which point a very long freight train came from the other direction. Our train had parked on a section of track about fifty metres from the main line. I could see the soft lights of the freight train as it clickety-clacked by; it needed a good ten minutes to pass, and I wondered what it was carrying.

I dozed a little, thought some more, wallowed in an ocean of self pity and wandered in a desert of loneliness. That was the overwhelming feeling; that I was lonely, that I had no one. I was almost twenty. I needed people around me, to reassure me, prop me up, make me feel good about being me.

Because I really didn't feel good about being me.

I was crammed into this wagon with sixty-something people, yet alone. Sitting next to my best friend, yet feeling like I didn't really know that person and that I might soon be friendless.

This also made me sad. Very sad.

Because the sixty-something people in this wagon seemed quite content with their situation, used to it and coping with it rather well, and this meant there was something wrong with me.

I'd been an unhappy, difficult child. More troublesome than troublemaker. A crier, not a screamer. Unsatisfied and demanding. My favourite saying was "It's not fair," which at the time was the best way I could express what I saw as the injustices of my world. This was my life? That couldn't be fair. There must have been some kind of mistake.

I hated school from day one. I tried to make friends only to blow them off in fits of pique. I sometimes worked very hard to win the allegiance of those deemed popular, only to fail and end up humiliated. I tried to be a good student. I tried to be good at sports. I was desperate to fit in, to sort of melt into the crowd and go unnoticed. I tried to run away. I was tormented and bullied by a couple of kids, and thought very seriously about doing them, or myself, harm. In primary school, I horded make-shift weapons like a prison inmate. In the drawer of my desk were pencils sharpened at both ends, a wooden ruler whittled into a spear, a rusty pocket-knife I'd found wedged in the grates of a drain, and ant poison stolen from my father's shed. I didn't really want to hurt anyone, and in the end wasn't brave enough to do it. I just wanted somehow to survive all of this until I was an adult and could do what I wanted.

Which was why I found myself floating through childhood, almost outside myself. I was killing the time, scratching off the years on my bedroom wall. I wasn't angry; I was disappointed, and bored. This was it? Perth, Western Australia, get a job, get married, buy a house in the suburbs. I floated through school. I would continue floating through university, then into some time-filling job. I'd float through love and marriage and parenthood. I'd float through mortgage repayments and Christmases. I'd float into old age, maybe even through an awful health issue that would bring about my demise. An entire life, but without me even having my feet on the ground. Without experiencing or engaging. Without looking at the stars.

Just slowly chugging forward on a single track, with no way to turn back or escape. No chance to take control. To open a window and breathe fresh air. To go at my pace. To find my own rhythm.

No. Come prepared for the plainness that awaits. Bring chips and a sleeping bag. Take a seat, settle in and wait for it all to be over.

As dawn broke on the desert, a sun blindingly yellow, I decided I would get off at the next stop, wherever it was. This wasn't a school trip to Kalgoorlie. There weren't any parents or teachers. I had a choice.

As daylight streamed into the wagon, the passengers started to stir. Curtains were pulled. Sleeping bags were rolled away. Crumbs of food fell to the floor. People yawned loudly and stretched in their seats. Down the aisle, separate lines formed for the toilet and the shower. Conversation was strained and people avoided each others' eyes. Having all spent the night together in this intimate wagon, breathing each others' breath, the morning after didn't really call for the usual small talk. It was like we all shared a dirty little secret and didn't want to talk about it.

At least, that was how I was seeing it. I also saw the resignation of long-distance commuting. And again, I envied these people, because I knew it would all be a lot easier for me if I could be as accepting.

The morning was quiet and people were slow to get going. I shouldn't have expected that they would sparkle with wit, cleverness and energy after such a night. And we were barely halfway through the journey.

Well, they were. I was getting off at the next stop.

This calmed me.

I was short with my answers to Simon's morning-after questions.

"How did you sleep?"

"I didn't."

"Have you had a shower yet?"

"No."

"Been to the shop for some brekkie?"

"I'm not eating that shit."

143

"Why do you always have to be such a downer?"

"Sorry."

That last question rankled. It was a refrain I'd heard many times before: me being unsatisfied with something, wanting more, and being labelled negative as a result. A downer. As if being critical was bad, and ordinary and plain should be more than good enough, and that there was something seriously wrong with me because I wanted something better than mediocre.

Simon joined the toilet line, then the shower line. He blended in well and interacted with others. He made people laugh and they enjoyed having him around.

At school, I'd often tried to copy his behaviour; to be well-liked and accepted.

I stared out the window, waiting for the train to pull into a station, wanting it to.

From the unchanging landscape of sand and shrub, it seemed the train wasn't moving.

There were no animals. No big red kangaroos in full flight. No meandering emus.

The hours passed. Breakfast blended into lunch, as the people ate almost constantly. I fell asleep.

The train finally stopped in Loongana, but there was nothing. I left my gear on the rack and got off the train. Lots of people went outside to smoke cigarettes.

I asked a conductor how far the Eyre Highway was from here. He laughed at me.

"Miles away," he said, blowing out cigarette smoke. "The train is all there is out here, mate. I suggest you get back on it."

The way he said it and the look he gave me made me wonder if I wasn't the first passenger to entertain the idea of getting off in Loongana.

Reluctantly, I got back on the train. And although I wasn't comfortable, and certainly not a good travel companion, I managed to somehow disassociate myself from this trip.

From which point, the trip became a blur. In the same way, when I think back to being a kid, much of my childhood is a blur.

I think the train stopped a few more times.

Simon gave up talking to me.

I ate nothing.

I tried to pretend I was in a coma.

Another night passed.

I sometimes felt myself outside of the train, watching it go past and looking at the person that was me silhouetted in the window. I didn't like the person I saw. But as the train passed, the me in the window became a blur.

We arrived in Adelaide at just after ten in the morning. Some of the passengers from my wagon got off too. They looked fresh and ready for the day, like they'd just done a short commute to work.

Simon took his time saying goodbye to a few people. He shook their hands and even hugged one woman.

I was tired, hungry and dazed. I felt absolutely filthy, and that not even an hour in the bath would remove the seediness that had sunk into my skin.

Adelaide was also a blur. Two days later, we were back on the train for Melbourne. At twelve hours, it was a breeze.

We went down to Lara to stay with Simon's family. While there, Simon and I had a long chat. I told him the trip wasn't working out for me; that this wasn't the way I wanted to travel. He convinced me to keep going, and despite having resolved somewhere near the border between Western Australia and South Australia to be less passive, I went along with it all.

We bought an old, tan-coloured Ford Falcon in Geelong and drove around Victoria. We went up to Bright and the Alpine National Park, where Simon wanted to go fly fishing. But we didn't catch anything, and ended up fishing at trout farms, where there were so many fish they could be scooped out with a net.

The Falcon had bench seats, front and back, which allowed us both to sleep in the car.

Simon was always a great spirits.

We drove on to Sydney. There, I found the courage to tell Simon I couldn't do this anymore. Selfishly, I left him with the car, bought a one-way ticket and flew home.

It was my first time on a plane. The flight took six hours.

Several months later, Simon returned to Perth, having travelled all around the country, hitch-hiking mostly, after selling the car in Sydney. I picked him up at the bus station and he stayed a night with me.

He'd changed. He seemed older, more evolved, and somehow more responsible.

I'd made new friends.

We didn't have much to say to each other. I think he wanted me to be sorry for leaving him in Sydney, which had pretty much ended our friendship.

I wasn't. It was the first time I'd made a difficult decision and taken control of my life.

The Herculean Ashtray

I'm crouching at the bar, as there are no seats. The locals must've been pretty short, because this bar comes up to about my knees. Built into the brick bar, which has a tiled surface of what looks like marble, are large pots. These pots held food and were heated from underneath. There are two more pots behind the bar.

There's something familiar about this place, the U-shaped bar and a wider area which could accommodate tables and chairs. Handed some bottles and glasses, I could quite easily start serving the people in here.

I wonder what the last barkeeper served to the locals. What did they eat? When did they eat? Did they use their hands? What did a meal here cost? Was the barkeeper the sort who engaged in conversations with his customers? Did they tell him their problems? What kind of problems did they have?

While I don't doubt the locals had similar problems to us today, including money, love, relationships, work and family, it turned out their biggest problem was Mount Vesuvius. None of the locals thought the volcano was a problem until it erupted on 24 August, 79 AD, burying Herculaneum and destroying nearby Pompeii as well.

It was just after lunch that Vesuvius began throwing ash into the sky. Were people eating at this bar when that happened? Did they feel the ground shake and hear the rumbling? Did it stop them mid-sentence, making them drop their utensils – if they used them – and look in the direction of the volcano? Did they panic and flee? Did mothers pick up small children and carry them as they ran down the street towards the water?

At the time, the city of Herculaneum was already a good seven centuries old. Legend has it the town was founded by Hercules, on his way back to Greece upon completing one of his Twelve Labours. A wealthy trading centre, it was first under Greek control and later under the Romans. The pyroclastic flow of ash and hot gases from Vesuvius buried the city. Rather than being totally destructive, the ash acted like a huge protective covering, so that when excavation began, as early as the eighteenth century, buildings, streets and houses were found to be remarkably well preserved. Wooden beams remain, houses have roofs and second floors, and decorative mosaics are intact.

While Pompeii gets all the visitors, it's Herculaneum that renders you speechless. The relatively few visitors wander around in a kind of daze, staggered by what they're seeing and not saying much. If anyone does speak, it's something along the lines of, "Come and look at this."

It's ghostly, impressive and surprisingly modern. This was what a Roman town looked like, and its basic construction and layout wouldn't be out of place in today's world. There are stone streets and footpaths, bars and baths, stores and water pipes. What is open to visitors is only one part of the greater ancient city of Herculaneum, much of which has yet to be excavated, but even here, the grid of streets is orderly and well-planned, sloping down towards the water.

It's clear that the people here had money. The houses are expansive and lavish, boasting beautiful frescos and elaborate floor and wall mosaics, many of which survived Vesuvius and can be viewed, even walked on. There are statues, marble furniture, tiled roofs, doors, beds and a remarkable array of the minutiae of daily life, including basins, candlesticks, rings, dice, bracelets, cradles, and even carbonised loaves of bread. Many of the artefacts are on display at the Archaeological Museum in Naples.

There are also several hundred skeletons, some found in 1981 in the boat chambers and on the beach, and more found during excavations in the 1990s. The poses of the skeletons show the people were caught by surprise and died instantly as the flow surged through the city, their joints bent by the intense heat.

Throughout the centuries, Herculaneum never rose from the ashes. It was buried under twenty metres of muddy ash that turned almost to concrete once it cooled. A new city was built on top, called Resina and renamed Ercolano in 1969. Now, this dug up time capsule is a UNESCO World Heritage Site, but despite its proximity to Naples, it's nowhere near as popular as Pompeii.

It is, however, surprisingly social.

Crouching at the bar, inspecting the pots, I get chatting with a few other people and we speculate on what life was like here some two thousand years ago. As they've got books and brochures, and some even tote audio guides, they have interesting information to share.

A man says that the skeletons found had excellent teeth, as the people then didn't have sugar. He adds that they also had traces of lead poisoning, possibly resulting from the use of lead water pipes. An American woman says she recently saw a report on television about lead poisoning in the city of Herculaneum, Missouri, coming from a huge smelter that had been forced to close down. We all find this a fascinating coincidence.

While some people drift away, I continue to hang at the bar, moving around to the other side, to where the server had stood. It feels quite natural for me to stand here, and I strike up conversations with others who stop for a look. Even among the ruins, people like to congregate at the bar; it's a shame I have nothing to offer them. The chatter turns to comparisons between Herculaneum and Pompeii, and this sparks debate over which site is more interesting. The consensus is that both are worth seeing: Pompeii for its size and impressiveness, Herculaneum for its preservation and tangibility.

I consider that last aspect to be of great importance. I can stand here, among the few visitors – and those visitors have chosen to come here, under their own steam and planning, rather than having been bussed here as part of a grand tour – at this bar or on that street or in that house, and imagine what life was like. At Pompeii, I stand there and think, wow, these ruins are amazing, but it's so large and overwhelming and full of people, I don't get a sense of daily life, personal stories or people dying. I'm a visitor, witnessing from afar under the blazing sun. At Herculaneum, I'm a citizen, both in shadow and light, projecting myself onto this place at street level, among the locals, soon to be charred alive and buried.

I see children on the streets, people gathered in circles and chatting, locals going about their business. I see dogs. I see people eating fish and drinking wine at this bar. The sun is out, but a cool breeze is blowing from the sea and up the east-west streets. I see trade and commerce, order and routine. Young lovers and families. Illness and health. Happiness and suffering. Festivals, births, celebrations, funerals, time marching forward. Seasons changing. Good years and bad years.

And then I see all of it wiped out. Because what Herculaneum shows so dramatically is the extent of the incredible natural disaster that occurred in 79 AD. No one saw it coming. The city was there one day, full of people and life, and gone the next. We stand in a ghost town, and its state of preservation makes it feel more abandoned than destroyed.

It's difficult to fully grasp a tragedy without bearing witness. We can try, by placing ourselves within the story, but imagining is never the same as experiencing, and historical sites that enable a certain interaction, or envisioning, are rare.

I get the sense at Herculaneum that all the townspeople are simply away; that they'll be back soon to resume life as it was.

Or, they're all still here, frozen in time, among us, with some of them sitting at this bar. But I don't have anything to serve them.

Junketeering

Ski maps, with their squiggly lines and happy piste names like Sundance and Moose Alley, always make the mountains look appealing. Even those tempting black diamonds don't look so difficult on the two-dimensional map. Cascade and Paint Brush sound like easy ones. This'll be fun and no one will get hurt.

I'm an average snowboarder. Somehow, I've managed to get down lots of ski hills, including the triple-black diamond Cliff at Big White in Kelowna, Canada. But I've never been keen on half-pipes or big air or being the fastest from peak to base. I prefer to stay away from crowds and to scoot down the hill at my leisure. Not so easy, given ski resorts can be busy, competitive places.

Jackson Hole is such a place. It's popular and difficult. Only ten per cent of the runs are rated for beginners. Looking up at the steep face of Rendezvous Mountain, knee-shaking piste names like Avalanche and Thunder spring to mind.

I was at Jackson Hole on a junket.

Travel writing and junkets have long gone together. The idea being that the writer would deliver a good story or glowing review if they are sufficiently pampered and looked after, and the story would then act as free advertising in whatever magazine or newspaper it's published. Companies, tourism organisations, hotels, resorts and marketing departments willingly spend money on junkets; writers willingly go on them. Given the nature of the exchange and often the pampering involved, it's a rather dirty, sleazy business, one that all participants seem to agree is integral to travel writing. A junket can be initiated by a writer, targeting a specific place and story (normally difficult to organise and only pulled off by writers with bulky portfolios and guaranteed publication), or set up by a company or organisation to bring many journalists to a place at once and maximise the output. The best times for junkets are in the off-seasons, or at the start or end of tourist seasons. A skiing junket often happens right at the end of the ski season, when the slopes are relatively empty and hotel rooms less expensive. It also means writers on such a junket can have stories ready to be published in advance of the next ski season.

Before Jackson Hole, I'd been on lots of junkets, for skiing, scuba diving, hiking and cycling. I seldom enjoyed them. One of the problems of junket journalism, apart from the seedy, whorishness of it, is that you get locked into the program you're on and the journalists you're travelling with, unable to do anything alone or at your own speed. With a ski junket, this can also include being taken off by guides to do dangerous stuff, then sitting in restaurants for hours afterwards talking about it, running up a huge bill with marketing people you wouldn't want to spend five minutes with.

The Wyoming junket I was on included skiing at Jackson Hole Mountain Resort, Snow King Resort and Grand Targhee Resort, and cross-country skiing in Yellowstone National Park. By day two, I was fully aware that I was in a situation that wasn't right for me and wanted to escape. Also, for the first time, I didn't feel good about being on a junket. This one reeked a bit too much of freeloading. A shame, because I was in some beautiful country.

It says a lot that the most fun I had on this trip was trying on cowboy clothes at Corral West Ranchwear in Jackson. That was on the first day, before the junket really kicked off.

On the slopes, as an average snowboarder, I was out of my league. I couldn't keep up with the others, and didn't want to. Off the slopes, I didn't want to be sharing hotel rooms with others and didn't want to wake up each morning with a hangover. But the junket demanded that we stay together; skiing all day and drinking in the restaurant and bar afterwards.

Granted, the first day at Jackson Hole was enjoyable. The weather was good, the snow fresh. In the gondola, guys talked about getting into deep powder and carving the trees. Gloved hands slapped high-fives. A silver flask was handed around. Helmets were put on.

I thought, helmets? Where are we going?

From the gondola, following a nip of courage, the runs didn't look so steep. At the top, it was a different story. The view of the Tetons and the surrounding valley was spectacular. I thought it best to sit down and enjoy the view. The others were already heading down. For journalists, they were very good skiers.

Rendezvous Mountain has a vertical drop of well over four thousand feet, and there's no easy way down. I was lucky that first day, as we had several guides with us. I managed to get through the first run and then, playing up a family angle for my story, talked one guide into taking me over to Apres Vous Mountain, where the drop was shorter and the runs tamer. There were also fewer people. At the base, my guide, under orders to please us, swapped his helmet for a pair of ear warmers and his telemark skis for a snowboard, and we spent the day working the Teton and Apres Vous quad chairs at my pace. That was good.

From there, things got progressively worse, with more challenging terrain the next day, followed by a long junket dinner, then trying to survive on the steep, icy pistes of Snow King Resort, followed by another drawn out dinner. As they ate and drank, the journalists I was with talked a lot about the work they do and the publications they write for, perhaps trying to justify their freeloading existence. They were all men, in the 35-50 age bracket, tanned, with longish hair, reasonably fit, but looking like they would be more at home on a tennis court than behind a desk. And while they talked a good game, I thought that few of them could actually lay claim to being full-time writers. They were successful hobbyists, like me.

Being close to downtown Jackson, Snow King doesn't get the same quality snow as up in the mountains, where it's dry and powdery. Needless to say, I fell down often at Snow King, and was lucky to walk away from one particularly bad crash, where the board's edge just would not carve into the ice.

I was still sore when we drove the next morning to Yellowstone, which included a long, bumpy and very loud ride in a snowcoach. During winter, no cars are allowed in the park, which was why we were crowded inside this smelly, overgrown snowmobile.

The bison meandering on the road boded well for what I hoped would be a more secluded, easygoing, nature-engaging few days. We were going to be cross-country skiing, and I was sure I could more than hold my own on the skinny planks. But there would be no skiing that first day, as the snowcoach wasn't much faster than a buffalo, taking forever to get to Old Faithful Lodge, one of only two park lodging options in winter. The afternoon was given over to a walking tour of the surrounding area, including the Old Faithful geyser, so named because it erupts every eighty minutes or so.

Despite the junket, it was great to be in Yellowstone in winter. The world's first national park, established in 1872, is also one of the most diverse. Towering peaks and dense forests go together with half of the world's geysers, while hot pools bubble next to ice cold rivers. Bison share the plains with elk and bighorn sheep, and bald eagles soar overhead. Coyotes stroll about, and yes, those prints in the snow could well be a wolf pack on the move.

Outside of winter, Yellowstone is very busy, with convoys of motor-homes, tour buses, station wagons and rental cars bringing the visitors in from every direction. But from November to around mid-April, the roads to the interior of the park are closed to vehicles. Snowmobiles are permitted, but there has been much debate over the years as to whether they should be allowed or not; they seem terribly out of place in this winter wonderland. Use is limited, however, with the park service running a lottery each year to distribute the permits. The snowcoaches, run by Xanterra Parks & Resorts and other tour companies, seem like utterly invasive species in this environment.

The first day's guided cross-country tour meant another couple of hours in a snowcoach, as Yellowstone's magical spots, like the Grand Canyon of the Yellowstone and the Old Canyon Bridge, are spread out. For me, it also meant waiting at meeting points, as the others in our group weren't quite as good on flat terrain as on steep terrain. I would have been very glad to take a map and plot my own course back to Old Faithful Lodge, but the junket demanded that the group had to stay together, as the marketing people weren't willing to risk journalists wandering off on their own and possibly having a negative experience. When the group was together, we were ferried back to the lodge in the snowcoach.

That evening, as more alcohol flowed, I really wanted to leave. When planning a winter in Wyoming writing trip, this was not what I had imagined. Stuck in this group and under the watchful eye of marketing people, I was having a filtered experience. I was also unable to contemplate things quietly or follow my instincts to where stories might be. So, while out in the park there were frozen lakes next to steaming geysers, volcanic pools of turquoise and aqua surrounded by snow, white ghosts for trees and an abundance of wildlife, I was bound to the itinerary of the group and the whims of whatever marketing person was in charge.

It was miserable.

Another day was required to get from Yellowstone to Grand Targhee Resort. On the rumbling ride south, I noticed that the snowcoach didn't appear to have an odometer. Or if it did, the lever never got above five miles an hour.

Those nursing hangovers managed to fall asleep despite the din. Those awake shouted conversation at each other, already talking up Grand Targhee. I wondered, not for the first time on this trip, how these people were journalists successful enough to be taken on a junket like this. Maybe they were convincing fraudsters; one-article wonders who parlayed that limited success into a career of junketeering; self-titled freelance travel writers who printed their own business cards and did more free trips than actual writing.

As a travel writer, I had done reasonably well, publishing enough stories to sustain as an interesting and lucrative hobby what was supposed to be my job. Though I despised them, the junkets did help, and they usually involved doing a trip worth ten times what I might get for a published article. Such was the case with this junket.

But I had the growing sense that my time was just about up. In early 2004, newspapers and magazines were not only paying less for features from freelancers, some were going out of print altogether. "Digital" was the catch-word all editors were using, features were being referred to as "content", and "online" was the most important audience of all. Travel journalism was being hit hard, as there were plenty of people prepared to write about their holidays, which they had paid for out of their own pockets, just to see themselves in print. Editors, constrained by revised budgets, were glad to get content for free. The travel sections of newspapers were basically turning into sponsored content and advertorials. And if there was no money for travel writing, there would be no more need for junkets.

Coming on this trip to Wyoming, I had the feeling it would be my last junket. Back home, I was already looking for another line of work, exploring options in advertising and corporate writing, following the money. Because my travel writing income had just about dried up. That was why this junket had such an archaic feel, like we were holding onto something that was about to disappear into history. The journalists involved seemed to be aware of that, though they seemed reluctant to admit it, and that was why they were trying so hard to get while the getting was still good; stuffing their pockets with freebies today before the new order comes into effect tomorrow. In a few days, we would return to our desks, write our articles and receive drinking money for them. I'd already noticed that the luggage of my junket group had grown, as they shoved towels, robes, slippers, hotel toiletries and the contents of every mini-bar into their bulging bags. It was pathetic and sad.

With two days remaining in Grand Targhee, I felt like I was in a relationship I knew was over. I didn't love this person anymore, we had no future together, yet we still had to keep up the pretence of our relationship for those around us, until we could leave and go our separate ways. So I tried to get excited about snowboarding Fred's Mountain, Peaked Mountain and Mary's Nipple. Bring on the challenging runs of Rock Garden, Lightning Trees and Nasty Gash. Yes, let's go cat-skiing outside the ski area boundary and find the deepest powder, and who cares about tree wells, steep cliffs and avalanches.

My feigned enthusiasm lasted all of an hour on the first morning. I couldn't keep the pretences up and simply went through the motions, detached from what I was doing, not concentrating at all. This was foolish. I was flying down hills, strapped to a board, with no helmet on, a very average snowboarder trying to negotiate black diamond runs beyond my ability and to avoid hitting people and trees, while also trying to keep up with the others in the group.

I broke my leg just after lunch on the last day. At the time, I wasn't sure if it was broken. I thought I'd just sprained my ankle, perhaps badly. I was glad to be rescued from the slopes and taken to the infirmary. There were no doctors present, but the emergency worker said I should go to the hospital in Idaho Falls and get an x-ray.

This was America: I wasn't keen on running up a massive medical bill. What I earned from travel writing wouldn't have been enough to get me past the door into an American hospital.

I asked him to strap me up and assured him I'd go to the doctor when I got home. He did so, giving me an old ski pole to use as a makeshift crutch.

By the evening, with my left ankle swollen and colourful, I knew something was wrong with it. When I tried to put weight on it, there was cracking and pain, and it felt like things were moving around inside the joint.

That foot and I had history, including an earlier break, several surgeries and plenty of sprains. I had arthritis in the joint when the weather was very cold, and a limited range of movement all through the year. The use of orthotics helped, but my problems with that foot had already brought to an end a (sort of) promising basketball career. It was rather fitting that the same foot would mark the end of my journalism career.

That evening at the Trap Bar and Grill, I got a lot of sympathy. More than one person remarked that I was lucky it happened on the last day.

Yep, I was lucky to break my leg.

It was a relief to get back to my room and sleep, knowing I would part from these people the next day and start my long trip back to Berlin. I was also very glad to be done with junketeering.

The next morning, my left foot was a brick. I could barely get my winter boots on, but once I did, the boot provided a modicum of support. With the ski pole as a crutch, I could walk, slowly and carefully.

I took a courtesy car to Idaho Falls, then a bus to Salt Lake City, the journey taking most of the day. In Salt Lake, I sat at Temple Square and prayed: that my foot would be okay, that I would find another job and that I wouldn't go to hell for being a junket journalist.

"Remember, God, I didn't steal any little bottles of shampoo."

At the airport the following morning for my flight to New York, I was relieved of my ski pole crutch, but I was given a ride to the gate on the back of a converted golf cart.

By this time, I'd become numb to the pain, but I had to be very careful not to put too much weight on the foot or to get it in the wrong position. I'd figured out a way to limp with the least amount of pain and discomfort, even while carrying my backpack. Though the joint was stiff and swollen, it felt like jelly. Things were disconnected and moving around. I was very worried.

I'd planned a three-day stopover in New York, to break up the return trip and perhaps search for a story. I managed to limp around and see some of the sights, but I was in no mood for researching or writing. I wanted to go home.

At JFK airport, my flight was delayed for six hours. We all sat around at the gate, at the far end of the terminal, like we were the last people at the airport. The delay meant I would miss my connecting flight in Amsterdam. I wondered if the travel writing gods might be enacting revenge.

When we finally arrived at Schiphol, a flight attendant, helping others with connections, told me I could make the next flight to Berlin if I ran.

Well, I couldn't do that.

The next available flight was several hours later. This gave me ample time to limp to the gate, which was on the other side of the airport and there was no golf cart to take me there. I limped the whole way, having to sit down and rest several times.

I got to Berlin in the evening and went to the hospital early the following morning. The x-ray showed the foot was broken in five places; a large piece of the lower tibia had broken clean off. The doctor didn't ask how it happened and I didn't tell him. I needed surgery to have two screws inserted, which would stay in for two years, and I would spend eight weeks in a cast and on crutches.

My junketeering days were over.

Escape to Colditz

Here's a typically outrageous and daring escape attempt. On 9 September, 1942, six officers were found to be missing. They had crept into the office of Sergeant-Major Gephard, where they had cut a hole diagonally through the back wall to the store room a few nights before. The hole was right under the Sergeant-Major's desk. When the time was right, the six escapees, disguised as two German officers and four Polish orderlies (in outfits they had made themselves), slipped through the hole. A German guard, fooled by a forged pass, opened the gate and the six of them marched out. Four were recaptured the next day, but Flight Lieutenant Hedley Fowler and the Dutch Lieutenant D.J. van Doorninck made it to Switzerland.

It had been heralded as the impenetrable fortress. All those troublesome chaps who had tried to escape from other camps were brought to the officers' camp at Colditz Castle. But these officers were not to be denied. Through their ingenuity, creativity and daring-do, the inmates of Oflag IV-C achieved small but important victories against the Germans in what was a surprisingly gentlemanly battle of wits that contrasted sharply with the brutal violence of World War II.

Colditz was no ordinary prisoner-of-war camp. It was controlled by the German Army – those noble Prussians, with their duelling scars and straight noses – and not by the SS or the Gestapo. There were no atrocities in this camp. The inmates were officers from Britain and the Commonwealth, France, Holland, Belgium and Poland, and thus received relatively good treatment.

Unlike other German camps, this one was run under the terms of the Geneva Convention, with the inmates not required to work. That gave them more time to sew uniforms in their secret attic workshops, forge passes, plan escapes and dig tunnels under the castle. One such tunnel, constructed by the French, actually started at the top of the clock tower and dropped down to the cellar below. It then ran under the chapel and towards the outside wall, for a total of forty-four metres. The Germans discovered the tunnel when it had only a few metres left before breaching the wall. Now, with Colditz Castle open to the public, visitors can view the entrance to the tunnel and chart its course through the chapel.

The castle itself, begun in 1046, is a brooding, off-white structure perched on the hill above the River Mulde in the village of Colditz, about an hour southeast of Leipzig, a city well worth visiting. Laid dormant during the communist era, much of Leipzig's old town has been lovingly restored since the Peaceful Revolution marched through the streets in 1989. Before and after that time, Leipzig was a place people wanted to leave, with locals hoping first to escape communist East Germany, then heading west to find work after the unification of Germany. However, from around early 2000, Leipzig has transformed itself into Germany's creative capital, attracting artists, designers and musicians, and earning the moniker Hypezig. It requires a train and a bus to get to Colditz from Leipzig.

Colditz's high structure made the castle the ideal place for a maximum security officers' prison, with an almost eighty-metre drop to the river below, but many of the inmates proved up to the challenge. Apart from many imaginative and brave escape attempts through tunnels, they also sought to use the height of the castle to their advantage. During the winter of 1944-45, British officers built a glider in three pieces in the attic above the chapel. Using wooden shutters, mattress covers and mud fashioned out of attic dust, the completed glider was to be launched using a bath filled with concrete and dropped through the tower as propulsion. While the camp was liberated before the glider could be finished, subsequent tests with a replica proved that it would have achieved its aim.

Guided tours take you through the castle, showing entry points to tunnels and detailing the clever attempts at escape. The small museum displays the means by which the inmates achieved their goals, with stamp pads and false documents, and the tools they fashioned themselves, including a hand-made sewing machine used for making fake uniforms. There are also photographs of inmates, and a replica of the Colditz Glider. The old guardhouse has an exhibition of paintings by British Major William F. Anderson, which offer a glimpse into the daily life of the camp.

The castle also has a fantastic history, having been burned completely to the ground, rebuilt, and used at various times as a hunting lodge, lunatic asylum and sanatorium. During the communist era, it was a nursing home, a hospital and a psychiatric clinic. The unification of Germany brought renewed interest in the castle, and it soon became a popular destination for people from America and Britain. Thanks to books, films, TV shows, board games and video games, the legend of Colditz in those countries is even more fantastic than the actual history. It started with *The Colditz Story*, the 1955 film based on the book by Pat Reid, who was escape officer for British POWs in the camp. Reid also devised the *Escape from Colditz* board game, released in 1973.

Recent renovations to the castle have unearthed a wealth of lost treasures, including a bag hidden under the floor which contained a fake German uniform and local maps. A secret radio room was also discovered, with a French officer then returning to claim his radio.

The castle now includes a youth hostel, housed in the German garrison's former headquarters, but there are no plans to offer guests the chance to escape.

Payback

Natasha was from Montreal, and was doing a trip around Australia. We met in Kalbarri, a small holiday town on the northwest coast. After three days together, she went north to continue her trip and I went south to resume slogging my way through university. I was a few months from graduating and wasn't even sure I'd make that.

We stayed in touched, exchanging letters and postcards for a few months. We had one aborted attempt to meet up in Queensland. Natasha wanted us to go diving together on the Great Barrier Reef, but I don't do well on boats. There was also the nagging fear of being stuck on a boat for five days, sharing a tiny cabin and being a dive buddy with someone I perhaps wasn't that keen on anymore. Months had passed since we'd met, and we'd spent barely three days together. Would we still click like we had in Kalbarri?

I wasn't sure, and used my dislike of boats to wheedle out of the Barrier Reef trip.

While it saved me an expensive cross-country flight I didn't have the money for, Natasha still wanted to meet up again before she left Australia. So, upon graduating a few months later, I bought a one-way ticket to Vancouver, making sure I passed through Sydney on the dates Natasha had given me. She was on her way to Fiji. We would have four days together in Sydney.

I took the red-eye from Perth and got to Sydney in the early morning. From the airport, I went straight to the giant youth hostel near the central station where Natasha was staying and which was the meeting point. It's an orange monstrosity that sleeps about six hundred and smells of floor cleaner and feet, and is about as inhospitable as a hostel can get. The people staying there were either just arrived, jetlagged and excited, or worn out, broke and about to leave.

I had no intention of spending a night there.

I took a seat in the lobby, with all my stuff next to me, and waited for Natasha.

Sitting there, I was overcome by the thought that this was all a very bad idea. I barely knew this girl. I wasn't even sure I could pick her out of this crowd of backpackers. And I couldn't help wondering how many other three-day guys had been with Natasha in the last six months? How many had there been before me?

While I was still very much a travelling novice, trips to New Zealand, the States and Canada had trained me to trust my instincts. This just didn't feel right.

I stood up and prepared to leave.

Then out of the elevator walked Natasha.

With a friend.

We had a hug – it seemed weird to kiss – and I was introduced to Terri. Natasha explained they'd met on the diving trip I'd bailed on, when they shared a room together as the only uncoupled divers on board. The two were about to go to Fiji together.

"I changed my plans," Terri said flatly.

"Great." I was unsure just how close this friendship was. There was something competitive in Terri's stare. "That's great. Fiji's nice, I'm sure."

"Have you been there?"

"Nope."

Terri didn't ask if I wanted to come with them. Natasha gave her a look and Terri wandered over to the rack of pamphlets advertising things to do in Sydney. While she perused the pamphlets, she kept looking in our direction.

"We travelled all the way down the east coast together," Natasha said. "She's a super travel companion."

"Great."

"So, what do you think?"

"About what?"

"The plan."

As had been decided through an exchange of emails, the plan was to move out to a hotel in Coogee for a couple of days. I was supposed to have booked it. I hadn't.

"Great," I said.

Natasha nodded slowly a few times, then went upstairs to pack. Terri followed, running so they got in the elevator together.

I paced a little bit, unsure what to do. The hostel lobby was very busy and loud, making it hard to think. There was a parade of backpackers, laden with gear, coming in to find a bed, or on the way out to their next destination. They looked weary and strained, as if the whole experience was getting them down.

They had the shambled, scruffy, annoyed look of people who had camped for a week in the rain.

They looked hungry, too, perhaps longing for the well-stocked refrigerator of their parents; for clean clothes and a bed in a room all of their own.

My feeling was that Natasha was about as uninterested in this return hook-up as I was. Yet we were both going to continue with it in order not to hurt the other person. And that, being cowardice, struck me as a stupid reason for intimacy.

Natasha and Terri came out of the elevator together, both carrying backpacks that towered over their heads and toting bed sheets.

Natasha said something about going out to Penrith to visit some friends, and I said:

"Great."

So, no need for the hotel in Coogee that I hadn't booked anyway, and now we were travelling as three.

"There's room for you too," Natasha said. "They've got a big house in Penrith."

I nodded, but none of this was great.

The girls handed in their keys and dirty linen at the reception desk. They got their passports back and their key deposits, and completed the other rigmarole that made youth hostels such an effort of administration.

I wanted no part of Penrith. This situation was all wrong and I started to panic. Fear made my imagination run wild. Would the house in Penrith be a kind of quasi-reunion of Natasha's three-day Aussie guys? Would I wake up the following morning with Terri's hands around my throat?

The only solution that presented itself was to run. And because I really had nothing to lose, I shouldered my backpack, picked up my guitar and walked straight out of the hostel.

Natasha was a bit slow in responding, but she eventually chased me down the street and got in front of me.

"Don't leave like this," she said.

I didn't think she looked terribly sad.

"Look, it's been great. Kalbarri was great. But I'm not going to Penrith. It doesn't feel right."

"Wait."

"I'm sorry. Have fun."

I walked around her and she didn't pursue me. I got to the next corner without looking back and asked for directions to the nearest bus stop. I had friends in Randwick; I could stay with them while deciding my next move.

It was an intense feeling: knowing I'd hurt someone (possibly), being so utterly selfish and callous, while also proud of myself for being forthright and honest. So often I just went along with things. Not this time.

I decided to leave Sydney and spent an enjoyable four days in the Blue Mountains. After that, I flew to Vancouver and hitch-hiked through British Columbia.

Thankfully, Natasha didn't send any hate emails or nasty letters, which made it easy to forget her.

As the weather got colder, I settled in Nelson, which was a nice little town in the Kootenays. The Steve Martin movie *Roxanne* was filmed there. I found a job, met some good people, took a room in a shared house, bought some cross-country skis and prepared to enjoy my first white winter.

The snow came early, and with it, snowboarders and skiers descended on the town; the seasonal workers who would check ski passes at the hill in exchange for minimum wage and a ski pass, and the young men and women who were tree-planters, fire-fighters and such through spring and summer, and spent their winters skiing and partying.

It was a lively place, thankfully without the pretensions I'd expected of a ski town.

There were lots of people my age and a little bit older, and plenty of girls. One after another, they all turned me down.

Michelle: I met her at the Critical Mass bike ride that happened just before the first snowfall. She was a pretty, kind of stringy, farm-type girl who dressed like a pseudo-hippy. She seemed interesting and interested. I asked her for coffee the next day and she brought four friends with her, including one guy, who was a lumberjack and dressed like one, and who turned out to be her boyfriend. He had huge hands, with palms like small plates. I chose to not make a scene.

Amber: I met her at the gym. I thought she was a bit young, but as it was lunchtime on a weekday when we started chatting, I figured she was at least old enough to have finished school. I asked her to meet for coffee later that evening. She agreed, but never showed. I found out later she was sixteen.

Sandy: a few years older than me, we got chatting at a party and got along rather well. She had a house outside of town, where she lived with her small son. After spending a bit of time together, I reached out at one point to hold her hand and she withdrew from me, saying, "I thought we were just friends," and walked away.

Stacey: we worked together at Overwaitea, the local supermarket where I was reluctantly working in the deli department for a very low wage, and eating much more than I served. She was very small, and only just out of high school. But she was fun to work with, and I hoped to take that fun beyond the deli service counter. We went for a drink. Some of her friends showed up as well. Stacey didn't seem to like me out of my Overwaitea uniform. Is a clip-on tie really such a turn on? After that one drink, she didn't talk to me at work anymore, and changed her shifts so we wouldn't work together.

Jessica: a morning swimmer, like me. We often found ourselves sharing the fast lane at Nelson's indoor pool. She gave me her number and we chatted on the phone a few times, but she never sounded terribly interested. I managed to get her to attend a charity basketball game where I was playing for the Nelson All-Stars against the Harlem Crowns, a lower-level version of the Globetrotters. I spoke with Jessica afterwards, but she kept looking around for her friends. I didn't try calling her again, and she seemed to stop swimming in the mornings.

Holly: about as tall as me, with blonde hair and a deep tan, she was a mountain bike racer. We lined up a date, and she stood me up. When we ran into each other at a party a few weeks later, she acted like she didn't know me.

Natalie: a very nice girl who I liked straight away and liked a lot. She was new in town, just starting to meet people and make friends. She worked at the bakery. I started going there regularly for lunch. We had a few dates, but nothing really happened. One morning, about two weeks later, I went downstairs for breakfast and there she was kissing my housemate Greg.

Andrea: we met at Ellison's Market, where she worked. She was lively and talkative, and said she was singing at a show that night. It was at the Fellowship Church around the corner from my house. I figured the church was just the venue. It turned out to be a rather serious religious gathering. On stage, Andrea was singing about God and Jesus. When we chatted afterwards, it only took a few minutes for her to deem me not worth saving.

Anna: we got talking at the gym one day. She had just come back from south-east Asia. I casually asked her for a coffee and she stared at me and said, "Let me figure you out first." I ran into her on the ski lift a few weeks later and I think she was still trying to figure me out.

Rachel: I recognised her from the University of Victoria, where I'd spent a semester the previous year. We'd been in a couple of classes together. Turned out she was from Nelson, and had come home for Christmas. We had a few drinks together at Mike's, and it was fun. But she went back to Victoria a few days later and never got too close.

A man should quit while he's behind. Far, far behind. I didn't.

Ashley: the whole thing with Ashley was bad from the start. I never knew where I was with this girl. We went snowboarding together a few times, and it was a lot of fun. She was a good snowboarder, plenty better than me. But our relationship was a strange one. Whenever I thought she was keen, it become apparent she felt the opposite, yet she still wanted to spend time with me. One minute we were just snowboarding buddies, the next minute she wanted to get close. It was like we were playing some bizarre mating game, the rules of which I didn't understand. After several false starts, I gave up.

Caroline: one of Greg's ski hill colleagues. I think he felt a bit guilty nicking Natalie from me and tried to set me up with Caroline. We went swing dancing a couple of times because I was writing a story about it for the local paper and needed a dance partner. She didn't have much rhythm and kept her distance when we danced together. She seemed very wary of me. Clearly, word had spread.

Nelson's a pretty small town.

Fiona: Towards the end of what had become a long winter, I found out that the girl who worked at the Beer & Wine store was very interested in me, and had actually been following me around the town in stalkerish fashion. A friend said I should go to the police and file a complaint. I called Fiona and asked her to meet instead, because it seemed I was such an unattractive, disgustingly horrid pariah, that all I needed to do to stop Fiona from stalking me was to spend some time with her, at which point she would gather that I was indeed an unattractive, disgustingly horrid pariah and lose interest. We met for a coffee. She told me all about the dreams she'd had of the two of us, how we were destined to be together. After less than half an hour of idle chat, the tide had turned and she wasn't interested in acting out any erotic dreams. She left. I paid the tab.

At that point, I did give up.

A few weeks after leaving Nelson, I was travelling through Colorado en route to New Orleans. I spent some time skiing with friends in Steamboat Springs, and regaled them with stories of my recent romantic misadventures.

"That's payback," one said. "For something you did."

Neon Pink

It's a cool, clear October evening on Hamburg's Reeperbahn, in the St. Pauli district. Raindrops aren't obscuring the view of the sinful mile, and the fog that rolled in off the River Elbe this morning is long gone. The sex stores, bars, souvenir shops and hordes of people are illuminated by an array of coloured neon, probing spotlights and flashing television sets showing naked girls dancing.

This is the Reeperbahn of today, relatively safe, a place for tourists, and not totally ruled by the sex trade like it was in the past. The genital zone is starting to grow up.

Walking the cobblestone streets of Hamburg by day, taking in the lakes, parks, boulevards and harbour, it's difficult to believe the city would even have a red-light district, let alone one as famous as the Reeperbahn. It seems too conservative and quiet. Hamburgers (that's what they call themselves), for the most part, follow the rules: they drive safely, keep the city clean, wait at traffic lights, and work hard. But on a half-mile stretch just west of downtown, pretty much anything goes, and always has.

Founded as a port, the harbour has dominated the development of the city. Successful in commerce and business, Hamburg is now home to more millionaires than any other German city. It remains the "Free and Hanseatic City", its own *Bundesland* (state). And with the exception of Napoleon in the early nineteenth century, Hamburg has never had to bow to a foreign leader. Freedom from tyrants, freedom of commerce and freedom of fetish.

The word Reeperbahn translates as "rope road", and not reaping as in the English sense. Until the 1880s, the road was used for the construction of the heavy ropes required by sailing ships. Because of this sea-faring connection and its proximity to the harbour, the Reeperbahn then was frequented by sailors and seamen.

When sailing ships were replaced by steamers and liners, the heavy ropes were no longer in high demand. As entertainment was banned from the city's mediaeval core, the Reeperbahn, being outside that area and still frequented by sailors, became the main strip of a new amusement area.

First popular were Hagenbeck's Dancing Bears, Red Indian displays and the hippodrome, the site of horse races. But the demand for waltzing bears decreased while louder and more voluptuous cries of "Hello, sailor" could be heard up and down the Reeperbahn. Prostitution increased and the streets became littered with open debauchery as moneyed sailors sought relief from months of seafaring loneliness.

Even though the city was ravaged by fire in 1842 and bombed extensively during World War II, the Reeperbahn's sex industry kept on pumping, with seamen and harbour workers bringing in enough money to maintain its constant restoration and reinvention.

Running off from the west end of the sinful mile is Grosse Freiheit (great freedom), a street famous for explicit sex shows. The first incarnation of the Beatles, with Pete Best on drums, played in the basement of the Kaiser Keller in the early 1960s. They shared the stage with strippers and bore the insults of rowdy sailors for the skiffle-influenced rock'n'roll they played, but mainly for keeping the girls off the stage. The Beatles time in Hamburg has been documented by the photographs of Astrid Kirscher, girlfriend of then bassist Stu Sutcliffe, and by the film *Backbeat*.

In the 1980s, it was thought AIDS, poverty and crime had brought the neighbourhood to its knees, but a new generation of young Hamburgers rediscovered the music clubs, discos and bars. Accordingly, the Reeperbahn changed, with restaurateurs opening modern bars, and with new theatres and venues for musicals taking the place of former brothels. This revitalisation brought gentrification, pricing many locals out of the St. Pauli area.

But even with all that, the sex trade remains vibrant, if only for its neon brilliance. The prostitutes can walk certain streets and stand on certain corners after 8pm. There are still peep shows, cinemas, sex shops, dangerous side streets, roaming packs of males, streetwalkers, dirty old men, fast talking peddlers, good time seeking sailors, and groups of men and women respectively on bucks' and hens' nights. But there are also wide-eyed tourists, villagers in the city for a night out, theatre goers and music enthusiasts.

The sex industry is not nearly as bad as it once was. Pimps no longer loiter and leer, or lower (via pulleys) flagons of whiskey to their hardworking street girls. The girls still sit in shop windows on the closed-off Herbert Strasse, but are required to undergo health inspections, hold insurance and pay tax. Streetwalkers remain something of a venereal roulette wheel, but come a lot cheaper.

In the centre of it all is the Davidwache Polizei, Hamburg's most famous police station. The neon Polizei sign is a comforting reminder that help is not that far away, though they impose no closing hours on bars and clubs, and their presence on the streets seems solely to be for intimidation and reassurance. They sometimes patrol on horseback.

A popular way revellers end a long Saturday night on the Reeperbahn, or perhaps to keep it going, is with a visit to the Fischmarkt. A five-minute walk from the genital zone and operating every Sunday morning from dawn, the fish market has been a Hamburg icon since it began in 1703. You can buy everything from fruit and fish to perfume and pyjamas. The drinking continues and rock music is played in the old fish auction hall. Vendors boisterously hock their wares, with some resorting to throwing pineapples into the crowd to get attention.

With about thirty thousand revellers on a regular night, the Reeperbahn is Hamburg's centre of nightlife and debauchery. It remains second to Amsterdam as the world's most famous red-light district and is Hamburg's number one tourist draw-card. But it's changing. The ever present sex trade is slowly diminishing in order to cater for a wider market. Good-time seeking sailors have mostly become a thing of the past, and the prostitution industry is suffering as a result.

It's all still there, though. It's hard to take the neon glint out of people's eyes, and as long as women are willing to take their clothes off for money, there will always be men happy to pay an exorbitant amount for a beer to watch them do it.

But it seems the hands-on nature of this business might also be fading away, as technology has men sitting in darkened rooms with their faces illuminated by the glow of their computer screens rather than watching Swedish films with the curtain drawn tight in soiled peep booths on the Reeperbahn. Perhaps this is how the sinful mile will evolve next, creating a sex trade based on cyberspace, where "downloading" is only a click of the mouse away.

Of course, the last thing I'd want to see is "internet" in pink neon on the Reeperbahn. Surely, some things can remain sacred.

Out of the Blue

Stupidly, I'd gone off the main trail, hoping to circle my way back to the Three Sisters. The narrow track got progressively narrower, until it closed altogether, ending in a thicket of thorn bushes that snatched at my clothes.

I was lost.

As I removed each thorny branch, I missed Rob, Toni, Lisa and Brian, my hiking buddies who had all left that morning. Given the situation I was now in, Lisa, the ever-prepared Canadian, was especially missed. She would have had extra food and water, and a map, and would sternly have told me to stay on the main trail.

I was without a map, and I'd finished all the food and water I'd brought on what had been a very long solo hike to Ruined Castle.

Unsure which direction to go, my imagination started to run wild. I envisioned being stuck out here for days, lost, hungry and thirsty. Which made me miss Scottish Rob, who always seemed to have the start of a grin on his face and was never rattled. He'd have calming words to offer. He'd find this amusing, as would Toni, who shared her countryman's sense of humour.

As for English Brian, he'd probably be deeper into the thicket than I was, or he had wandered off on another trail and we would be searching for him.

Out of the thicket, I couldn't quite discern which direction I'd come from. There were several narrow tracks that ended here. I'd walked downwards to this point, so it made sense to take the track heading up hill.

After five minutes, this track came to a dead end. I turned around and found my way back to the thicket.

I missed Toni and the old compass she said her grandfather had given her.

It was strange to miss people I barely knew.

We had met at the Katoomba Youth Hostel four days ago, arriving from Sydney on different trains. I met Rob and Toni first; we shared a pot of tea in the hostel kitchen the evening I arrived. Lisa and Brian, who were sitting by the fireplace, tagged along for a walk down to the Three Sisters, a formation of rocks that extends out from a cliff. The Sisters are floodlit until midnight.

That evening, as we walked to the end of Echo Point Road, we bonded over our collective dislike of Sydney. Though touted as one of the most liveable cities in the world, I found it too busy, hectic and unwelcoming. The locals struck me as carrying themselves with a snobbish superiority; as if this was Australia's one city, and all the other places were just big country towns populated with country hicks.

Katoomba, two hours east of Sydney's urban sprawl and the main entry point to the Blue Mountains, is very much a world away. It has a population of about eight thousand, and is a day place. There aren't many hotels. The visitors are most often day-trippers from Sydney, coming by tourist bus or rental car.

The hostel was comfortable and hospitable. The people staying there actually talked with each other and did things together, which hadn't been my experience staying in various hostels in Sydney, where most of the travellers were actually residents, living in the hostel while working temporary jobs.

Rob, Toni, Lisa and Brian were all travelling separately, around my age and good company. It was Brian's idea that we all go hiking together, which we did for three days straight, exploring a different area of the Blue Mountains each day and ending in front of the hostel's fireplace toasting marshmallows.

It was also Brian who had the habit of just wandering off when we were hiking, seeming to forget that we were with him, making us follow him down a trail he had spontaneously selected and, one time, spend an hour searching for him. He was profusely apologetic each time, but appeared torn between staying with us and wanting to go at his own speed and follow his own instincts.

While I felt the same, in this situation I was happy to follow more prepared and organised hikers. Through past experiences and lucky escapes, I'd set a low standard for preparation and forward planning when wilderness was involved, heading off on long hikes without the right gear, provisions or maps. Like the time I did a nine-hour hike up to a glacier near Arthur's Pass in New Zealand, in a pair of shorts and a raincoat, with just a small bottle of water and an apple, and no map.

And now I'd gotten myself lost somewhere in the Blue Mountains. I tried another track, and came to an area where several tracks met. This place looked vaguely familiar. I rued not having a map. I felt very alone.

At the Three Sisters the first evening, there was too much fog, so

173

we sat down on a bench, all five of us, and waited for it to clear. We chatted. Brian had a dry sense of humour, and Lisa laughed at just about everything he said. Rob had a platonic arm around Toni, with the two Scots behaving a little like brother and sister. Lisa was next to Toni, while Brian and I book-ended the bench. Toni asked why the mountains are blue. As the only Australian in the group, it fell on me to answer.

"You haven't read about it or heard it from someone else?" I asked.

Toni smiled and shook her head. "Nae."

"Well, I guess it's a bit like your grandma's hair. For as long as you can remember, it's always been blue. It just is like that."

Toni, Rob and Brian laughed.

Lisa then talked knowledgably about eucalyptus trees, oil and water vapour reflecting rays of light, or something, which combine to cover the mountains in a haze that appeared blue from a distance.

"Oh, okay," Toni said. "But I think I like the hair version better."

A wind blew up from the valley, dispersing the fog as if lifting a veil, and the Three Sisters were suddenly revealed. We stood up and went to the railing. The spotlights accentuated different colours on each sister, more shadows than light. I thought I saw a flying fox gliding over the valley. Owls hooted.

The pointy-headed, squat middle sister is certainly the least attractive of the three, while the youngest, tall and lean and almost with her back to the other two, has separation, from the cliff and her sisters. She appears to stand alone, yet also reluctantly with the other two.

As the youngest in my family, I could relate.

I also thought that the youngest sister had her back turned to Sydney and was looking west; away from the known and towards the unknown, from the faux to the real.

The lights of Sydney glimmered in the distance. Even from here, the metropolis looked like it was posing: hey, take a gander at my big city lights, shining from such a very long way away, because no other lights shine this bright and look this stunning.

"It's really good to be out of Sydney," I said.

"You sound traumatised," Brian said. "What happened to you there?"

I started to formulate an answer, one that would justify my actions and hopefully make me feel less guilty, but Lisa said the cold was getting under her base layer and motioned that we start walking back to the hostel, to hot cups of tea in front of the fire. She added that we, meaning she, needed to plan the next day's big hike to Govett's Leap.

Coming to the Blue Mountains, I'd had no intention of meeting people and hiking with others. I'd expected more situations like the one I was in: me, on my own, doing a ludicrous hike, somehow getting through it unscathed, but unable to share the experience with anyone.

On the first day, Lisa, with her maps and supplies, asserted herself as our leader. She marked the hiking route on several maps in red pen, carried a Swiss Army Knife and claimed to know how to make fire. She also had the best hiking boots of any of us, and would have left us behind if she hadn't been so nice. Hiking with Brian made her frustrated, but the two seemed to like each other anyway. Searching for an ambling Brian each time presented her with a challenge she seemed glad to take.

We took the 8:26am bus to Blackheath – Lisa had the bus schedule from somewhere – for the starting point to Govett's Leap. Being the only Australian in the group, I was chosen to point out scenery, spot wildlife and give lessons in bush survival. Like I had any clue. They dubbed me the Bushman of Blackheath, with the moniker used more in mockery than reverence.

Not even into the first hour, we had the banter of old friends.

"Bushman, are we going to some famous place to commit suicide?" Brian asked.

"Not that I know of. Lisa?"

She was already too far ahead of us to hear.

"Leap is a Scottish word for waterfall," Rob said. "We'll see leaping water, not leaping people."

The conversation continued as we went down into the valley. It had the ease of friends catching up, and not that of people getting to know each other.

We negotiated slippery rocks, old concrete stairs and narrow, winding tracks. The scenery was beautiful, but there was no wildlife, which was disappointing. It was a long undulating hike, which included an ascent to a cliff that offered fantastic views of the valley.

Into the sixth hour, we saw Bridal Veil Falls tumbling over the cliff on the other side of the gorge.

It started to rain just as we reached the bus stop. We had fifteen minutes before the bus back to Katoomba, with Lisa happy that we were on time to catch a bus that came just once every hour. Exhausted, we sat under the bus stop's shelter and didn't say much.

Back in Katoomba, we cooked dinner together and sat by the fire afterwards.

The next two days passed in similar fashion. We did hikes to Leura Falls, Weeping Rock and the car graveyard, where a dozen cars had been "retired" into the valley.

There were no sad goodbyes when the other four left. I had one more day in Katoomba. I used it to hike on my own and get lost.

From the intersection of narrow tracks, I tried each one in turn until I finally got back to the main trail. For the rest of the way, I felt like a fool. Fortunately, as I was alone, I was spared having my foolishness pointed out to me. But I wouldn't have minded Lisa berating me for getting lost, or for Rob to offer some calming words, or for Toni to give me a warm smile, or for Brian to say all would be better after a cup of tea.

I knew I wouldn't see any of them again, but I didn't think that was so bad.

As I walked back up the long staircase to Katoomba, I thought about the last four days; the hikes with Rob, Toni, Lisa and Brian were far better than the one I did today.

It's not easy travelling alone. Perhaps the five of us took so quickly to each other out of loneliness, enjoying the comfort of being part of a group. Travelling alone means making every decision yourself, and this is a glorious type of freedom. But it can be something of a relief to defer decision-making to others, tag along and not get lost. And there's something special about shared experiences.

A Beautiful Corpse

Vienna looks exactly as expected, all romantic, theatrical, nostalgic and imperial. The horse and carts are quaint and fitting. The cellar bars are warm and cosy. The palaces are impressive. The cafés are crowded, the cakes excellent and the schnitzels plate-sized. There's music everywhere, whether it's coming from a concert venue, drifting through a thick baroque wall, being played on the street, or is a ghostly echo heard in your ear.

The general feeling in the Austrian capital is that the locals live well and that life is good. Yet the vibrancy and old-world beauty of this city masks a curious obsession with death.

Firstly, a confession: I believe in ghosts. Not those ethereal, floating things of white light, as depicted in films, but a kind of residual spirit. A leftover. A remnant. Something that is more felt than seen, and something that might require a bit of my own imagination, knowledge and inference. Which makes me party to this creation of ghosts, and that's fine.

In Vienna, there are a great many deathly remnants, physical and spiritual, seen and felt. They trigger my imagination, bringing out the ghosts.

One example is the Kaisergruft, the imperial burial vault on Neuer Markt, far below the Capuchin Church. The Habsburgs, almost a hundred and fifty of them, have been interred here since 1633. Well, parts of them. The hearts of the leading Habsburgs are in the St. Augustine Church, placed in silver urns, while their organs are in the catacombs below St. Stephan's Church, in copper urns.

This crypt is not for the weak.

The opulently ornamented sarcophagi, particularly the statue-adorned bronze pressure-cookers of Karl VI (with four skulls wearing crowns) and his wife Elisabeth Christine (with four young women with heads covered by cloths), and the magnanimous sarcophagus of Karl VI's successor Franz Stephan and his wife Marie Theresia, are borderline frightening. But more devastating are all the sarcophagi of children, some raised on talon-like feet and others so small you could almost pick the sarcophagus up and rock it in your arms. They're like fully enclosed cribs, for the royal babies and toddlers who didn't survive infancy. The heirs who weren't. Somewhere, up in the

Hofburg, Schönbrunn and Belvedere palaces, these little aristocrats are still playing, forever infants, dashing through the halls or crying for a parent and being nursed by a maid.

These little boxes are tragic. They say so much more than the massive enclosures the emperors and archdukes are in.

As I pass through the crypt, going forward in time, there are fewer dead children, as eras became healthier and medicines were discovered. Still, I'm haunted by those little boxes. I feel as if those children are following behind me, pattering tiny, ghostly feet, and when I turn to look, the pattering stops.

It's a relief to go back up the stairs and leave the ghosts behind. On the street, the city is alive and beautiful, bathing in soft afternoon light. Everyone's walking, looking good.

But I'm curious. If the Kaisergruft is how it was for the royal family – huge, ornate sarcophagus, heart in one place, organs in another – how was it for everyone else?

At the tourist office, I ask this very question. The knowledgeable woman at the counter explains, rather brightly, that in the catacombs far below the city streets, the dead were once stacked on top of each other, including the masses of people who died from Black Death, buried in the "plague pits". Most of the catacombs are now closed to the public, she says, but there are rumours that hidden tunnels connect them to the main sewer system and to other crypts.

On a map of the city, she marks with crosses – in thick black pen – certain places that might be of interest for me.

The first I get to is the Cemetery for the Nameless, where almost five hundred people have been buried since 1854 in unnamed graves. They were fished out of the Danube, having died in accidents or committed suicide. I imagine these ghosts wandering slowly along the river, always alone.

Vienna has over fifty cemeteries, and also a museum dedicated to funeral and cemetery culture of the last few centuries. The Funeral Museum was in an innocuous building on Goldeggasse, open only by appointment, but has since moved out to the Zentralfriedhof in the Simmering district. Which is the right spot for it, given the central cemetery not only has the largest number of people interred in Europe, but also a host of celebrities, even if not all of them were actually buried there, while others have been moved.

Interestingly, tourists come out here to see the graves of composers such as Beethoven, Schubert, Brahms, Schoenberg, Salieri, and the prodigious Strauss family. The Austrian pop singer Falco, of *Rock Me Amadeus* fame, is also buried here. There's a monument to Mozart, but he was actually buried in nearby St. Marx Cemetery, in a common grave. A cemetery makes a strange tourist attraction, with cameras clicking and some inappropriate laughter. These tourists are seeing the sights, not paying their respects.

To get here, you take tram 71 from the Innenstadt, which is why there is this local expression for dying, one of very many: *er hat den 71er genommen* (he's taken tram 71).

Vienna has some great museums, including the Albertina, the Leopold Museum, the amusing Museum of Art Fakes, and the interactive and entertaining House of Music. One to avoid is the Funeral Museum. Like the Kaisergruft, the weak should definitely give it a miss.

The exhibits cover funeral customs, burial rites, the cult of death and the very particular Viennese perspective of dying: the desire to be a beautiful corpse, which has as much to do with an elaborate funeral as with living an impressive life. Of the curiosities on display, there is a "flap coffin", which opened on the underside allowing it to be used again, and examples of the strange methods employed to avoid being buried alive, including a sword to stab the dead person through the heart, and a cord leading from the coffin to the surface to ring a little bell. A guide informs me that some hospitals, even today, administer lethal injections into dead people, to ensure the person isn't buried alive.

After twenty minutes, I've seen enough. I take tram 71 back to the Innenstadt, to rejoin the living.

There weren't many ghosts at the cemetery. I think the spiritual remnants of those buried out in Simmering are more likely to be lurking in the centre of Vienna, perhaps at old haunts.

Or if that spirit is Beethoven, then he's all over the city. He lived in no less than sixty different places during his thirty-five years in Vienna, and was known to be a cantankerous tenant: loud, argumentative, unconventional and self-serving. No doubt, more than one landlord, fed up with Beethoven's behaviour, cast him out onto the street. Two residences are now memorials: the Pasqualati House on Mölker Bastei and the Heiligenstadt Testament House on Probusgasse, where he admitted his deafness in the famous Heiligenstadt Testament, written in 1802 and found twenty-five years after his death. A number of other houses have plaques, signifying that Beethoven was here, but the house in which he died on Schwarzspanier Strasse is no longer there.

I feel Beethoven's ghost is as restless as the man was, still moving from place to place, trying to find peace. But I hope he's sitting in a cellar bar with Mozart, developing a formidable spiritual partnership, the two superstars of the Viennese orchestra of the dead.

Like Beethoven, the other famous composers have birthplaces and residences scattered around the city. Schubert has his birthplace on Nussdorfer Strasse. Here, sixteen families were crammed into sixteen bed-sits, with Schubert's family residing in two tiny rooms in which eleven of sixteen children died in infancy. Strauss has his Donauwalzerhaus on Praterstrasse, where he composed the *Blue Danube*. Haydn's house is on Haydngasse, and it also features a Brahms Memorial Room, meaning those two ghosts are probably hanging out there, forming another formidable partnership. And there's Mozart's apartment on Domgasse; the museum there makes it appear he lived his whole life in the apartment when it was only three, albeit productive, years.

But those are the all-stars. What about the musicians who didn't reach stardom? For several centuries, Vienna was Europe's most prominent music and theatre city, drawing aspiring composers, musicians and singers from across the continent. It was the Hollywood of its time. How many journeyed here, with just a handful of shillings in their pockets, hoping to make their name, their mark and their fortune? For every Beethoven and Mozart, there must have been hundreds who came here and failed, thousands even. The tough city of Vienna would have chewed these people up and spat them out: for not having enough talent, not making the right connection, not knowing the right person and not having the required luck.

I imagine their ghosts fill the crowded ranks of the unknown orchestra and the choir of failure, grinding out sorrowful tunes and performing operas that really were best left unmade.

Perhaps some were driven to madness by their failure, and thus ended up in the circular Narrenturm. The "Fools' Tower" was one of the first insane asylums ever built, near the old general hospital. The building now houses the Anatomical-Pathological Museum, and once again, this is not for the weak. Not just the cabinet-of-horrors human and animal exhibits, but being in the tower itself, with its many residual spirits and nightmarish remnants. I really don't want to imagine how they treated crazy people in the eighteenth and nineteenth centuries.

Funeral museums, crypts, cemeteries, anatomy museums, catacombs, not to mention the bones, coffins and mummies in the crypt of St. Michael's Church, or the (fake) skeletal remains of Saint Ruprecht behind glass in Vienna's oldest church, named for the saint.

Meanwhile, out on the cobblestone streets of the old town, there are ghosts everywhere. Students, peasants, composers, failures, traders, the insane, thousands upon thousands of Jewish people transported out during the 1930s and World War II. They are all here, jostling for space.

It's the lingering spirits of the old town that make Vienna stunning and morbid, thriving and shrivelled, brightly lit and shadowy; living well but also frozen in time. The Imperial City, a beautiful corpse.

There's Something in the Wasser

I've swum laps in lots of pools around the world, but swimming in Germany takes the gold medal for idiocy. It's bizarre to the point of farce. For a country that excels at organisation and efficiency, they just can't get a pool set up properly and for the benefit of everyone. Swimming is such a strange and chaotic experience that it actually becomes funny.

When an indoor pool is built in Germany, it's normally twenty-five metres long and it might have one lane rope, way to the side. That will be just a divider, perhaps even an old garden hose, and not one of the proper lane ropes that spin and absorb the water waves. German pools, for the most part, don't use proper lane ropes, which is why the water can become as rough as being out on the open sea.

The one lane set for lap swimming never lives up to its name: *Tempobahn*, *Schnellschwimm* (fast swimming), or whatever. Everyone uses it, even those not swimming laps. They swim all sorts of strokes at all sorts of speeds. The result is no one is happy, and no one swims in their own rhythm. It's all made worse by the complete lack of pool etiquette: keeping to the lane rope, waiting at the wall for faster swimmers, actually swimming and not crowding the wall. There's none of that. In fact, the general feeling in the lane is one of animosity. The swimmers don't like each other, and there are more than a few who are determined not to be passed. They'll give everything, including swerving and kicking in your face, to keep you from passing them.

While frustrating, swimming in a German pool makes fascinating viewing. This small microcosm of behaviour, sociology and cause-and-effect is made all the more interesting when compared to how Germany so brilliantly runs everything else. It seems in the water, anything goes and chaos reigns.

Very few swimmers wear caps. Some women, and some men, are determined not to get their hair wet, and will complain to you if your kick is sending water too high into the air. People dive in without looking. People swim pretty much wherever they want, and get angry with each other when their swimming paths cross. The predominant stroke is breaststroke. The pool is packed during the dedicated times for actual lap swimming and training. But schedules change often, and you might have fifty school children take over the pool, or an aqua-aerobics class will churn the water into a Jacuzzi froth, or there'll be an unusual rehabilitation class featuring blue floaties tied around waists. Or you might get unbelievably lucky and have the pool just about to yourself, but this is extremely rare.

From many years of observation and research, I've managed to divide German pool swimmers into the following types.

The Whale: this swimmer is a little blubbery around the middle and perhaps was once a decent swimmer. He (and it's usually a man) normally takes forever just to get into the pool. It appears he's getting back into swimming after a very long break: on doctor's orders, to lose weight, or for enjoyment. He has brand new trunks which are far too tight, and goggles straight out of the packet. Once in the water, he struggles mightily, swimming reasonably fast, but creating a lot of splash and waves, and seeming to go quite a way above and below the surface to breathe. The effort normally requires a rest after every lap, meaning the Whale "beaches" himself at the end of pool, elbows hanging on the side, breathing heavily, and possibly in need of some kind of rescue effort. When starting another lap, he really launches himself from the wall, creating another wave of water. With each lap, he gets slower and slower, and the time spent beached at the wall gets longer and longer.

The Eel: a slender, long-limbed woman who swims a strange kind of breaststroke, normally with a very wide kick, with each leg going through the water like an eel swimming. She even looks shiny and slippery. She's extremely hard to get around without getting a foot in the face, and appears to be unaware that anyone is trying to pass her, or even that there's anyone else in the pool. Her head never moves, her eyes stare straight ahead and she acknowledges no one. She swims only breaststroke, without taking a break, and monopolises the middle of the lane. When she hits the wall, she turns without looking. It's an absolute nightmare trying to share the lane with an Eel.

The Rusty Robot: a curious swimmer who does a bit of everything, changing strokes every lap, sometimes halfway through. He or she swims slowly and mechanically, like his or her joints are rusted stiff. When swimming freestyle, the Robot breathes on one side, in a two stroke rhythm, as if programmed. But that programming doesn't extend to having any sense of direction, so the Robot simply follows the black line on the bottom of the pool, regardless of where said line is in relation to lanes and other people swimming. And like a robot, he or she lacks social skills, ignoring everyone and just staring at the black line. Robots are very anti-social swimmers and never seem to get tired. The longer they are in the water, the rustier they get.

The Wriggler: this swimmer really puts the "free style" into freestyle. Wrigglers use their whole body to swim, contorting and bending with each stroke. It appears the Wriggler is trying to gain forward propulsion by using the spine. The arms are bent and cross over each other with every stroke, the feet come way out of the water when kicking, and the body is often sideways or curved in the water. Despite a lot of stroking and effort, Wrigglers make very slow progress, "slaloming" through the water rather than swimming straight. Watching a Wriggler swim is a bit like passing a car accident; you don't want to look and you know you shouldn't, but you can't help staring. There's something hypnotic about it.

The Dodgy Brothers: two guys, swimming reasonably fast, often side-by-side. They take over and dominate whatever lane they're in, do a lot of sprints, some kicking drills, and they swim most of their laps using hand paddles. Every lap is timed. They both have large watches on their wrists, and possibly heart-rate monitors around their chests. They also spend so much time talking at the end of the pool, you feel the need to quietly tell them to take it to a bar or café so they can discuss things in more apt surroundings. There's also something about them both that's not quite right: that they don't look like swimmers at all, don't have the right technique, aren't really so fit, yet they can swim quite fast. Maybe they're getting a bit more help than the hand paddles are offering. Their swimming looks chemically enhanced.

The Tank: beware of this swimmer. He (usually a man) makes a big splash jumping into the pool, diving in without looking, then ploughs through the water (without looking), making everyone get out of his way. Then, he hangs on the wall, with his back to it, and starts kicking slowly (without looking). Setting off for another lap, he explodes from the wall (without looking), swims with his head under the water and gets very angry if someone is in his way. It's not the nicest metaphor, but German pools have a lot of Tanks, and there doesn't seem to be anything to combat them.

The Jellyfish: similar to the Eel, but swims on his or her back, using two arms at the same time to get some movement. Legs like tentacles, all over the place and not appearing to do anything coordinated, and the whole movement resembling the pathetic progress of a jellyfish.

It happens so slowly and with such little forward momentum, you wonder if the person is actually swimming or simply floating and going with the movement of the water. Jellyfish have their faces set in grim determination, making you think that they just might be poisonous to touch. They don't look very happy to be in the water, and they seem aware that everyone else is not happy to see them in the water.

The Gorilla: a very, very hairy man. With hair that moves in the water like a sea anemone. You see him and want to get out of the pool straight away. But the guys at the other end of the scale, who are completely hairless, are just as off-putting. And also concerning hair, because so few swimmers in German pools wear caps, it's not unusual to swim straight into gritty strands of hair, or to see clumps of it at the bottom of the pool.

The Slash: no matter what swimming stroke, the Slash swims with severely weighted feet, so his or her body is diagonal in the water. For breaststroke or freestyle, it's a forward slash. For backstroke or jellyfishing, it's a backward slash. These swimmers have a very weak kick, to the point it's almost imperceptible. If you happen to know a Slash, do them a massive favour and buy them a pool buoy for Christmas.

The Surveyor: swims with effortless ease and is faster than anyone in the pool, but has to keep looking ahead to be sure he or she doesn't swim into someone else. They also need to regularly look up in order to navigate from one end of the pool to the other without causing collisions: around, over, under or through all the other swimmers. Regardless of these difficulties, and while seemingly not well-liked by others in the pool, Surveyors are clearly the happiest swimmers in the water. They have the right technique, they love swimming, it's easy, and there is perhaps the satisfaction of swimming well while everyone else is floundering, struggling, stressed out and hating it. Surveyors also appear to swim faster the longer they are in the pool. They are rare in Germany.

The Bademeister: the person patrolling the pool and ensuring everything is all right is the Bademeister (literally "pool master"). That first "e" can be removed from the job title, because this person is so unbelievably bad at their job. They don't look able to swim fifty metres. They don't mind if people run around the pool or if swimmers take a running jump into the water without looking. It's not clear what

185

purpose these people serve, beyond sitting poolside in a high-chair and looking incredibly bored. If you try to point out ways to make the pool safer and easier to swim in, they will become rather hostile towards you.

However, swimming against the tide of all these types is Berlin, where things are slightly more organised and structured. Unlike other German cities, Berlin has an abundance of fifty-metre pools, not to mention swimming lakes, and Berliners are more than capable in the water.

The rest of Germany just can't figure pools out.

Red Island Cricket

It's proving difficult to see the ball. The pitch is dark green, like boiled seaweed, while the field is ringed by bushes of a green not quite as dark, and there's a huge red cliff as the back drop at the north end. When the red ball is bowled and hit, there's a brief frozen moment, with all the fielders trying to ascertain where the ball has gone. Then, a fielder chases the ball, the batsmen take a run, or not, and the procedure repeats, in various forms. Maybe a wicket is taken, or the ball goes for four. Maybe the batsman swings and misses, or the ball hits a dead spot and fails to bounce.

No one has got hurt yet, which is good, because the hard leather cricket ball can sometimes morph into a dangerous missile, especially when struck firmly or bowled quickly.

All the players are enjoying the game immensely. There's a lot of talking on the field, much of it humorous banter. And more than once, a player remarks to another that it is truly a unique and glorious setting for cricket.

That setting is the North Sea island of Heligoland, some fifty kilometres west of mainland Germany and around five hundred kilometres from England. The red sandstone island has an area of just one square kilometre and rises sixty-one metres above sea level. Seals lie on the beach, tourists walk along the cliff top, and there are an inordinate number of birds, circling the air or squawking from the other side of the cliff.

The two teams playing include the Heligoland Pilgrims Cricket Club, made up of members from throughout Germany who journey once a year to play on their home turf, and Andorra Cricket Club, who have made the arduous journey from the principality land-locked between Spain and France all the way to the red outpost in the North Sea.

Ages and skill levels vary. Both teams have numerous nationalities and also a pair of female players. A few hamstrings have been pulled. Knees are sore. But the sun is out and the smiles are broad.

Yes, it's a great day for cricket.

I'm playing for Heligoland, and I'm wearing my baggy red and green cap with pride, though it's bloody hot with the thing on. It's my first time on the island, as I don't do well on boats. The club president managed to twist my non-bowling arm, and this meant taking a plane from the airport near Büsum, an hour's drive from Hamburg, while everyone else lurched from starboard to port on the Friday morning ferry. The plane was basically a passenger van with wings. It was incredibly loud. For the twenty-minute flight, I sat up front with my knees under my chin, expecting at any point to be handed a parachute and ordered to jump into enemy territory. But no, I was on course for hospitable land. The plane was surprisingly steady, and the milk-coffee froth of the water below made me very glad I was airborne and not seaborne. As the island came into the sight and the plane descended, I thought there was something unreal about the place. The plane swayed with the wind, like in a film, with us approaching some villain's lair. The buildings were out of focus or hidden by low clouds. The runway shot towards us, seeming far too short. And suddenly, we were on the ground. The rain was sideways, splattering against the windows; it would eventually ease, allowing for a warm-up match to be played later in the afternoon.

It was a friendly game, which the Pilgrims won.

Things are a tad more serious today; enough for the game to have a competitive edge, which is often a requirement for banter and friendly heckling. While the focus is on having fun, both teams want to represent their clubs well and give their best. Because a tiny island like Heligoland is not a place a player wants to be found wanting, as there is nowhere to hide and the last ferry has already left for the day, and any unglamorous acts and epic cricketing fails will be retold and laughed at through the evening and into the early hours of the morning.

This is not to say there hasn't been good play. One batsman from Andorra made a fine century, cleverly angling his bat to the short boundaries square of the wicket and taking the honours against me as we battled bat against ball; he couldn't score against my dodgy leg-spin bowling, but I also failed to get him out.

By the end of a fabulous day's play, Andorra have a deserved lead of twenty-seven runs, and the players adjourn to a barbecue held at the local youth hostel to talk and laugh about all that has so far transpired.

Some context is required here, not only because cricket is played on Heligoland, but because cricket is played in Germany at all. It's hard to believe, but cricket was once a popular sport in Germany. The first club was founded in Berlin in the mid-nineteenth century, and towards the end of that century, Berlin had dozens of cricket fields. The first organisation to run a national football league in Germany, with its main office in Leipzig, was even called the German Football and Cricket Federation.

What happened?

Football became the national past-time and obsession. Cricket disappeared. Ask a German about cricket and they'll allude to mallet-wielding royals on horseback, hammering a ball towards a goal, or to mallet-wielding estate owners, hammering balls through small hoops on manicured lawns.

In Germany, cricket lags far behind football, handball, ice hockey, basketball, motorsports, boxing, tennis, winter sports and swimming. While there are well over a hundred cricket clubs in Germany, with that number rising thanks to the influx of refugees from cricket-playing countries like Afghanistan and Pakistan, membership numbers fluctuate, clubs come and go, and the sport has retained something of an underground status. Few people know cricket is actually played in Germany and that there is even a ranked national team.

For the most part, cricket goes over Germans' heads. While the sport's particular code of behaviour, countless intangibles, relaxed rhythm and relative air of mystery (people play for decades and never quite figure the game out) appeal to players and aficionados, they strike the majority of Germans as downright weird. They see it as a bizarre, sedated sport, but this doesn't stop some Germans from playing. The Pilgrims boast many German members among their blazered ranks.

When seen for the first time, cricket can be difficult to grasp. It's hard to know what's going on without someone talking you through it. And then you've got the jargon: the silly mid-offs and fine legs, the backward points and first slips, the yorkers, bouncers, googlies, flippers, snicks and cover drives. It's like learning a new language, or even trying to grasp a unique culture, one with a long and storied history. What kind of sport features a complete stop in play in the middle of the afternoon so the players can have a cup of tea? Why does the guy in the lab coat sometimes raise his finger when everyone shouts at him? What on earth is a baggy cap?

While the Pilgrims' founder is German, cricket in Germany is very much driven and dominated by ex-pat players from India, Pakistan, Sri Lanka, Afghanistan, Australia, South Africa, New Zealand, and the country that gave cricket to the world, England. Sure, the clubs are gaining more players, but the problem remains that these players have learnt their cricket elsewhere. The real challenge is youth development. Other imported sports have faced similar problems in Germany, including American football, rugby, lacrosse, Australian rules football, ultimate Frisbee and hurling. There are normally enough players for a league or some dedicated ex-pats to get a game going, but it's much harder to get children and teenagers to switch from another sport and start playing a new, relatively unknown sport. As the majority of sport is played in the summer months, the sports vie with each other for participants, with football most often the winner.

For cricket to really grow in Germany, it needs to take hold at the grass-roots level and not simply be a league for ex-pats and temporary residents. The Deutscher Cricket Bund (German Cricket Federation) is working hard to develop the game at the youth level, but despite the good work done by the DCB and some clubs, not all the clubs in Germany are interested in developing the game. They just want to don their whites and play.

That's not so easy, as finding a suitable location to play is difficult. What should be a very large oval, ideally one hundred and fifty metres in length, is often a smallish square or rectangle, or something like an oblique circle fashioned to include as much ground as possible. The fields are either permanent and not terribly well looked after, or temporary and hazardous, set up on the day of a match. On Heligoland, the field is a sloped, Astroturf football pitch, with a running track down one side, goals galore and a small, tiered concrete grandstand on which the entire population of the island could sit. When the ball bounces, it leaves a sprouting of white sand, as if ants have dug a hole.

On the mainland, you'd be hard-pressed to find a cricket field. The few permanent fields are normally tucked away somewhere on a city's outskirts, on an oddly shaped ground, with bowling often from just one end; proper cricket requires the bowling to switch from one end of the pitch to the other after every over. As they say, bowling from one end "is just not cricket." The permanent fields are subjected to a variety of mistreatment, from people using the Astroturf pitch as a base for barbecues and campfires, to dog-owners allowing their pets to shit all over what they think to be an abandoned field. Then there are the rabbit holes and mole hills, the shards of broken glass and piles of trash. Vandals have also cut Astroturf pitches to shreds or poured acid on them to make them unplayable. A pre-game warm-up often involves cleaning up the field and making it safe for play. The pitches on the permanent fields are consistent in being utterly inconsistent. When a ball is bowled, anything can happen. Batting can be treacherous.

For the non-permanent fields, a pitch gets placed onto a playing area normally reserved for football or hockey. Clubs use coconut fibre pitches, Astro mats and do-it-yourself decks which all offer unique playing conditions. With foundations like wooden planks, sheets of rubber, bumpy concrete, rolled grass or pressed clay, the ball may not bounce at all or it may go clear over your head. Again, batting can be treacherous. A pre-game warm up on such a field often involves several hours building the pitch and making the playing area look something remotely like a cricket field.

Despite the lack of playing fields, a lot of cricket is played in Germany from the middle of spring to the end of summer, with men's, women's and youth leagues. Throughout the winter, cricket is played in large, all-purpose sports halls. The outdoor league cricket is called the Bundesliga (national league), yet this rather grandiose name doesn't quite match the quality of the cricket played.

The DCB is organised into six regions: Bayrischer Cricket Verband, Berliner Cricket Verband, Hessischer Cricket Verband, Norddeutscher Cricket Verband, Westdeutscher Cricket Verband and Baden Württemberg Cricket Verband. That might sound impressive, especially with the youth development done by some clubs, but training facilities and playing space remain a concern.

Most interesting is that arguably the country's best club, Husum CC in northern Germany, which boasts a wonderful ground with sightscreens, top-notch training facilities, impressive youth development and a swag of talented players, doesn't even play in the German league, preferring to compete in the higher level Danish league.

Playing for the Pilgrims is a lot of fun. It is village cricket, with crates of beer on the sidelines, and all the players walk off the field smiling and laughing, regardless of the result.

Playing in the Bundesliga, on the other hand, remains something of an adventure. Matches are fifty overs, to be completed in one day. Travel is often required. Because of the varying fields and pitches, an away game is bit like heading into the unknown. A field may have its own particular set of rules as well. Teams show up late, even when playing at home, and can struggle to get the required eleven players together. Each team usually has three or four players that do all the batting and bowling, while seven or eight players simply field and watch. Over rates are slow and a lot of wides get bowled, meaning a fifty-over innings can take up to an hour longer than it should. The umpiring can range from just okay to utterly dreadful. There is excessive appealing, with players attempting to bully the umpires and sometimes marching on the batsmen when appealing, which is not done in cricket. Players who walk without needing to be given out by the umpire are rare. More common are players who, when given out, don't move, and sometimes need to be escorted from the field. A lot of time can be spent searching for a ball hit out of the small ground. The legality of the ball used is occasionally called into question, players get suspended for abusing umpires, clubs sometimes protest results, fights have broken out, and players have walked off the field in the middle of matches for unclear reasons. The matches seem far too serious and important for the level being played. Yes, these players take their cricket very, very seriously, even if their ability doesn't come close to matching their ambition.

Thankfully, the Pilgrims don't take their cricket as seriously. And in this regard, the smiling, joking Andorrans make fitting opponents. The Saturday evening barbecue is a pleasant affair. Beers are drunk and sausages consumed. The rain holds off until it's dark, at which point the players head indoors. After Friday's trip to the island's centre of nightlife, Disco Krebs, no one seems keen for another night out, and there's much talk about strategy for Sunday: which batsmen to get out, how many runs to make, who should open the bowling. Because cricketers never tire of talking about the cricket. Around ten in the evening, players start to drift away, keen to rest up for tomorrow. There is a collective sense that the game will go down to the wire.

I find it difficult to sleep in the musty hostel. As I did on Saturday, I get up at dawn and wander the island. The fresh air does me good. It's supposedly richer in iodine and oxygen than anywhere else in Germany, even than at the top of the Alps. Save for a handful of service vehicles, there are no cars on the island, which means no pollution. There aren't even bicycles. Locals push themselves along on large, two-wheeled scooters.

When yesterday I was "Unten", exploring the bottom section of the island, which included sneaking behind a fence to get onto the beach at the north end and walk around the cliff for some unsuccessful seal spotting, this morning I am "Oben", first strolling the east-west streets on top of the cliff and seeing how the houses are singularly numbered, with no two houses having the same number, then hiking out to Lange Anna, the rock column at the island's northern point. I pass a crater made by a 5,000-kilogram bomb. During the Second World War, Heligoland, as a strategic naval outpost, was bombed. In 1947, 6,700 tonnes of explosives were detonated on the island by the British, to destroy the remaining fortifications and submarine base. The Guinness World Records lists this as the world's largest single non-nuclear explosion in history. The rebuilding started in 1952, with much thought being given to harmonise the new structures with the location. Just fourteen colours can be used to paint buildings.

On the cliff-top walk, I lean into the wind and do not dare open my umbrella, despite the rain. The heavy clouds make me worry that the cricket will be washed out today, which would be a shame, given how much fun it was yesterday and with the match evenly poised.

Along the path, there are small, white pyramids with information about local history, nature and developments. I learn that the island once belonged to the Danes, and from 1807, it was a British colony and hotbed for smuggling. The informative pyramids tell me the lighthouse was the only building to survive the Second World War relatively intact, that 10,000 pairs of sea birds breed on the island every year, and that the 1,600 hours of sunshine received each year makes Heligoland one of Germany's sunniest places.

This morning, I'm finding that difficult to believe. The clouds are ominous, seeming to fold on top of each other in different shades of grey. The strong winds – flags are seldom limp – mean the weather moves quickly, but today that looks like it's going from bad to worse. I return to the youth hostel damp to be informed that play has been suspended until further notice. The Andorrans trek to the local museum. A few Pilgrims play cards, while others don their green and white blazers and head into town to do some duty-free shopping. The island doesn't belong to the EU customs union, so all goods are sold free of duty and value-added tax.

I go along with the shopping party, feeling very comfortable in my rather garish blazer. It suits the island, when on the mainland I feel more like I should be selling hot dogs or ice cream when wearing it.

The streets are quiet, the shops having only just opened. The ferries and boats haven't arrived yet. Heligoland is very much a day place, busy by lunchtime, bustling in the afternoon, and dead at night. While the others shop, I stand under an awning and think about the island. Cricket is furthest from my mind as I imagine how Heligoland might have been through the centuries. A pyramid had earlier informed me the island was first mentioned in the year 700, and that a storm in 1720 had swept away the stretch of land connecting Heligoland to the Dune, which is the smaller second island where the airport is and where all the seals hang out.

I decide Heligoland is less a place to live than somewhere to be marooned. A castaway, trying to survive. Or it's a place of exile, to send aristocrats and former leaders, as with Napoleon on St. Helena, off the coast of Africa. Or it would be a prison, where no one could escape and where the worst criminals were sent, a bit like Australia's Norfolk Island, in colonial times. The way the island came into view through the small cockpit window on Friday morning has stayed with me: foreboding, mysterious, and somehow scary.

The rain has eased. We are summoned back to the hostel to begin the day's play some two hours late. My flight is at five in the afternoon, while everyone else will board the stomach-churning ferry at four. With time short, the play begins in a hurry. Andorra wants to score fast runs. The Pilgrims need to take wickets. The rain holds long enough for two hours of exciting play, with Andorra able to pull off a victory with just two balls to spare.

What should be heart-breaking and disappointing is laughed off by the Pilgrims, with the consensus being that Andorra deserved to win and that it might have been an injustice if the Pilgrims had somehow won or held on for a draw. It's not long after the presentations that the rain starts again, but that doesn't stop everyone from repeatedly saying what a great weekend it was.

"Cricket was the winner," is said more than a few times.

On the plane back to the mainland, I think that when playing in the Bundesliga in Germany, cricket is seldom the winner. The clubs play to win, and don't seem too bothered by the means of how victory is achieved. I'm glad the Pilgrims can find refuge on their North Sea island.

For cricket in the rest of Germany, there's still a long way to go.

Winter Sting

For my sole white winter in Canada, I chose to base myself in Nelson, British Columbia. A fine little town in the Kootenays, about eight hours drive east of Vancouver. There, I eked out a living playing music, working at a supermarket and writing an entertainment column for the local paper. I was also lucky to have a travel article published in one of Canada's national newspapers. With that and my clips from university papers in Australia, I was starting to put together a bit of a journalist portfolio; albeit, a rather thin one.

With its two rickety double chairs and mountains of powder, Whitewater, the local ski hill, was something of a well-kept secret. I decided to write a travel article about it.

I went to the Whitewater Resort office and told them who I was and what I wanted to do. The marketing manager was suspicious, and rightly so. I wasn't anywhere nearly as professional as I should've been. So, I said I'd come back the next day with some samples of my work. I also drew up a story outline, which listed the newspapers which had published my work and explained why the story would be good publicity for the ski resort and the town. This seemed to satisfy the Whitewater Resort marketing people and I was given three free day passes.

Later that evening, it dawned on me: if I could do it with one ski resort, why couldn't I do it with them all?

So I started researching the ski hills in British Columbia. There were eight worth visiting, including Whistler, North America's number one resort.

But would anyone believe me? Was it stealing? It seemed like that, because I didn't have any guarantee of publication.

I decided to try it; the worst thing they could do was say no.

The next day, I sent emails, thinking maybe half of the resorts would reply. By the end of the week, all eight of them were ready to host my skiing. I remained professional, kept it straightforward and simple. I asked only for two days skiing and a snowboard. I would cover my own accommodation, travel and expenses, because the story was about skiing, I explained, and not about where to stay or where to eat. That probably made it easier for the ski hills to say yes. The free rentals meant I wouldn't have to carry a snowboard, and that was good, because I planned to hitch-hike.

Some hills were nearby, so I could go to them and then come back to Nelson. It was February and my rent was paid up for the rest of that month. I also had a few more gigs to play and a few more columns to write. I couldn't leave town for good until March.

The trip started when I hitched down to Red Mountain, near Rossland, which was the next closest resort to Nelson. I started early and got there when the lifts opened. The resort's marketing manager was ready for me, having put together a hefty press kit. It was full of photos with blue skies and smiling families. But it also had some good information about snowfall, prices, opening hours and terrain. I decided to ask all the resorts for such a press kit.

I stayed that night at the youth hostel in Rossland, where every bed was taken by a member of the travelling ski tribe. The hostel was an unloved mess and reeked of the musty smell of old ski boots.

I had two enjoyable days snowboarding at Red Mountain. The best thing was that it had all worked out and been so easy. I got everything with very few questions asked and was treated like a travel writer. If I could keep the charade going, the next few weeks would be great.

I decamped back to Nelson, to stack supermarket shelves and sing songs, then headed east to Kimberley the following weekend. It was a miserable day, cold and wet, but I had good rides and splurged on a cheap hotel once I arrived. I didn't mind paying a little extra for the hotel because I was skiing for free. And after all, I was (supposedly) a professional journalist on assignment.

I met up the next day with a representative from Resorts of the Rockies, an organisation which owned several ski hills in western Canada. She was very friendly and accommodating, having already brought a group of sports store owners from Calgary out for a few days skiing. I tagged along with them, but stood out a little given I wasn't wearing the latest in ski-wear. I had a hand-me-down ski jacket that was more suited to being worn in a Duran Duran video, bright red ski pants I'd bought at the Salvation Army Store in Nelson, my old blue longshoreman hat, woollen gloves, and a pair of ill-fitting scratched goggles, again from the Salvos. I looked a sight, especially because skiing can often be more about fashion than anything else. My pants had red tape around one leg, to fix a tear. I looked anything but professional. I looked homeless.

But one of the guys from Calgary actually complimented me, saying I was skiing grunge.

I gave myself the day to get from Kimberley to Fernie, which was further east. I arrived just after lunch and had a small problem: the hostel was full. They told me to come back later in case anyone with a reservation didn't show up. I sat in a coffee shop and read the papers.

The hostel opened for new arrivals at 5pm. The staff were unhelpful to the point of being rude, and I felt like throwing my credentials in their faces, threatening to bag them in my big ski story. But I reminded myself that they'd been dealing with the ski crowd all winter. It was most probably serving selfish, big-air skiers and powder-hound snowboarders that had made them rude and disgruntled. I paid for a bed for the next night and sat down, waiting to see if some others showed up without a reservation and who I might split a hotel room with. I waited about an hour, then gave up. I found a hotel room that had two double beds. I phoned the hostel and told them I had an extra bed, in case anyone came in without reservations.

Within ten minutes, two guys showed up. Brad and Matt from Toronto. They were driving cross-country in a converted van and wanted to sleep in a real bed for a change. They were good guys and I was glad to take their money. But we had to sneak in and out of the hotel so the management didn't know there were extra people in the room. We got away with it and snowboarded together the next day before parting ways in the evening.

I moved into the hostel that night and spent a pleasant evening with some people from Calgary.

Two days at Fernie weren't enough. The ski area is just huge, with five bowls. I found the runs I liked and stuck to them. The snow was fabulous. More dry Rocky Mountain powder.

After the second day's skiing, I decided to hitch-hike back to Nelson in the afternoon, which was rather an ambitious undertaking given it was about a three-hour drive. That meant it was about a six-hour hitch-hike, and I had maybe two hours of daylight left.

I had great rides and made it to Creston quickly. I thought I was home, as all the cars from there were going to Nelson, or at least to Salmo, which was half an hour from Nelson and there were buses from there, if necessary.

I was wrong.

I had to walk three kilometres out of the sprawl of Creston just to get to the Nelson turn off. It was bitterly cold and I was tired from snowboarding all day at Fernie.

I waited for almost two hours at that damn turn off. It was -15°. Creston is in a valley and the wind chill was like nothing I'd ever felt. It went right through me, even though I was wearing pretty much all the clothes I had with me. I felt the cold inside my bones. It hurt.

Every time a car came, I had to take off some of my gear so the driver could see my face.

I was just about to give up, because it was pitch dark and I wanted the warmth of an expensive Creston hotel room, when a car pulled over. The driver looked at me in the fading light and opened the boot. I threw in my backpack and got in. I was shaking.

"Where ya headed?" He was pretty rough around the edges, which made me wonder if the ride would be okay. I was in no condition to defend myself; one punch and all my fingers would snap off. I couldn't even make a fist, let alone use it.

"Nlsn." I could barely get the word out.

"Well, ya there." He cranked the heat up for me.

What a relief. I was going to make it. Of course, I had to spend the next hour listening to this guy talk about the mine in Kimberley he worked at, and that his father had worked at, and his father's father, and how it was closing down, and that this was the worst possible thing for the town. I listened and nodded as I was expected to. People often pick up hitch-hikers for company and conversation; part of being a good hitch-hiker means being a good listener.

I was already planning my recovery in Nelson. First, a long, hot bath. Then, a cup of tea in front of the fire.

A few weeks later, I left Nelson for good and headed west. I had five ski resorts left to visit. The first was Apex in Penticton. I was treated well there, and even had a ski-guide for one day. After the second day, I hitched to nearby Big White, the resort on the outskirts of Kelowna. What I hadn't reckoned on was the distance between the town and the resort.

Kelowna is a large, mostly industrial town of petrol stations, malls and car yards, and I had to walk through it all after getting dropped in the centre. It was snowing heavily, which boded well for tomorrow's snowboarding, but it wasn't so nice to walk through.

A man in a blue pick-up truck took me out of town, dropping me about five kilometres short of the turn-off to Big White.

It was dark, still snowing hard, and I was standing in the middle of nowhere. There wasn't a single car, from either direction. No streetlights either.

I started walking. I didn't think I had any other option.

The first car that came along stopped and I got in, covered in snow. The nice man took me to the turn-off to Big White. He pointed at the lone streetlight and suggested I stand under it so I could be seen. He seemed reluctant to leave me out here. I told him I had a tent. What I didn't tell him was that my tent was just a big sheet of plastic with a rope in the middle, more suited to being a castaway on a deserted island; not the kind of thing for surviving a blizzard.

As he drove away, I took my position under the streetlight, my gear on the ground covered by the orange tarp. After a few minutes, the orange disappeared, with my stuff on the way to becoming a mound of snow. I was cold, tired, hungry and feeling very foolish.

The snow was relentless; the kind of snow that closes roads and highways. When school gets cancelled.

Good day's skiing tomorrow, I thought, trying to stay positive. A major powder day, if I ever get up to the hill.

I looked at the road. It was covered in snow. There were no tracks or tire marks. I figured maybe an hour had passed since the last car took the turn-off.

I was starting to get very worried, that I would be stuck out here for the night, freezing to death under a pathetic excuse for a tent. Free skiing wasn't worth this hassle and risk.

Two sets of headlights turned off the highway. The first car slowed down as it approached me, looking like it would stop. Then, there was a flash and the car drove on.

They slowed down enough to take my photograph.

The second vehicle came to a lurching stop. It was a truck. A man got out, beer in hand, and almost fell head first into my mound of snow and gear.

"We thought theys was gonna stop for ya," he said.

"Yeah, me too. It looked like they had plenty of room."

"We gotta full load, but we'll squeeze you in."

"That's great, guys. Thanks a lot."

We threw my gear in the back, stashing it on top of a fridge or an oven or something. I didn't care if anything broke; just get me to the ski village.

We climbed into the cab. There were two others, making it a squeeze to get all four of us in and comfortable. The drunk guy was almost sitting on my lap. I looked out the windscreen. The snow was so thick, I couldn't see anything beyond the first few metres.

The driver then said that he'd never driven a truck like this, and they all laughed.

Great.

After forty-five minutes of swerving and sliding – and the guys laughing a lot and leaning with each swerve, like they were on an amusement park ride – we reached the village. I was very glad to be out of that truck. I thanked the guys. The truck went lurching off towards the main resort hotel. I walked up the hill to the hostel.

I had two really good days at Big White, with lots of powder runs. You could ski from the hostel to the lift, and there were floodlights for night-skiing. On the second day, I did the famous, very dangerous "Cliff" run with a German guy who seemed to have learned all his English from listening to hip-hop.

I went to Vernon after the second day without much trouble. It was there I stayed in the best hostel, did some of the best snowboarding and was treated the worst by resort management. The Silver Star marketing manager was so suspicious, it made me wonder if someone had pulled a scam on them recently and this was why they had their guard up. Or maybe he was just making me earn it. He relented in the end, and I got my pass and snowboarding gear.

On this trip, I was learning that the ski hills in the lesser known towns were the best. This was certainly the case with Whitewater in Nelson, and it was the same at Silver Star. Fewer crowds, good snow, challenging runs. I really enjoyed my two days there, and skied right up until closing time on both days.

After six straight days of snowboarding, I gave myself the day off. It was a Sunday and I was headed for Kamloops, a hundred plus kilometres north-west of Vernon. It was the best hitching day of the trip. One ride out of town and then one ride all the way to downtown Kamloops.

I met some nice people at the hostel and felt very comfortable there. The hostel was in the old Kamloops courthouse, replete with court room, gavel and wigs. Hitching to the hill the next morning was a bit of an ordeal. I walked a long way to what I thought was a good hitching spot, but couldn't get a ride. A salesman drove me out of town and I eventually got a ride to the hill from there.

Despite being late, the marketing staff received me well and I had two ordinary days skiing at Sun Peaks. There were just too many people. I did find one secret run that required a little hiking to get to, and that was pretty rewarding.

Only Whistler remained. That resort has quite a reputation in Australia. Everyone knows it. The drunken exploits of snowbound larrikins are the stuff of legend to most down under.

I didn't want to stay at the hostel in Whistler and booked a bed in nearby Squamish instead. I hitched to the hill and back both days.

The Whistler people treated me well, but I had two days of crowded, forgettable snowboarding. For a ski hill, Whistler is Disneyland; more about fashion and reputation than good snow and quality skiing. I didn't realise how spoilt I had been, skiing at all the little hills in the interior, where you could count on one hand the number of people on each ski run.

And then the Great Ski Swindle was over. Ending with Whistler made it seem like a non-event, but I'd had some fantastic days and really felt like I'd pulled off a good one.

But it wasn't a swindle in the end. Because I did write a story, titled *Mountains on the March*, and the Canadian national daily ran it.

Fire and Water

I spent the morning snorkelling dangerously on my own, going far from the beach and duck-diving down in the deep water until my lungs hurt and the pressure in my ears squeezed and popped. I saw a shark, which was gone as soon as I'd spotted it, and a large, nasty-looking jellyfish that had a mess of tentacles trailing behind and fanning out as the long hair of a girl swimming underwater does.

Sections of the coral reef had been destroyed from dynamite fishing; snorkelling over this was like passing through a battlefield, with casualties. The bits of coral were white, like bones.

I found a cave about six metres down and dared myself to explore it, eventually just making it through and kicking hard to the surface for air. That triggered another coughing fit, and I had to float on my back to regain my breath and calm the coughing.

It had been nearly two months since the fire, but still my lungs felt full of smoke. Coughing hurt, and the memories were also painful.

While snorkelling, I'd taken no notice of the current, and so ended up far from the beach where I'd left my gear. I tried swimming against the current, but it was too strong and I was too tired. The only option was to swim to the nearest beach and walk all the back, and hope that my gear would still be where I left it.

Which is how I now end up walking on this deserted part of Gili Meno, mask on my forehead, snorkel dangling and one enormous dive fin looped around each wrist.

Meno is a small island, part of the trio of Gilis at the north-west tip of Lombok, Indonesia. It's only partially settled and, in 1998, rather primitively at that. The huts look like they get destroyed by every cyclone and are rebuilt the day after, using the same materials. There's no electricity. In the evenings, the island hums with generators. Pretty much everything has to be brought here in small boats. Gili Trawangan is more advanced, with a resort, electricity, more accommodation options, dive shops and even a road. As a result, it is the most popular Gili, its restaurants showing movies every night to entertain guests, who are mostly young backpackers taking breaks from shoe-string swings through south-east Asia. They come predominately from Europe and the U.K, and many seem to be happily in limbo between university and starting a career. The key phrase to describe this situation, as dropped by almost everyone I meet and speak with, is "gap year".

I fit this bill as well, a directionless, recent graduate of twenty-two. I'm not sure what career to embark on and have no job to go home to. I don't even have a home to go home to, as it burnt down and I lost everything.

Fortunately, the gap year crowd stay away from Gili Meno, as it lacks the relative comforts and status of Trawangan. I'm spared the conversations about futures and options, and don't have to listen to travellers talk about cutting costs so their money goes further and they can continue on to Vietnam and Laos.

I walk alone, following the dirt track that goes around the rim of the island. I'm not quite game enough to head inland, as I don't want to get lost, but I also stick to the water-side path because I can't remember exactly where the beach with my gear is. I'm hoping to see my blue sarong spread on the sand and my little backpack next to it, both purchased in Denpasar, like pretty much everything I have with me.

I'd flown to Bali with just my snorkelling gear, which had been in storage at the time of the fire and was one of the few things that remained. I planned to sell it once the Indonesia trip was over. The idea being to get as much money together as possible to go to Canada.

My lack of possessions and abode will make it easier to leave. But there's also the hurt from having been seriously let down and disappointed, after the fire, by people I thought I could rely on. Meaning, it's fine to leave these people behind, for now, and I hope the distance will help me to get over the hurt and allow me to forgive. I had no plan for Canada, except that it might offer the chance to start again, from scratch, with possible reinvention.

I was very lucky to survive the fire.

Walking around Meno is making the island feel huge, though it's not. At two kilometres long and about one kilometre wide, it's the smallest of the Gili islands. While not exactly a tropical paradise, the island has a certain rustic charm, giving me the very slight feeling of being a castaway. Even as a tourist, a level of ingenuity and improvisation is required to get along with things and to keep from running back to civilisation, which can be seen as just a boat ride across the water to Trawangan. My accommodation is a rickety bamboo shack that costs less a night than a chocolate bar back home, and includes a light breakfast of fruit and tea. The bathroom is a hole in the ground with a hose that has a weak trickle of salt water. My bed is a hammock. The island is teeming with insects, because of the inland Meno Lake. I'm not taking my anti-malaria medication, because it gave me horrendous nightmares. I've rigged my mosquito net, also bought in Denpasar, over the one in my shack, which is full of holes. On my first night, my can of condensed milk, which I'd picked up on Trawangan to sweeten the bitter breakfast tea, was completely overrun by ants. The can also attracted the mosquitoes; they got stuck in the liquid and died, which is why I haven't thrown the can away.

A girl comes from the opposite direction, a small basket of pineapples on her head. I ask her for one and we go through the usual bargaining routine. She puts the basket down, allowing me to choose. After agreeing on a price and a pineapple, she deftly cuts the skin away with a rusty machete longer than her arm, and trims the stalk so that it becomes a handle of sorts. Her work done, the basket goes back on her head and she walks off in the direction I've come. I wonder if she circles the island all day, repeatedly calling out "Ananas, ananas" in a sing-song voice.

Sitting down, I hold the stalk and eat the pineapple. Since arriving on Meno, I've been eating at least three a day, because they are delicious, cheap and plentiful.

As I eat, I watch two locals unloading a boat; although, calling their vessel a boat is somewhat of an exaggeration. It's actually a very large outrigger canoe. There's an outboard motor at the back and a canopy across the middle to provide shelter from the sun. The boat's light weight enables the men to park it up on the beach and reduce the distance they have to carry their cargo.

They're unloading plastic crates which I assume are full of fish. I hope they're not dynamite fishermen, as I'd hate for the locals to be so destructive of their own area. A dive instructor on Trawangan told me a few days ago that the blast fisherman come mostly from the Philippines. But the proximity of the damage to the island, which I saw today while snorkelling, makes me wonder.

I finish the pineapple, toss the stalk and core into the bushes, and continue walking. I see the fishermen struggling to push the boat off the beach and out into the water. The tide has also gone out, exposing old bits of coral and rocks.

I drop my snorkelling gear on the sand and run over to give them a hand.

They don't notice me at first, but look around when their boat starts sliding more easily across the sand and coral, and they stop pushing. One is on the left side, the other at the back. They share a suspicious glance, then the one at the back says something to me in Indonesian that sounds rather accusatory.

I smile, say "*Salamat sore*," the Indonesian afternoon greeting, and continue pushing from the right side. They join in and we start making progress.

The water is barely above my ankles, not nearly deep enough to drop the outboard motor into. It's difficult to get purchase in the sand, as some of the coral pieces are sharp. I can hear them scratching at the bottom of the boat, threatening to put holes in it.

I wonder if the fishermen have insurance for their boat. Probably not.

In the preceding two months, a lack of insurance had ruined my life; I had none and neither did my housemate. It turned out there was insurance covering damage to the building, which was owned by my father, and a certain amount of contents coverage for the main occupant: me. My housemate's contents weren't covered, and despite a lot of arguing over this point with my father, he refused to let me list my housemate's possessions as mine in order to claim the insurance for them. I didn't tell my housemate this, and instead assured him he would be covered. So, when the minuscule refund came for the listed contents, I gave the check straight to my housemate to cover his losses. I had the feeling he was aware of the transaction that had taken place, and that I would end up with nothing, but he still took the money as if it was his due.

The most disappointing thing was to have some necessary relationships put into dollar values. I needed support, not to be wrangling over insurances and the estimates of contents. And I needed help, especially as I was doing my final university exams at the time and coming close to death had really put me on edge.

I got little of either, and even ended up spending a week in a youth hostel, in my hometown, because no one stepped up and came to my rescue.

All that made it easier to escape to Indonesia after I graduated. And it will make it easier to leave for Canada. My home was scorched earth and my relationships were casualties. From it all, I would withdraw.

As we continue pushing the boat, I think that it's maybe not so bad: to lose everything, to cheat death, to be cut free from the security bonds of my parents, to know which people I can't count on and which friendships aren't worth keeping, and at the end, to stand alone, with nothing.

The boat makes a horrible grating sound as it slides along the coral. As we get further from the beach, there is much more coral than sand. I see the two fishermen are wearing some kind of makeshift black rubber booties to protect their feet; they look to be made of car tires. I can feel my soles getting raw and the skin cutting in some places. But I'm not going to walk away and leave these two men stranded here. I know other people could, and that wouldn't be wrong, but I can't.

Despite the pain and the cuts on my feet, and the exhaustion from snorkelling all morning, I keep pushing.

I feel like I've been doing exactly this for the last two months. When can I stop pushing? When will the real friends stand up and help? When will family mean more than the meagre figure at the bottom of an insurance refund? When will people stop putting themselves first?

Relationships are hard work, and I know I will have to repair things with my family. But right now, I want to get over the fire, which was my fault and also not my fault, and get away from the people who hurt me.

My final semester of university was hellish. I'd had enough of studying, felt that my history degree would get me nowhere, and couldn't decide which direction to go in. The best I could come up with was: away. I was working at a supermarket, just about full-time in order to get money together for a long, post-graduation trip, which would start in Canada. I was single, lonely and unhappy, and tired most of the time – constantly pushing.

After working a ten-hour shift on a Saturday at the supermarket, I came home and decided to have a bath. I had to study that night for an exam, and needed to relax before digging in for that cram session. I lit some candles, blowing out the match and dropping it in the trash, and placed them in the bathroom. I got in the bath while it was still filling. At some point, the hot water turned cold. It was then I saw smoke coming from under the door and I started coughing. With the bathroom door open, I saw that the kitchen, dining room and living room were ablaze. There was so much smoke, I couldn't breathe.

Jumping through some flames, I somehow just got out of the house without losing consciousness. From the driveway, I watched the house burn. A neighbour had called the fire department. Someone gave me a blanket to wrap around myself, which stuck to the places where the fire had burned skin away.

It was the kind of thing I thought happened to other people. It was what you read about in newspapers or saw on the news. But I was the one in the middle of it, blackened by smoke, burned, coughing profusely and lucky to be alive.

The water becomes deeper and the boat starts to float. The man at the back jumps in and drops the outboard motor, the propeller half in the water. He gets it going and the other man climbs aboard. They smile and wave at me as they roar off.

I walk slowly back to the beach, picking my way across the shallow water so that I step on more sand than coral. The salt water cleans my cuts, and it doesn't feel like there are any pieces of coral stuck in my feet. Those small wounds should heal quickly.

On the beach, I leave behind faint traces of blood with each step. I pick up my gear and head back to the water's edge, thinking that walking there will be better for my cuts than on the dirty, dusty track.

Further down the beach, I locate my blue sarong and backpack. I take a long drink from my bottle of water; it's warm from being in the sun.

Sandals on, I trudge back to my shack. Away from the beach, I can smell smoke. The locals keep their fires going all day, enshrouding Meno in a smoky fog. I assume this is to ward off the insects, though it doesn't help much. All it does is get me coughing and remind me of the fire.

I'm struck by the desire to go to some place very cold. It's still summer in Canada, but I decide to use that time to find a nice place to spend a white winter.

Maybe the crisp cold air will remove the smoke from my lungs.

Auschwitz-land

The cat scampered along the side of the ditch, its coat shiny black from the morning rain. I followed, stumbling over mounds of weeds and sinking my shoes into spongy mud. Every few metres, the cat stopped and twisted its head around, focussing its yellow eyes on me, checking to see if I was still in pursuit. It ducked under the barbed wire, once electric, and sashayed across the ruins of crematorium III. Seeing me stuck at the fence, the cat's ears lowered and it sat there staring at me, smirking.

"Is that you, Höss?" I asked quietly. "Have you trapped me like you trapped a million others?"

Unfair to the cat of course, but there was something sinister about a black cat stalking the grounds of the Birkenau concentration camp, also known as Auschwitz II. Satisfied it had cornered me, the cat strutted across the field of ruins and settled under the shelter of one of the wooden observation towers, the old commandant surveying what remained of his domain.

Auschwitz. What can you say that hasn't already been said? Journey seventy-five kilometres west of Krakow and you will learn just how extreme and vile the hate of humankind can be. There is nothing uplifting here, no tales of heroic resistance, of individual sacrifice to save others; there are only fences and towers, barracks and blocks, chambers and crematoria. It is such an important place, but I worry that it does not get the necessary response from visitors.

That is by no means the fault of the museum and the caretakers. Auschwitz is devastating, but I spent a day there, watching the groups flood in, trying to gauge their collective response. It made me wonder if time has already removed many of us from this history, reducing Auschwitz's impact and meaning, rendering it just another historical site.

The Auschwitz-Birkenau complex is made up of four camps, but only two are visited. To be more precise, Auschwitz gets the most visitors. Birkenau, a much more distressing experience because of its overwhelming size, is less frequented. It is the lack of tourists, and the resulting solitary feeling one has walking around, that etches the Birkenau experience into your mind.

But it seems few visitors to Auschwitz get that feeling. For most, there is a rush to get inside, pass through the famous gate, see the mounds of suitcases, the puzzle of entangled spectacles, the rolls of cloth made of human hair, take a few photographs and then rush back out again. The tourist buses jam the car park like baguettes in a French baker's window. They sport number plates from all over the Europe, as do the assorted cars and campervans. They have all travelled so far, but why?

The morning is grey, with intermittent drizzle causing people to constantly open and close their umbrellas. This fluttering and ruffling is my soundtrack as I sit at the Auschwitz gate, that gruesome gravestone-shaped entrance adorned with *Arbeit macht Frei* (work brings freedom). Everyone gathers here, to have their photo taken in front of it. Groups come together for portraits. The people grin and laugh. I imagine these people back home several weeks from now, showing the photos from their Europe trip: "Here's me at the Eiffel Tower, in front of the Berlin Wall, at the gate of Auschwitz, on St. Mark's Square."

The prisoners passed through this gate twice each day. I hope the day will not come when there will be re-enactments, with actors dressed in blue and white striped uniforms marching through the gate every hour on the hour. Tourists could have their photos taken with an emaciated prisoner or, worse, with a strapping blond-haired SS guard, or worse still, with someone dressed up as Commandant Rudolf Höss. I really hope it does not come to that.

I venture inside the camp, passing with a sickening shudder through the gate. Before the war, this was an abandoned army barracks. The buildings are solid brick, but the place has the feel and look of a lunatic asylum, one with a difference: here, the crazy people were in charge and all the prisoners were sane.

Blocks 4, 5 and 6 are where the tourists flock. The rooms are crowded with groups, with leaders talking loudly about the camp, and eventually moving aside to let the cameras zoom in. These blocks give details about the camp (maps, blueprints, plans, documents, shipping manifests – the efficiency of it all is numbing) and display samples of the masses of personal effects the prisoners had brought with them.

While standing in front of the pile of hairbrushes and toothbrushes, a young man approaches me. He has a youthful face and, unsure of which language to use, holds out his camera to me. I take it. The young man locks arms with two others and they all smile, like they are being photographed at a football game. What beautiful white teeth they have.

With the boys gone, I turn back to the toothbrushes. There's something about them that is really disturbing. Such a personal instrument. There are piles of them, each telling a particular story of cavities, root canals and impacted wisdom teeth, but the toothbrush does not know the story's end: gold teeth yanked out after the person was dead, melted down and added to the piles of Nazi loot.

I station myself outside this popular row of blocks, this morbid amusement arcade where all the important exhibits can be seen in a quick twenty minutes. There are animated conversations, the rush-rush of tourists groups, the jingle and blare of mobile phones, and lots of shiny, healthy teeth.

A large group of middle-aged Americans pass en route to the gas chamber and crematorium I. This group seems like two joined together, with the people interacting and getting to know each other. I hear one woman remark to another, "After the camp, we're hittin' the castles near Krakow."

And so it goes for the rest of the afternoon. More groups, more canned laughter in the face of such distressing exhibits, more itinerary discussions, more ducking down the side of the block for a quick cigarette stubbed out against the red brick, more people shouting into their mobile phones, "Yeah, I'm at Auschwitz."

Perhaps this is how people deal with such a difficult place like Auschwitz – act normally and try to smile through it.

I leave the Auschwitz part of the camp and walk the three kilometres over to Birkenau.

The car park here is small. There are no tourist buses, and no place for them to park. It is quiet, barren and isolated, and the atmosphere is much more sombre. The camp's most striking feature, aside from its immense size, is the railway track cutting down the middle like a dividing line. Here, the cattle cars jammed with the innocents of Europe came in and amid confusion the selection process began. The SS doctors chose those fit to work and sentenced the others to death. Standing on the railway siding, I can almost hear the murmur of low voices, the mumbled, stuttered fear, the clatter of suitcases and the snap of jackboots.

The camp stretches far in all directions. Most of the buildings were destroyed by the retreating SS in January 1945, but enough remain to give you an idea of the layout and the conditions of the camp. Words cannot capture this place. It strikes an emotional chord in a way that Auschwitz completely fails to. Standing alone in one of the blocks, a converted horse stable that held over a thousand prisoners, I see the triple bunk beds, walk the earthen floor and breathe the old stench. I don't know whether to fall to my knees and weep or to run from the block screaming.

I spend an hour wandering the mossy field where the outlines of a dozen warehouses remain. It was here that the worldly possessions of all the people brought here were sifted of valuables and stored. The SS destroyed the buildings, but even now, more than sixty years on, you can still find rusted cutlery and other small items. Chancing upon such personal possessions hits close to home. One and a half million: that's a lot of people, and it's difficult to imagine each one's individual existence. What was it Stalin said about one death being a tragedy and one million being a statistic?

If you can breeze through Auschwitz in twenty minutes, Birkenau requires much longer. Take time to sit by the ruins of one of the four crematoria. Try to imagine the systematic destruction of one and a half million people: the work involved, the administration, the quotas to keep, the ashes to dump, the SS guards mundanely complaining to each other about their work. "Come on, Hansie, just another hour of this and then our shift is finished."

It's too hard to picture: violence as lifestyle, the stench of burning flesh the normal smell, the annihilation of a people the routine, mundane day's work. But that's what happened. It is ghastly. Where does that leave us?

I am Australian. While living in Germany, I have discovered the Germans to be humorous, honest and loyal. And yet, Auschwitz-Birkenau is much more a part of them than it is of me. The modern Germans are not responsible, but they cannot ignore the connection. Or is it that we are all responsible? While the Holocaust was a horrific event, it was not the first of its kind. Our history is full of attempts to wipe out racial and ethnic groups; I could quote the Bible extensively, and include my own country's history.

To that end, Auschwitz-Birkenau is a memorial to all the nameless victims of genocide, a symbol of our propensity for evil, which counter-balances our attempts at benevolence. We are not perfect, we are not all-powerful. We are weak creatures who succumb easily to violence (often when it is government policy – the persecution of Indigenous Australians is an excellent example) and we are able to commit unimaginable crimes.

But then again, perhaps it's better to smile for the camera, turn your back on the pile of toothbrushes, jump back on the bus and hit the castles near Krakow.

Digital Enlightenment

Is the overload of information in the modern world derailing the quest for transcendence?

As a child of the 1970s, I'm old enough to remember a world without mobile phones, internet, mp3 players and GPS, but young and tech-savvy enough to have easily adapted to and utilised these new technologies. Given the choice, I would prefer to live in a world without them, to live independent of digital dependence. That's not necessarily nostalgia, but more a yearning for a return to simplicity. All this information, all these phones ringing, all these headphones blaring; I just want to turn off the noise.

I feel bombarded, overwhelmed, and I can't possibly process all this information nor make sense of all these distractions. Do you feel the same? And why must almost all of our information come from a screen? Is that how wisdom now gets passed? With virtually everything ever said, known and done on the internet, is there nothing left to learn?

I can find out anything in just a few seconds and go on the quests for digital enlightenment offered by thousands of websites and online programs. Yes, transcendence is a click of the mouse away. But is that what we want?

The digital age, for all its simplifying of tasks and lifestyle betterment should be renamed the difficult age. It has become nearly impossible to find peace, while inner peace has become a slogan for selling cosmetics, shampoos and luxury retreats. We are surrounded by information, immersed in it, and have to utilise filters to separate our favourite information from that which doesn't interest us. Can't find what you want? Feeling disillusioned, lost? Relax. Google can help you find your path. Perhaps Google has become part of your path. And all these digital tools have made it easier to find and communicate with your spiritual teachers and guides. No need to sit down and learn together though. Text each other or speak via Skype. Don't have a teacher? Then log-on to an online forum. There are a multitude of enlightened people floating around online who will readily advise you. If all else fails, Google "self-help" and watch the hits roll in.

"We have to learn to adapt to the technology," says Dan Millman, author of more than a dozen books, including the best-selling Peaceful Warrior series. "I think there will be a movement back to simplicity, back to quality."

Perhaps, but until then, we remain swamped with emails to read, phones to answer and information to digest. Even when everything is turned off, there is still the lingering sense of what is waiting for us when we switch it all back on.

I first read *Way of the Peaceful Warrior* long before the internet, before the yoga-Pilates boom of the nineties, before a spiritual life meant an hour every Wednesday in the gym with bank tellers and office assistants desperate to relax and stay in shape; who want to look good and not necessarily feel good. And before New Age became a million dollar industry with a billion Google hits. And before Self-Help morphed from learning about yourself and growing to getting what you want and fulfilling desires; namely, money, success and attention, the "secret" to wealth dressed up as the quest for inner happiness. Success is now our most important goal and understanding the world normally entails understanding economics.

"Successful people are suffering along with everyone else," Millman tells me at a special screening of *Peaceful Warrior* the film in Hamburg, Germany. "More than anyone, they find out that being successful doesn't make you happy."

This is right, but that doesn't explain why self-help has moved from improvement to attainment. The digital world has made getting our goal. We live in an age of instant gratification, and spirituality has been as much affected by this as all parts of our lives. For many, inner peace, or even happiness, is too often linked to financial security and to the gratifying of desires. All the external noise and information, our goals and expectations, have drowned out our inner voices.

But don't despair, because online you can find answers to questions that not even history's greatest philosophers could reconcile. On the internet, everyone can be enlightened if they want, and there are thousands of would-be sages ready to dispense wisdom and to help you as much as they can with your self-help.

Interestingly, the turning of *Peaceful Warrior* into a film sums up our current spiritual world. A book about a quest for self-improvement and enlightenment spawned a sports film with a few wisdom catchphrases dulled down for mass consumption. "The time is now. We are here." Everyone can understand that, and it's short enough to send as an SMS to all your friends. But at the screening I attended, the closest most of the audience came to living in the moment was when they convened outside to meditate in a nicotine fog.

Through the teaching of wisdom, concentration and focus, the Dan Millman of the film becomes a successful athlete, but he is far from enlightened. Which brings us to the here and now: the digital world where success is inexplicably linked to a higher plane of existence. This can be seen in our fixations with celebrity, media and bling. Showing off has become proof of exceptionalism, while modesty, etiquette and the humble search for a bigger picture have been replaced by quick fixes like pharmaceuticals, gym classes and, of course, attainment.

What is thought of as a meaningful, happy life is being redefined, as is our search for spirituality. Millman thinks of his books as "reminders for living" and has cause to feel perturbed that his practical and applicable works sit on shelves next to UFOs, the occult and ungrounded magical thinking. There's nothing esoteric about eating well, trying to breathe right, exercising and attempting to find your place in the world. Best of all, Millman's books remind us to pay attention, to notice the spiritual all around us and to be aware of where we are, to be fully in the moment.

It seems that this concept of constant awareness has become lost in this current world of distraction and gratification. Just look at those around us: barking into mobile phones, hypnotised by screens, or staring dumbly into space while music pours into their ears. All of them tuning out with the aid of technology. If you walk while talking on the phone, chances are you won't remember anything you passed while walking; the same goes for those listening to music. As entertaining, communicative and informative as it all may be, this technology has succeeded in removing us far away from the moment. We experience the world with our heads down, looking without really seeing while always listening to something else.

Even the aware and attentive can be thrown off course. Millman readily admits that today there are "interminable distractions. One can stay distracted just by playing with a mobile phone. I find myself doing it sometimes, too."

So, what does all this mean? Will there be a return to simplicity? Will we eventually turn away from all the technology and information which fills our lives and start again with learning how to eat, breathe and be happy? Or is the search for the transcendent soon to be lost in the digital quagmire? There are already countless websites that will guide you step by step towards enlightenment. YouTube can show you how to meditate, Amazon will recommend all the books you need and bring them to your doorstep in twenty-four hours, while Wikipedia explains all the eastern philosophies.

But all the noise, all the devices, all the content that overwhelms our lives, and all the media telling us what we need to attain to achieve happiness and success, just drowns out the voice we should be listening to – the voice coming from ourselves, from within. But in the digital din, can we hear it anymore?

Vainglorious

London in September, wet and cold. An official in a clear plastic poncho tells me the water is twelve degrees, and that because of the low temperature, the swim has been reduced from 1,500 metres to 750 metres.

After several days of rain, Hyde Park is more mud heap than park. The Serpentine looks putrid, oily brown. Even the ducks and swans have stayed away today.

The triathletes haven't. About two hundred drop into the water every ten minutes and set off for the first red buoy. They're lining up near the start, gathered in their waves, specific-coloured swim caps on, and shivering; from the cold, nerves, excitement, or all three.

I'm one of them, starting in the second wave of age group 35-39. While we all qualify as middle-aged, the guys around me look incredibly fit and motivated. They are the best amateur triathletes from around world. They've trained all year and travelled to London for the World Age Group Championships at their own cost. A little bit of cold weather is not going to stop them.

I think I'm the only one in my starting group having second thoughts. As we're herded towards the water, I'm hanging at the back, trying to decide if this is worth doing or not.

It's only about twelve minutes of swimming, I tell myself.

However, following that would be two hours of riding and running in the cold. And after all of that, I'd probably have the joy of finishing last in my age group.

I was lucky to even qualify for this race, taking one of the last places from the twenty made available for Triathlon Australia in this age group. While I've been racing for over ten years, I've never been serious about it, and the sport has simply remained a way to stay healthy and in shape.

Through the years, I've watched triathlon expand quickly and change dramatically. Races that started out with small groups of people having fun on a Sunday morning have evolved into crowded, ultra serious affairs, with super-fit guys riding very expensive bikes and racing aggressively. Gear improved, training became more structured, triathlon clubs grew, athletes spent more money and performances seemed to get better each year, even with athletes getting older. It became common for triathletes in their mid-forties to win races with hundreds, if not thousands of starters, posting professional-level times, and no one questioned how that could be.

There's no drug-testing involved in amateur triathlons, not even at the World Age Group Championships, which are held every year in a different location. And why should there be? At this level of sport, there is absolutely nothing to gain by using performance-enhancing drugs: no prize-money, no sponsorship deals, no accolades, no gold medals.

Yet as my fellow starters edge towards the short pier that is the start block, I'm certain a fair chunk of them are on the juice. Maybe not all, but certainly some of them.

A study by the University of Mainz in 2013, involving anonymous interviews with the participants of races in Frankfurt, Wiesbaden and Regensburg, estimated that almost twenty per cent of starters in amateur triathlon use performance-enhancing drugs. Which would mean that about forty of these two hundred guys I'm now in the water with are enhanced. As we start swimming, I think that number might be higher, because these guys are flying through the water. And these are amateurs, with full-time jobs and families and responsibilities, who would struggle to find time during the week to train enough to race this fast.

It's all very dubious.

And this water is really cold. It's hard to breathe.

I'm one of the last to reach the first buoy. There's a rescue boat nearby. A couple of swimmers have already been pulled out and wrapped in blankets; they're grey, prison-type blankets, and not those special silvery, emergency thermal blankets. I plough on, alternating between freestyle and backstroke because it's too cold to keep my face in the water. My feet and hands are numb.

Rounding the second buoy, I look towards the swim exit and see some guys have already finished and are sprinting for the transition area, peeling their wet-suits off as they run.

I regret not taking the testosterone when I had the chance.

That was earlier in the year, when I got the news I'd qualified to represent Australia in the sprint and Olympic distances at the world champs in London, and I visited some doctors to be sure my health was okay. The urologist I saw commented that my testosterone was low, which wasn't uncommon for a man my age, and offered me a course of prescription medicine that would raise my level. It would give me more energy, he said, increase my sex drive and help me train and recover. When asked about taking testosterone and being an athlete, he said that everything was fine because I wasn't a pro, it was a medical condition and I'd have the prescription.

It was very tempting, but I declined, not wanting to be one of those T-men, to join all those drug-takers who were ruining triathlon. Though my urologist saying how easy it was to get testosterone did explain why I so often get beaten in races by guys in their fifties and sixties, and why so many of the races I compete in are won by middle-aged men.

No T for me. I would train hard, go to London, give my best and represent my country with pride, but I would not cheat. I decided that even if I finished last, it would be me that finished last; taking something and finishing first or in the top ten would mean that the drug had finished first, not me.

I'm just about last out of the water. It's hard to get running because my feet feel frozen. It's hard even to get out of the wet-suit, as my hands are like arthritic claws. But once I've got the wet-suit down to my waist, and my Granny Smith green triathlon suit is showing, people start to cheer loudly. They wave Australia flags and call out my last name, which is printed on my suit.

This is great. I never thought I'd get the chance to represent Australia; that I'd have a moment like this, wearing the green and gold, with people cheering for me and shouting my name. I feel lucky and privileged.

The support continues throughout the race and spurs me on. I give absolutely everything on the forty-kilometre bike leg and somehow make it through the ten-kilometre run. At the finish line, I collapse. Place 132 in my age group is more than satisfying, even though I'm a long way behind the top athletes, who post times good enough to be professionals. I find it difficult to shake their hands, congratulate them and be impressed. I even think that I catch a glimmer of shame in their eyes. A wonderful effort, tainted. A winner with an asterisk next to his name. The top twenty per cent, all with asterisks against their names.

A sport rotting from the top down.

~~~

It took a few weeks to physically recover from that weekend in London. But I haven't really mentally recovered, and I have an aversion to cold water. I still race triathlons and enjoy the competition, yet I look at some of my fellow competitors with an increasing amount of suspicion and resentment. In London, the sport changed for me, and I'm fed up with being beaten by guys who are old enough to be retired.

For a lot of middle-aged men, completing a triathlon, whether it's a sprint, Olympic or Ironman distance, has become a kind of rite of passage. Something to tick off the bucket list. Using performance-enhancing drugs can shorten the way to achieving that goal. For the serious triathletes, drugs help them improve each year when the natural slide of ageing should take over.

There's so much talk about the use of drugs in professional sport, but no one seems to care about what happens at the amateur level. A few journalists have experimented to see and understand the impact of performance-enhancing drugs, and have written articles and books about it, but they haven't quite garnered the attention they deserve. And again, no one is bothered by weekend warriors who are on the juice.

I'm bothered by it, because it's ruining the sport and creates an unlevel playing field.

I can understand why professional athletes take drugs. At the pro level, there is a huge financial difference between finishing first and fifth, between winning a gold medal and not even qualifying for the final. But I'm curious as to why amateur athletes take drugs. With no money, prestige or fame on the line, why dope?

A weekend triathlete taking testosterone, human growth hormone (HGH) or erythropoietin (EPO), or combinations thereof, or whatever course of "vitamin D", to improve his or her own performance with absolutely nothing to gain beyond a faster time, is really no better than those guys at the gym who are pumped more with air than muscles.

It's vanity.

Applied to amateur triathlons, the vanity comes from training hard, racing fast and feeling good about yourself; winning some small village race where a handful of people clap you to the finish line and you stand on a dais made of chipboard as they hang a ten-cent medal around your neck, and you can think of yourself as king of this very tiny world, while in the back of your mind you know full well it's the vitamin D that got you there, and you also know that your vanity is rather shameful.

There could also be the vanity that comes not from fast times, but from victory. A bit like: if you can't beat the twenty per cent, join them, so you can beat them, or at the very least compete with them. And, the drug-taking triathlete says, while we're talking about victory, please look at the trophies on my wall, the photos of me hitting the finish line first and me drinking from the big glass of beer. Look at what a hero I am. Admire my cups made of tin, my ribbons and medals and finisher shirts. But please, don't look in my trash, and please don't ask me to explain how I can be so fit when I have a full-time job, three children to raise and a mortgage to pay.

Then there's the physical vanity. From the shaved legs and skin-tight suits to the sculptured, greyhound-lean physiques, triathlon has vanity written all over it. The drugs can help you look the part. Testosterone and HGH and whatever-the-latest-generic-crap-available-online can make you look younger, leaner and more muscular. And that's just the kind of thing that might appeal to men in their forties and fifties who are determined to stave off middle age, or at least get back their feelings of youth. It used to be guys having mid-life crises bought red sports cars and tried to date younger women. Now, they also ramp up the T, put on the Lycra, train themselves as hard as they can and set about dominating the amateur triathlon and cycling scene.

As the sport of triathlon has grown, it has become increasingly popular with alpha types: driven, ambitious, competitive people who are willing to make sacrifices and do whatever it takes to succeed. They invest in the latest bikes and gear, and maybe even a personal trainer. They put the hours in, running at dawn and grinding out kilometres on stationary bikes after work. They want to do well in the races, to benchmark their improvement, see their gains and have something to brag about. Why wouldn't they seek any advantage they can get? If they are ruthless at work and use all the means at their disposal to get ahead, why not do that in triathlon as well?

It's the addition of such competitors to weekend triathlons that has greatly changed the sport. They stand out, because they normally do well, they rarely smile and they seem to gain little enjoyment from participating. These are the grimacers. They're the ones elbowing you in the swim, shouting at you to get out of the way on the bike, pushing past you to get a cup of water at an aid station on the run, and looking so fresh at the finish line that they could do the whole race again. Roid rage, anyone?

Fortunately, triathlon still has a lot more grinners than grimacers; those who are out there for fun, looking like normal people, with just water in their bottles and riding affordable bikes.

The rash of drug-takers dominating the sport at the amateur level hasn't diminished my enjoyment. Rather, I find it fascinating. I'd really like to see the World Anti-Doping Agency test an amateur race and publish the results. It will never happen, and in some ways, it's not necessary. Those who race clean have a pretty good idea of those who don't.

The Uggstralian Diaspora

The two girls come out of the Erotica Boutique Bizarre clutching small, jet-black string bags. I can only imagine what frilly, lacy, racy nothings are in those bags, what sexual gadgetry. The girls lock elbows, giggle in a guttural German way and head west down Hamburg's infamous Reeperbahn. Their bag contents remain unknown to me, but their footwear is very familiar. Uggs.

Sorry. Strike that. I can't actually say that, because ugg is a registered trademark of UGG® Australia, the brand owned by the American outdoor clothing company Deckers. I fear their wrath. I don't want a cease-and-desist letter. Outside of Australia and New Zealand, you aren't allowed to call an UGG® an ugg, thanks to a court decision in 2006 which ruled against Deckers, meaning the trademark was removed from ugg in Australia and New Zealand. It was successfully proven that ugg, ug and ugh were generic terms for such a boot and long used down under.

In Germany, and many other places, the word is copyrighted, registered and owned, and there's the litigation to prove it, from court cases in the USA, Belgium and the Netherlands, all of which Deckers won. An ugg is only what is made by UGG® Australia. Thus, everything other than an UGG® is a fake, and everything has to be called something other than an ugg.

Here in Hamburg, it's 2012, and I'm entering another German winter. The air temperature is two degrees Celsius, and there's slushy, exhaust-fume and dog piss-covered snow on the ground; the kind of conditions that require good sturdy, waterproof boots made in places that know about slushy snow and slick ice. But the two girls are in, um, let's say sheepskin boots (SBs), fake ones at that, those not actually made with real sheepskin or wool, but synthetic versions which can be bought here in bargain shoe shops for about twenty Euros, while the UGG® goes for around two hundred a pair. The two girls in their knock-off SBs venture onto the busy footpath, sexy shopping bags a-swinging, elbows locked, a confident, shoulders back line defying all the realities of the financial downturn. Crisis? What crisis?

The girl on the left loses her footing first, the smooth rubber sole of her right SB catching a piece of ice after just a few steps. She goes down like a demolished tower, losing structural integrity from the ground up, until she's listing far to the left and heading right bottom-cheek first for the well-churned slush. It all happens soundlessly, slowly. Elbow still locked with her friend, she brings her down too, leaving both floundering on the footpath, dignity lost, their damp and mattered SBs kicking in the air.

Schadenfreude. To take pleasure from another's failure or misfortune. The German language has a word for everything. Wonderful economy, to capture a myriad of situations, sensations and reactions all in one word. German efficiency at its best.

My first inclination is to help the girls up, to talk to them in thick "Strine" and make jokes about European winters and Aussie footwear. But the girls are German, and they probably have no idea that uggs (so sue me, Deckers) are Australian. I have already made this mistake several times, starting conversations in overseas locales with ugg wearers who looked at me perplexed, convinced that uggs are American. The whole UGG® Australia thing is just some kind of marketing ploy. They first saw Americans wearing uggs, so that's where it started, for them.

The girls struggle to their feet. One girl goes down again, her grey-blue pipe jeans now splotched and crusted with snow. It's a rather evil, pleasurable sensation, this Schadenfreude. It tickles my toes, which are snug and dry inside my wool socks, ensconced in a sturdy pair of hiking boots bought eight years ago in Jackson Hole, Wyoming. Uggs are the single most impractical winter footwear. What would we Australians even know about making winter footwear, for real winters, beyond sewn-together reversed sheepskins worn for trudging up cold beaches after surfing? More, how did the ugg become the most sought after winter footwear? From bogan slipper to American celebrities in frump mode to the Milan catwalk to downtown Hamburg, where every second girl is slipping, sliding, sloshing and falling in the snow just for the sake of fashion. How did the ugg, which my parents refused to buy me based on the social norms of 1980s Western Australia and what I (and they) might get labelled for wearing a pair, get here? How did the ugg become the one thing that Australia has given to the world?

The Theory of Uggolution

It gets cold in the south-west during winter. Not on the coast, but inland, in the small towns that insignificantly dot the Albany Highway and its less-prominent arteries. Farming land, sheep and wheat, where the football teams used to have names like Rovers, Railways and Towns, before they folded; where the August frost would crackle under my socks and sandals as I walked across the neighbours' lawns on the way to school; where nearly a hundred years ago the shearers stuffed wool into their boots to keep their feet warm.

I remember, in year one at Williams District School, wanting very badly a pair of uggs. My parents refused. I cried. I'm sure of it, because a lot of things ended in tears in those days, often in direct connection to getting and not getting. When I was older I would understand: the ugg was the shoe of the bogan, the lower classes, what Americans call white trash, what Germans call *Prols*. My firmly set middle-class parents didn't want their children growing up bogan. As a freshly-minted teenager, I saw the mulleted bogans at the Kalamunda Roller Rink in the Perth hills: in their skin-tight black jeans, packets of Winnie Blues tucked under the sleeves of AC/DC shirts, swapping their uggs for roller skates and unleashing an incredible cacophony of odours as Lionel Richie sang about dancing on the ceiling.

Australia in the 1980s was a society very much defined by location; you were where you lived. In many ways, it's still like that. In Perth, there were no bogans in Cottesloe, Scarborough or Nedlands. They were in the outer suburbs: Armadale, Kenwick, Midland and Kalamunda. The social classes of Australian cities were set by the suburb inhabited, the tiny circle moved in, and the accoutrements of a life accessorised; yep, love the fuzzy dice and the shiny mags. If you wore uggs, whether around the house, to school or down the shops for a carton of milk and the paper, that meant you were a bogan. Simple.

What we've given to the fashion world is something many of us grew up deriding. It may be hard to believe, but the ugg is beyond huge in North America and Europe. On university campuses, in high schools and on the streets, once the leaves start to turn and fall, the uggs come out. In 2009, Deckers sold over seven million dollars in sheepskin footwear.

The ugg was long the butt of jokes for us, from the Mazda Sharon sketch from *Full Frontal*, with the ugg boot slipper for an accelerator, to the pair of uggs that Daryl Kerrigan wears in *The Castle*. But it went overseas to become a star beyond imagination: the way Nicole Kidman went from BMX bandit to Oscar winner, Mel Gibson from Mad Max to William Wallace, Foster's from last choice to Australian for beer, Peter Carey from ad writer to Man Booker Prize winner,

225

Heath Ledger from clown to joker, and a host of other examples – they all reached much greater heights by leaving Australia.

Now that the ugg is so popular, fights have broken out over its ownership and origins. With this being the twenty-first century, the fights are all about money, no matter how they get twisted and reconstructed. The 2005 case that pitted Uggs-n-Rugs (based in Kenwick, Western Australia) against Deckers was quickly labelled by the Australian media as a David-versus-Goliath scenario, with the ugg morphing in short media shrift from punch-line to Australian icon. The bogan slipper suddenly was to be held in the same regard as lamingtons, Vegemite, meat pies and the Hills Hoist, and people at all levels of Australian society started screaming "Hands off our ugg."

Interestingly, no such Aussie icons have been appropriated and turned into profitable products overseas quite like the ugg. The attempts to export Drizabone coats, Akubra hats, and even Victoria Bitter have all fallen flat. Foster's Beer has done well, but no one drinks it in Australia, and the Foster's you get in various parts of the world is actually just beer produced locally under license in a Foster's bottle or can (which means in Germany it's drinkable).

Products aside, the most successful Australian export by far is the Australian: soldier, singer, actor, athlete, writer, barman, nurse, teacher, and a host of other occupations and positions that Australians have taken up overseas.

But back to the bogan slipper. Uggs-n-Rugs successfully challenged the registration of ugg as a trademark in Australia. Deckers lost the UGG® trademark in Australia and New Zealand, while keeping the trademark in over a hundred countries where ugg was never a generic term, including the key markets of the USA, the UK and Europe. The Kenwick company could keep its name, and all of us down under could continue using ugg in everyday speaking. The story is well-documented in the film *The Good, the Bad and the Ugg Boot*. While it's clearly presented as the battler taking on the evil American conglomerate (replete with western-themed music, OK courtroom showdown and triumph of good over evil), there is no mention in the documentary of how the multi-million dollar marketing campaign implemented by Deckers made uggs so sought after in the first place, opening up huge, lucrative new markets for small manufacturers like Uggs-n-Rugs. Deckers bought the UGG brand in 1995 and implemented a very clever marketing strategy, getting a swathe of celebrities into them, including Pamela Anderson on *Baywatch*, Oprah Winfrey, Heidi Klum, Kate Moss and Sarah Jessica Parker. Pamela Anderson, a PETA advocate, has since renounced the boot after finding out they're made from sheepskin. Of course, she could now choose from a host of uggs made from synthetic materials, including, rumour has it, the UGG®.

The ugg was first brought to America in the late 1970s by Australian surfer Brian Smith. Uggs had been a mainstay among the Aussie surfing set since the 1960s and soon caught on in small numbers on the California coast. Smith would eventually sell the UGG brand to Deckers.

UGG® Australia is marketed as the real ugg boot, which is far from the case; they are made in China, and the quality and authenticity of the materials used remains under scrutiny. When the ugg craze first caught on in the late 1990s, customers who couldn't get the sold-out UGG®s bought uggs from Australian sellers and then sent them back claiming they weren't real uggs – which meant the uggs didn't have the UGG® Australia label on them – but the "Made in Australia" ugg could claim to be the real thing, with the UGG® being the fake, and if you're confused now, that's all right, because I am too. Basically, the boot that calls itself real and everything else a fake is actually not the real thing, but is marketed as the real thing and, more importantly, is known by customers in mega markets like North America and Europe as the real thing. So, the uggs made for decades by Australian hands in the back workshops of companies like Uggs-n-Rugs using real Australian wool are considered by many to be fakes. Consumers want the branded UGG®. And to drum home that they are the real thing, UGG® Australia added a counterfeit education page to its website in order to inform its customers about counterfeit goods, how to spot them and how the UGG® is the only real ugg.

The incredible popularity of UGG®s, and uggs, in Europe and North America has spawned a whole posse of poseurs. Shoe manufacturers, seeing the trends, introduced cheap knock-offs (with a variety of names) to cater for those unwilling to pay a hefty price for the so-called real article. The majority of the uggs on the streets of Hamburg, Vienna, Paris, Milan and elsewhere are cheap fakes, made with synthetic materials and prone to stink, fall apart and provide an inner haven for a world of bacteria. And the wearers have little to no clue of the ugg's place in Australiana. Of course, those same people don't know that Nicole Kidman is Australian, or that Mel Gibson is Australian, and so on.

What is interesting is that the ugg today has been completely reinvented. From Sydney's western suburbs to a coveted pair of "Made in China" genuine UGG®s, to now being a fashion item seen at Coogee Beach. The ugg went overseas, became popular and has been imported back to Australia to be worn by everyone, not just bogans. Indeed, the bogans are probably shunning the ugg as being too commercial and uppity. But bogans too are evolving. According to the blog and book *Things Bogans Like*, bogans are no longer just in the outer suburbs or in the Collingwood Football Club members area. Like many aspects of Australian identity and culture, the meaning of bogan has been twisted and reshaped to fit certain contexts. In some marketing circles, bogan has become cool. Bogan chic, it's referred to. And "cashed-up bogans" is a defined target group.

The popularity of the ugg has resulted in a new generation of Australian wearers; girls who are following the celebrity ugg wearers of the USA. These girls are taking back the ugg as their own, disregarding its history and former social status, and stepping out in sheepskin style, regardless of the season.

But no matter how much something is reinvented, rebranded or redefined, it never loses its roots. For many Australians, the ugg remains the bogan slipper, and we find it both amusing and confusing that people the world over think of it as high fashion.

The Coming Uggstralian

Around the time of Federation, a few decades before Australian fighter pilots would don massive thigh-high sheepskin boots (flying uggs – fugs) to stay warm in freezing, unpressurised cabins during World War I, there was much discussion and debate about what it meant to be Australian. This was tied in with growing nationalist sentiments, the work of Banjo Paterson, Henry Lawson, C.J. Dennis and other Australian writers, as well as with the rising Boy Scouts movement and the writing of Rudyard Kipling. Then, the Australian was mythicised as the ideal specimen of manhood, and there would pass a clear evolution over the course of the twentieth century: from bushman to digger to lifesaver to larrikin, each with its own cult, myth and application.

The ugg is now an Australian icon, thanks to its popularity overseas and the David versus Goliath court cases that followed. It doesn't matter if the world doesn't recognise uggs as Australian, because we do. The ugg has become important to us because we like to think it's one of those uniquely Australian things that define who we are: laid back, unpretentious, funny, off-beat, battlers, etc. The Uggs-n-Rugs court case was billed the same way: the little Aussie underdog battling and punching above his weight to get a fair go.

True, we love an underdog and like to see people given the chance they deserve. We value honesty, hard work, fairness, independence and egalitarianism, and have a general disrespect for authority. Interestingly, these were the characteristics, arising from the same debate and writings at the turn of the twentieth century, which comprised what was known then as the Coming Australian. This highly evolved specimen would be sent overseas for mettle-testing, exported as military hardware for fighting in the Boer War and World War I. And as the history goes, the Coming Australian was not found wanting. Indeed, the Coming Australian proved his worth overseas and came back a hero, offering up the clear-cut identity the young nation craved, even if it was contrived, constructed or idealised, as historians have argued. The argument of the historical construction of Australian identity is well outlined in Richard White's *Inventing Australia* and John Pilger's *The Secret Country*, among others.

The early wars of the twentieth century mark the first instances of Australians finding out who they might be and what they can do, and they make those discoveries by leaving their country to take on greater challenges on markedly bigger playing fields. Joe Digger (b. 1896) may have been an ordinary farmer or worker, possibly with convict roots, but when he signed up to fight in 1915, he became an ANZAC, along with all that that would come to mean. If he managed to survive the war, he came back a hero, much more of a man than when he left.

Why is that? We built this country, from staggered beginnings of penal settlement and land theft, but we still built this country, and that is an incredible, impressive effort, one we should be proud of. Though we should not be proud of the land theft.

Why do we have to go overseas and prove to ourselves, our countrymen and everyone else just what we're made of? Sir Donald Bradman was a great cricketer, but he only became a legend by making runs against England in England. Beating our overlords at their own game on their own soil: that mattered.

The list of Australian heroes, celebrities and icons heading overseas is long: Errol Flynn, Dame Joan Sutherland, Germaine Greer, Rupert Murdoch, Clive James, Eric Bana, Steve Irwin, Kylie Minogue, Foster's, Billabong, Speedos, uggs, and on and on. There seems to be the need for our brands, singers, actors, lawyers, doctors, businessmen, etc, to prove they are just as good if not better than everyone else, and to do it abroad. In Australian society today, this happens from top to bottom, thanks to globalisation, reduced visa restrictions, improved transportation and greater working mobility. The last quarter century has seen increasing numbers of Australians heading overseas for work, for greater opportunities and for adventure. Global Swagmen they're called. But this is romanticising a deeply ingrained insecurity: to be tested, to not be found wanting, to be a successful underdog, to waltz Matilda all the world over, to go and fight and come back a hero.

The Going Uggstralian

The ugg went to America in 1979, slowly built a market, was sold to Deckers in 1995 and became the boot of choice for the rich and fashionable, and thus for much of America. As it is for members of the Australian diaspora, success and achievement for the ugg took some time. It needed establishment, settling in, adaptation and local acceptance. The ugg had to make friends abroad, build networks, work hard, show warmth and win fans. There were certainly rough periods, when the ugg was unwanted and lonely, felt so different and outside, and surely came close to packing it in and going home. But the ugg had friends abroad, other Australians who could vouch for it, support it and draw it into the local expat scene.

In the mid 1990s, I saw Aussies in uggs in Canada, upraised on foot stools near fireplaces in Whistler, Banff and Big White. I saw more trudging through the snow in Steamboat Springs and Aspen in the States, and Kitzbühel in Austria. Then, the uggs were part of the Aussie expat's travel survival kit, like the reserved-for-sporting-events inflatable kangaroo and the much-travelled jar of Vegemite that gets passed around at breakfast, a spread which the locals screw their mouths up after a sample taste, much to the delight of the Aussie. Vegemite, owned by Kraft Foods, an American company, hasn't had any of the success abroad like the ugg. Maybe Kraft needs to get Oprah Winfrey and a few other Hollywood stars eating it. If only one of the girls from *Sex and the City* had smeared it on a guy's donger and licked it off.

In winter settings like a Whistler youth hostel or a shared trailer in Steamboat, the Aussies could wear their uggs with pride and be whoever they wanted to be. If they were from Kenwick, they could say they were from Perth, and this wouldn't be a lie. Or better still, they could tell the truth, say Kenwick, because all the people present, including many Australians, wouldn't know where Kenwick was and wouldn't be able to draw all the conclusions and stereotypes based on it. Basically, bogans from Perth's eastern suburbs, or Sydney's western suburbs, could go overseas and completely reinvent themselves. The bogan could simply become a larrikin while also playing to and fulfilling all the stereotypical expectations of the locals they met. This idea of self-reinvention in a foreign land was the subject of my first book, *The Bicycle Teacher*, where a young man from Perth's lower class moves to East Berlin in the 1980s and as a result becomes much more than he could ever have been in Australia. In communist East Germany, he gets the chance to fulfil his potential.

Australians are widely travelled, having started in known quantities like London, New York, Hong Kong, Singapore and Vancouver, then branching out to other places around the globe. Jafas they're called, "just another fucking Australian", and they're not just singers and actors. They cover the full spectrum of occupations and often get the chance in the foreign country to do something different than before: uni dropouts become English teachers in South Korea, trainee nurses become highly desired and respected medical professionals in Botswana, and so on. We are everywhere, populating the expat circles, building cliques in European cities, getting games of touch rugby going, starting Australian rules football leagues in Germany and Denmark, packing multi-lingual kids off to international schools, firing up the barbecue in Chicago and explaining to the locals that we eat prawns not shrimps, while also laughing away the claims that we wrestle crocodiles, spar with kangaroos and have koalas for pets. Deconstructing the Australian stereotype was the subject of my third book, *True Blue Tucker*, where two Australians open a restaurant in Munich that tells the true history of Australia.

From the statistics gathered by the Southern Cross Group in 2001, there are close to a million Australians living overseas. I'd venture to say that number is now much higher. More students are studying overseas, there are more working holiday agreements between Australia and other countries, more employment opportunities, and employers are more open to having an international workforce. Doing time abroad somewhere has become part of an Australian's development, so much so that it's quite normal from an Australian to have been to Paris, London or New York, but not to Darwin, Launceston or Esperance.

Some of us then, essentially, are like the ugg. We head overseas, work hard at reinventing ourselves, try to find people in new markets who have a greater appreciation for us, all with the goal of coming back to Australia a hero or heroine, better than before, or perhaps simply better than the people we left behind.

Leaving the homeland for some place foreign offers escape, challenge, difficulty and the chance for success. It also means you're suddenly more interesting, regardless of your background, location or education. An Australian in Australia is just another person; an Australian in, say, Barcelona, as ubiquitous as jafas are, is something of an oddity, and thus more interesting.

It seems, though, that this time spent abroad is temporary. While living in Germany, I have seen a lot of Australians come and go, and plenty of them were bogans. We're heading overseas for short-term challenges and new work experiences (and now because all our friends are doing it and it's expected of us too), but we don't appear to set our feet firmly in those lands. We are always just visiting. In our heads and in our speech, Australia is always the place to be. Of those almost one million Aussies abroad, how many have made permanent homes in other countries?

The ugg has already come back home, replete with new identity, new history and new status. The ugg is the bogan made good. And when the fashion trend of the UGG® passes for the rest of the world and attention is focused on something else, we will still be wearing them, even more so than before.

The Uggly Truth

I've learned that being outside Australia allows reflection, distance and the chance to see things from a different perspective. It also offers the opportunity to learn what other people think about us and our country. I've concluded that Australia has a mash-up culture, which is not necessarily a bad thing. This mash-up incorporates lots of different elements, fusing influences from immigrants with colonial narratives, and nationalist sentiments with Indigenous cultures, all the while still trying to define the essence of what Australian culture really is: to construct it, brand it and package it. Nice and neat, easy to identify and sell.

I have come to question those concepts ingrained in me that we are supposed to hold in high stead, like fair go, equality, honesty, mateship and hard work. We may agree on a set of principles and ideas about what it means to be Australian, and maybe have a vague sense of what our culture comprises, but these often get challenged and nullified by history (no matter how much we choose to ignore it), current events (both at home and abroad), swings in national mood, and the rally cries of those who consider themselves more Australian than others. To cite a few examples: the White Australia Policy, native title, the One Nation Party, Australia First, the Tampa Crisis, the Cronulla Riots, Aboriginal reconciliation, Stolen Generations, Forgotten Generations, Aboriginal deaths in custody, refugee camps, boat people, Palm Island, Come Walkabout advertising campaign, WorkChoices, etc.

Overseas, Australia is criticised for having no culture at all: a place of beaches not Bach, of pools not poetry, of innocence not intellect, of lifestyle not life. But even a mash-up culture is a culture. That mash-up includes the ugg, which is also derivative. We can try to claim it as our own, but really it's an animal skin boot the kind of which humans have been wearing since we came down from the trees. They're called mukluks by Canadian Inuit, moccasins by Native Americans, and lots of other versions from different native peoples. The animal skin or fur boot is as old as fire.

The word ugg only has long-term meaning in Australia and New Zealand. The judges ruling in favour of Deckers in various trademarks disputes were right when they said ugg was not a generic term, outside of Australia and New Zealand. But now that the ugg is huge, it's definitely ours. It wasn't an Aussie icon when it was floundering in the American market in the early 1990s, nor when bogans were swapping them for roller skates at the Kalamunda Roller Rink in 1986. But it is now.

Ours is a mash-up culture of appropriation and derivation, one that has drawn – and continues to draw – on the outside influences of immigration, wars, television, foreign trade, and from Australians going abroad and bringing their experiences and influences home.

233

Australia, the colonial settlement, was born from the imported culture of Ireland and England, and grew later with the arrival of immigrants from European, Asian and Middle Eastern countries. Those who came across the seas to share these "boundless plains" brought with them their culture, reference points, backgrounds and beliefs, and planted these in the new soil of Terra Australis. The convicts, settlers and (self-titled) landed gentry were the first Global Swagmen, heading overseas to start anew, even in chains, to reinvent themselves and maybe go back a hero, better than before, or even free. This is ingrained in us: that there is always the chance to start again; that after the drought the rains will come; that after the bushfire the trees will grow; that everyone deserves a fair go; and that given the opportunity, Australians will always show their worth. There is always the chance for redemption, forgiveness and homecoming. Our mash-up culture allows us to take an old song and blend it with a new song to make our own song, then sing it as loud as we want, with a chorus of Oi, Oi, Oi.

The ugg has been forgiven. It has been welcomed back into the fold and remashed into our culture. It is the bogan slipper no more. It went overseas and has come back an icon, a hero, an essential part of us we once derided and joked about. And this is the key to our mash-up culture; it includes the constant revising, reworking and remashing of our own narrative. The convict stain is a stain no more. We are sorry, as former Prime Minister Kevin Rudd said. The Mabo decision rewrote history and Australia was in fact invaded.

This mash-up needs more outside influences, more time abroad, more reflection, more filling of job vacancies in farther flung places. It needs the continued appropriation of culture, and the reappropriation of the parts of our culture that we once found shameful or laughable. The narrative is ours, and we change it to fit the context of our time. There's no Shakespeare, Galileo or Newton. Ours is a culture under construction, never to be finished because it never really started. It can be unpicked and sewn together again, like an animal skin boot. The ugg is now part of our narrative. The girls in Hamburg slip and slide in the snow in their uggs, but for them it's just a fashionable boot, an UGG®. The ugg is ours. We have made the ugg an icon. We are the ugg.

Travel Page (cont.)

Lightning Source UK Ltd.
Milton Keynes UK
UKOW05f0319191116
288008UK00002B/14/P

9 783981 624946